Welcome to the EVERYTHING® series!

These handy, accessible books give you all you need to tackle a difficult project, gain a new hobby, comprehend a fascinating topic, prepare for an exam, or even brush up on something you learned back in school but have since forgotten.

You can read an *EVERYTHING*® book from cover-to-cover or just pick out the information you want from our four useful boxes: e-facts, e-ssentials, e-alerts, and e-questions. We literally give you everything you need to know on the subject, but throw in a lot of fun stuff along the way, too.

We now have well over 100 *EVERYTHING*® books in print, spanning such wide-ranging topics as weddings, pregnancy, wine, learning guitar, one-pot cooking, managing people, and so much more. When you're done reading them all, you can finally say you know *EVERYTHING*®!

E FACTS

Important sound bytes
of information

E SSENTIALS

Quick handy tips

E ALERT

Urgent warnings

QUESTIONS?

Solutions to
common problems

EVERYTHING
Series

Muy estimado lector (Dearest reader),

　　As a boy, I loved listening to the Ecuadorean "melody" that accompanied my relatives' Spanish dialect. Soon I realized that my Spanish-speaking friends "sang" their own ancestral tunes. Needless to say, I borrowed these tunes every chance I had. In my world of pretend, I was a Mexican cowboy, an Argentine sportscaster, a Spanish bullfighter, and more.

　　Learning a new language is all about pretending. It's about pretend -ing to live in a familiar yet refreshingly foreign world. I have kept this in mind while writing the book you now hold. While I'm sure you will want to travel at some point, keep in mind that an external Spanish world may be discovered in a cultural center near you. Thinking in Spanish can create an internal world right in your own home. I hope that as you progress, you will feel as though you are in the middle of all things Spanish.

　　Thank you for considering this book; but most important, thank you for being open to making a language I love dearly your own. I hope you find as much pleasure as I have in exploring it and the many cultures that employ it.

Respetuosamente,

Frank H. Zambrano

THE
EVERYTHING®
LEARNING
SPANISH BOOK

Speak, write, and understand
basic Spanish in no time

Frank H. Zambrano

Adams Media Corporation
Avon, Massachusetts

EDITORIAL
Publishing Director: Gary M. Krebs
Managing Editor: Kate McBride
Copy Chief: Laura MacLaughlin
Acquisitions Editor: Bethany Brown
Development Editor: Julie Gutin

PRODUCTION
Production Director: Susan Beale
Production Manager: Michelle Roy Kelly
Series Designer: Daria Perreault
Layout and Graphics: Paul Beatrice,
Brooke Camfield, Colleen Cunningham,
Michelle Roy Kelly, Daria Perreault, Frank Rivera

An Everything® Series Book.
Everything® and everything.com® are registered trademarks of F+W Publications, Inc.

Published by Adams Media, an F+W Publications Company
57 Littlefield Street, Avon, MA 02322 U.S.A.
www.adamsmedia.com

ISBN: 1-58062-575-4
Printed in the United States of America.

J I H G F E D

Library of Congress Cataloging-in-Publication Data
available from publisher.

This publication is designed to provide accurate and authoritative information with regard to the subject matter covered. It is sold with the understanding that the publisher is not engaged in rendering legal, accounting, or other professional advice. If legal advice or other expert assistance is required, the services of a competent professional person should be sought.
—From a *Declaration of Principles* jointly adopted by a Committee of the American Bar Association and a Committee of Publishers and Associations

Illustrations by Barry Littmann.

This book is available at quantity discounts for bulk purchases.
For information, call 1-800-872-5627.

Visit the entire Everything® series at everything.com

Contents

Introduction

Welcome to *The Everything® Learning Spanish Book* and the exciting and diverse world of Spanish! Perhaps you chose this book because you want to be able to communicate with some of your coworkers, neighbors, or clients. Perhaps you want to feel more comfortable traveling in countries where Spanish is the national language. Maybe you enjoy listening to Latin jazz and would like to understand the lyrics to some of your favorite songs. Whatever your reasons for learning this popular language, you've come to the right place.

Don't be surprised when at some point in your mastery of Spanish you are rewarded in ways you had not even considered. When you find yourself in Mexico City and need to ask for directions, imagine the sense of accomplishment you will feel as you approach the first person you see and say confidently, *"¡Perdón! ¿Dónde está la calle San José?"* (Excuse me, where is San Jose Street?) Imagine how subtly transformed your life will have become when the person answers in Spanish and you are able to understand the directions!

Learning Spanish will expand your intellectual horizons. You will be in a position to learn about Spanish culture from the inside—by listening to Latin music, reading books in Spanish, and conversing with native speakers. You will have more personal opportunities to witness how other people live day by day in your own neighborhood, on their own terms. Not only will you be able to listen to their opinions on family, life, work, and society in general, but you will be able to come to mutual understandings by sharing your own.

Knowing Spanish might even get you a promotion! Given the trend toward globalization, you will be able to take advantage of many opportunities that already exist, but that you currently know nothing about. The business opportunities are obvious—a larger market for you to sell to or for you to find employment in.

Learning a new language is a difficult undertaking. Succeeding will mean not only that you have command of some foreign words, but that you will have discovered the power within you to tackle any other situation that requires patience despite uneven progress. As you can see, you may have a good idea of why you want to learn Spanish, but what you will actually get out of it will most certainly be tenfold what you expected. You may or may not notice the transformation, but it will certainly take place.

Take a quick look at the chapters of this book. I'm sure you'll recognize a few words or phrases here and there. Perhaps you've studied Spanish in high school. Perhaps you've never heard a word of Spanish, but you are quite familiar with French, Italian, or Latin. Even if you've never studied a foreign language before, you'll discover that you already know more than you had realized. Don't feel like you are starting from scratch. You'll see that even those years of studying English grammar will be helpful.

You are about to embark on a very exhilarating and at times frustrating journey that will lead you to look at your own life differently and will reward you with experiences as yet unimagined. Again, whatever your interests are in learning Spanish, this book will help you achieve the goals that you have set for yourself. *Buena suerte* (good luck) in your endeavor!

CHAPTER 1
Starting with the Basics

This chapter will introduce you to the Spanish language and start you off on the right track with advice on how to study. Remember, to be rewarding, learning a new language should always be enjoyable, but you must dedicate attention and time to studying.

Developing Basic Study Skills

If you are full of enthusiasm to sit down and learn *español* (Spanish) at one go—*¡relájate!*—stop and relax. Learning a language is not like crash dieting; it's a gradual process that requires planning and concentration. Here is what you should know as you incorporate learning Spanish into your everyday life.

Some Do's and Don'ts

Self-fulfilling prophecies are your biggest enemy. Don't think that you will never learn the language, or that there is just one way of saying something. And if you don't know a word, remember that you may know a synonym, or how to explain what you intend to say.

Use new phrases as soon as you have learned them and as many times as possible. Don't wait until you have everything down perfectly before you begin using Spanish in conversation. Remember: When it comes to languages, perfect fluency and pronunciation are myths.

The expressive potential of a sentence is often more than the sum of its parts. Don't just concentrate on memorizing words. Individual words have a breadth of meaning that you should come to know. However, the purpose of speaking is to take one of those meanings and make your point. Learning whole phrases will help you make your point quicker.

Invest in an English-to-Spanish/Spanish-to-English dictionary. There are several good ones—written with many learning styles in mind. Do you work better with pictures, or with themes? Choose the one that best suits you, the one you will have completely dog-eared within a month.

Do try to speak in "long words." You might have noticed that native speakers don't make a point of separating each word when they speak. Think about it—do you say "Hello. How. Are. You. Today?" Or do you say, "Hello, howareyoutoday?" Learn to string along the elements of a sentence so that they flow together.

Don't force yourself to spend hours at a time learning Spanish—you don't want to make studying a chore. Set up study periods of about fifteen to twenty minutes a day, five days a week, and take the time to review instead of rushing on to learn new material. And if you feel that you prefer longer study periods, don't forget to include minibreaks for every thirty-minute stretch of study.

Do set up a "Spanish-only" zone in your home, apartment, or office. Within this zone, you must think and speak in no other language but Spanish. It should be a space that you enter every day, not the attic that you see but once a year. A curious feature about the zone is that it tends to be contagious and will slowly spread into adjacent areas.

Use your dictionary to look up the objects in the zone and label them in Spanish. When you enter the zone, name all the items you can within two minutes or so. After a while, you'll discover that you don't need the labels and are ready to expand your zone.

Do use the Internet. Online, you will find free instruction, opportunities to practice, reference materials, and cultural information, as well as paid online Spanish courses (use your favorite search engine to browse through thousands of Web sites). For those who have yet to master the World Wide Web, the library can be a good source of additional information.

Do immerse yourself in the world of Spanish. Eat at Spanish and Latin American restaurants. Listen to Latin music: *boleros, cumbias, flamenco, merengue, pasillos, pasodoble, salsas, sevillanas, son, tango, rancheras,* and *rock.* Go out to Latin dance clubs—you'll have fun dancing the night away, and will have the opportunity to meet Latin Americans from many diverse backgrounds and cultures. Go to Spanish movie festivals, and rent Spanish films on video or DVD—most will offer subtitles or dubbed tracks in Spanish. Read bilingual books and magazines (check to see if your area has a local *Extra Bilingual Newspaper*). Try watching Spanish television—at first you won't understand it, but it might be fun to make it a game and try to guess what is happening.

FACTS

There are at least four major Spanish-language networks available in the United States: *Galavisión* (cable), *TeleFutura*, *Telemundo*, and *Univisión*. Check your local listings for these and other offerings.

Do combine your hobbies and interests with the study of Spanish. If you love playing tennis, learn how to say everything you know about the game in Spanish. Religion, politics, work, and recreation all have their Spanish vocabulary.

Don't panic. Take your time to learn new material, find somebody to answer your questions, look up words in the dictionary, and don't allow yourself to be intimidated by anything. Make mistakes and learn from them. When you goof up, you can either look mortified or just laugh about it—the choice is up to you.

Making the Most of the Spanish Environment

The do's and don'ts list emphasizes regular practice and immersion in the language. Focus all your attention on all things Spanish that you find in your daily life. Put yourself in situations where you have no choice but to use your Spanish. Begin to think in Spanish.

When you are in the thick of things, listen for key words. Try to identify the verb. Are there any pronouns you can hook some meaning to? Does the word vaguely remind you of a word in English? Forget about trying to decode every single word—getting the main ideas first will help you fill in the details.

Listen for familiar intonation patterns and pay attention to the speaker's gestures. Think charades. When you speak, don't be afraid to gesture as well. Nod your head and smile when you understand or agree. Twist your flat horizontal palm back and forth for "so-so."

Use your thumb and forefinger to indicate "a little bit." Cover your nose when something smells mighty awful. Some gestures seem universal, others are tied to the language, culture, or region. Be observant and proactive in investigating what common gestures are appropriate in any region you visit. You should be aware that some gestures might be misinterpreted—be especially careful with the "okay" hand sign.

ESSENTIALS

To ask someone to clarify or repeat something, use the following phrase:

¿Cómo? Perdón. ¿Me lo repite más despacio, por favor?
(COH-moh? pehr-DOHN. meh-loh-rreh-PEE-teh MAHS dehs-PAH-syoh, pohr-fah-VOHR?)
What? Excuse me. Can you repeat it (what you said) for me more slowly, please?

Remember to relax and smile *(relájate y sonríe)*. Your audience is having as much trouble understanding you as you are having speaking. They want you to succeed. Take a deep breath and have a sense of humor about your mistakes. Remember: A smile goes a long way.

What You Already Know

In many places around the United States, Spanish is encountered at every turn—on street signs, on buses, at banks, at restaurants, even in your junk mail. Did you realize that the names *California, Florida,* and *Los Angeles* all come from Spanish? As soon as people begin learning it, they discover that they know more Spanish than they had originally thought. In fact, Spanish is all over the world. Given the number of countries where Spanish is the official language, it most certainly ranks as one of the most widely spoken languages.

RECOGNIZING SPANISH-SOUNDING WORDS

To prove that you know more Spanish than you think you do, take a little quiz. Take a look at the following list, and see how many words you can understand.

accidente	cereal	famoso	información	respetable
actor	ciclista	favor	inventor	
adorable	color	físico	local	simple
animal	conductor	fútbol	motor	
asistir	convertible	honorable	musical	taxi
atractivo	criatura	hospital	natural	
auto	criminal	hotel	plan	teléfono
autor	cruel	humor	popular	
bagaje	doctor	idea	potente	usual
catedral	elefante	importante	presidente	
central	error	inevitable	radio	visible

That wasn't too difficult, right? Are you convinced that you do know a lot of Spanish already? Although you might not yet know how to pronounce these words in Spanish, you should be able to figure out what they mean, because all of these words are cognates.

QUESTIONS?

What are cognates?
Cognates are words in different languages that share a similar meaning and spelling because they originated from the same word. True cognates share the same meaning. Pure cognates are spelled identically in both languages. False cognates share a common origin and spelling, but have completely different meanings.

Words such as *actor, animal, central, error, hospital, idea, natural, radio,* and *taxi* are true pure cognates. (Note that even though these words are spelled the same way in English and in Spanish, the pronunciations are different. See Chapters 2 and 3 for pronunciation guidelines and accents.) Words like *accidente, autor, elefante, presidente,* and *teléfono* are true cognates—they share similar but not exactly identical spelling.

Many cognates between English and Spanish originated from Latin—hence the words "Latino" and "Latin America." Over time, these words gained new meanings in each language, and ended up evolving in completely different ways. These words are called false cognates; don't be misled by their meanings in Spanish. As you can see, "Latin" is no longer the language of the Ancient Romans, but an adjective describing Spanish-speaking people from Central and South America.

- *anciano*: "elderly man" (not "ancient")
- *asistir*: "to attend" (not "to assist")
- *carta*: "letter," when referring to a form of written correspondence (not "cart" or "card")
- *chanza*: "joke" (not "chance")
- *constipado*: "congested," as when suffering from a cold (not "constipated")
- *delito*: "crime" (not "delight")
- *embarazada*: "pregnant" (not "embarrassed"—though misusing this word could certainly lead to embarrassment!)
- *fútbol*: "soccer" (not "football")
- *recordar*: "to remember" (not "to record")

Also keep a wary eye open for "Spanglish"—combinations of Spanish and English that might "sound" like Spanish, but that would make little sense to people who don't speak both languages. Here are some examples:

TABLE 1-1

WHEN MEANING . . .	SAY . . .	RATHER THAN . . .
to block	*obstruir*	*bloquear*
to brake	*frenar*	*brekear*
business	*negocio*	*bisnes*
to check	*revisar*	*chequear*
to look (at), watch	*mirar*	*wachar*
to park	*estacionar*	*parquear*
to quit	*renunciar*	*cuitiar*
to touch	*tocar*	*tochar*

SSENTIALS   Because Spanish shares common roots with other Romance languages, like French, Italian, and Portuguese (all Romance languages originate from Latin), knowing any one Romance language will help you recognize and understand cognates in Spanish.

Learning the Common Suffixes

From the true pure cognates, you may notice a one-to-one correspondence in Spanish and English of the following suffixes: *-al, -ble,* and *-or.*

–al   **(pertaining or related to; an extension of; a place)**

criminal	pertaining to crime
hospital	place for hospice and treatment
usual	an extension of use, usual

–ble   **(having the ability or aptitude to or capacity of; this suffix transforms verbs into adjectives)**

| *adorable* | adorable, capable of being adored |
| *convertible* | convertible, capable of being converted |

–or   **(agents that are or do; abstractions)**

| *inventor* | inventor, one who invents |
| *amor* | love |

Suffixes often clue you in on the meanings of the words that use them. A complete list of examples would be rather lengthy. Here are a few:

TABLE 1-2

SPANISH COGNATES WITH SUFFIXES *–BLE, –AL,* AND *–OR*		
–BLE	*–AL*	*–OR*
accesible	abdominal	ardor
aceptable	anual	auditor
acomodable	astral	censor

admisible	beneficial	compositor
afable	comercial	confesor
biodegradable	cordial	destructor
blasfemable	cultural	detector
calculable	educacional	editor
comprensible	emocional	fervor
curable	esencial	inferior
digestible	fatal	inspector
durable	federal	instructor
evitable	fundamental	mentor
explicable	ideal	opositor
falseable	ilegal	pastor
incomparable	nacional	profesor
lamentable	neutral	protector
miserable	oficial	reflector
negociable	original	rumor
organizable	parcial	seductor
ostensible	racional	superior
pasable	sensacional	tenor
presentable	tradicional	valor
preferible	universal	vigor

From the other cognates, you see various suffixes that are familiar, but just a little off:

–aje **(pertaining to, particularly broadened to a collection; similar to English "–age")**

bagaje military baggage
equipaje baggage

–ano/–ana **(pertaining to origin, location; relating to beliefs and affiliations; similar to English "–an")**

americano, americana American (male, female)
anciano, anciana an elderly man, woman

–ante/–ente (related to an event, the nature of, or an agent; similar to "–ant" and "–ing" in English)

accidente an unexpected event
importante something of great effect
potente of powerful nature
presidente one who presides

–ción/–sión (abstraction of an act or state of being; similar to the English "–tion" and "–sion")

atención attention
confusión confusion

–do/–da (relating to, an agent of, or the result of an action; characteristic; similar to English "–ful")

embarazada pregnant
sufrido person resigned to suffer

–ico/–ica (relating to; being similar to; similar to the English "–ic" and "–al")

físico physical, physicist
idéntico identical

–ista (pertaining to one who does; similar to English "–ist")

ciclista one who rides a bicycle
periodista reporter, one who writes for a newspaper

–ivo/–iva (relating to an action; expresses tendency, disposition, or function; similar to English "–ive")

atractivo attractive
extensivo extensive

–oso/–osa **(relating to possession or characteristic; similar to English "–ous," "–ful," and "–y")**

asqueroso disgusting
futuro future

–uro/–ura **(abstraction of an act or state of being; similar to English "–ture," "–ure," and "–ness")**

criatura baby, small child
cultura culture

Try guessing at the meanings of the words in **TABLES 1-3** and **1-4**. Use a bilingual dictionary to check your answers.

TABLE 1-3

COMMON SPANISH WORDS WITH SUFFIXES
–AJE, –ANO/–ANA, –ANTE/–ENTE, –CIÓN, –ICO/–ICA

–AJE	–ANO/–ANA	–ANTE/–ENTE	–CIÓN	–ICO/–ICA
herbaje	californiano	abundante	admiración	alegórico
lenguaje	cristiano	alarmante	anticipación	Atlántico
linaje	jerosolimitano	brillante	invitación	científico
marinaje	luterano	constante	confusión	democrático
plantaje	presbiteriano	agente	decisión	drástico
plumaje	republicano	frecuente	inversión	orgánico
porcentaje	vegetariano	prudente	posesión	pacífico

TABLE 1-4

COMMON SPANISH WORDS WITH SUFFIXES
–DO/–DA, –ISTA, –IVO/–IVA, –OSO/–OSA, –URO/–URA

–DO/–DA	–ISTA	–IVO/–IVA	–OSO/–OSA	–URO/–URA
decorado	artista	abusivo	ambicioso	agricultura
delegado	capitalista	consecutivo	contagioso	bravura
emigrado	dentista	defensivo	curioso	fractura
enamorado	moralista	explosivo	delicioso	futuro
estado	novelista	incentivo	generoso	literatura
invitado	optimista	negativo	meticuloso	obscuro
tornado	turista	progresivo	nervioso	postura

Other suffixes to remember include the following.

-ario **(pertaining to the subject; relating to an act or thing; similar to English "-ary")**

millonario millionaire
voluntario voluntary

-ncia **(relating to an act or state; result of an action; abstraction; similar to English "-nce" and "-ncy")**

abstinencia abstinence
elegancia elegance
insistencia insistence

-dad **(relating to an abstraction and a state of being; similar to English "-ty," "-ness," and "-hood")**

brevedad brevity
claridad clarity
enfermedad sickness, disease

-ismo **(pertaining to an action or practice; state or condition; similar to English "-ism")**

atletismo athleticism
idealismo idealism

-mente **(pertaining to the manner, the timing, and the place of an action; similar to English "-ly")**

afortunadamente fortunately
relativamente relatively

You've just read pages and pages of Spanish words and were probably able to understand most of them. As you can see, you already know so much Spanish! Take a look at all the words you know again. Look up the words you're not sure of. There will be times when you find words that are so obviously close to the English, that you wonder why you didn't figure it out on your own. Take heart. When that happens, you probably will never have to look that word up again.

CHAPTER 2

Pronunciation I: The Alphabet and Vowels

N ow that you're convinced that you already know a lot of Spanish words, the issue comes down to injecting that certain Spanish flavor, that secret salsa, into them. In this chapter you will learn the Spanish alphabet and then take a look at the Spanish vowels. Then, after a break, go on to the next chapter, to work on your consonants.

Sounding Native

Because Spanish is spoken in so many countries, from Spain and the Philippines to Mexico, Cuba, and Argentina, sounding native is hard to define. If you were asked to teach someone to sound like a native speaker of English, which native speaker would you choose—an American professor of English at Harvard or a police officer working on the south side of Chicago? A Londoner who speaks with a cockney accent, or an Aussie from Melbourne?

FACTS

Español (ehs-pah-NYOL) means "Spaniard" (from Spain, Spanish), and *Castellano* (kahs-teh-YAH-noh) means "Castilian," the language you call "Spanish," the official language of Spain.

Whether you speak a particular Spanish dialect or not, if you were not born within the boundaries of Spain or a Latin American country, you will always be a *gringo* (GREEN-goh). In most places, "foreigner" is all that it means, so, for example, a person born in Vermont to a Chilean couple is still a *gringo*. His Chilean family, however, may actually use the term *gringuito* (green-GEE-toh) to demonstrate affection.

Learning the Alphabet

In Spanish, the alphabet is called *el abecedario* (ehl ah-beh-seh-DAH-ryoh). If you take a look at the alphabet in **TABLE 2-1**, you will see how similar it is to the English alphabet. For the most part, the Spanish letters, *las letras españolas* (lahs LEH-trahs ehs-pah-NYOH-lahs), are the same graphically as those employed in English. What's nice about them is that, unlike their American English counterparts, their pronunciation is consistent (most of the time!), so learning them should be easy—as long as you take the time to practice.

TABLE 2-1

EL ABECEDARIO (THE SPANISH ALPHABET)

LETTER	PRONUNCIATION	SAMPLE SPANISH WORD	PRONUNCIATION	ENGLISH TRANSLATION
a	ah	*abierto*	ah-BYEHR-toh	open
b	beh	*blusa*	BLOO-sah	blouse
c	seh	*calabaza*	kah-lah-BAH-sah	pumpkin
		cerrado	seh-RRAH-doh	closed
		cierto	SYEHR-toh	certain, true
ch	cheh	*chiste*	CHEES-teh	joke
d	theh	*débil*	DEH-beel	weak
e	eh	*edad*	eh-DAHD	age
f	EH-feh	*fuerte*	FWEHR-teh	strong
g	hheh	*gracioso*	grah-SYOH-soh	amusing
		gente	HHEHN-teh	people
		girasol	hhee-rah-SOHL	sunflower
h	AH-cheh	*hambre*	AHM-breh	hunger
i	ee	*Latina*	lah-TEE-nah	Latin
		igualdad	ee-GWAL-dahd	equality
j	HHOH-tah	*jabón*	hhah-BOHN	soap
k	kah	*keroseno*	keh-roh-SEH-noh	kerosene
l	EH-leh	*ley*	LEHY	law
ll	EHL-yeh, EH-yeh	*lleno*	YEH-noh	full
m	EH-meh	*madrugar*	mah-droo-GAHR	to rise early
n	EH-neh	*nadie*	NAH-dyeh	no one
ñ	EH-nyeh	*niño*	NEE-nyoh	child
o	oh	*obra*	OH-brah	work
p	peh	*pájaro*	PAH-hhah-roh	bird
q	koo	*querido*	keh-REE-doh	beloved
		quiero	KYEH-roh	I want
r	EH-reh	*pero*	PEH-roh	but
rr	EH-rreh	*perro*	PEH-rroh	dog
s	EH-seh	*sala*	SAH-lah	living room
t	teh	*terciopelo*	tehr-syoh-PEH-loh	velvet
u	oo	*útil*	OO-teel	useful
		igual	ee-GWAHL	equal
v	veh	*vocal*	voh-CAHL	vowel
w	DOH-bleh veh	*Wáshington*	VAH-sheen-tohn	Washington
x	EH-kees	*exigencia*	eh-gsee-HHEHN-syah	demand
		México	MEH-hhee-koh	
		extraño	ehs-TRAH-nyoh	strange
		Ixtapa	eesh-TAH-pah	(town in Mexico)
y	ee-GRYEH-gah	*yerno*	YEHR-noh	son-in-law
z	SEH-tah	*zarzamora*	sahr-sah-MOH-rah	blackberry

Introducing the Vowels

Vowels, or *vocales* (voh-CAH-lehs), are distinguished from the other letters in the alphabet in that they are generated in the vocal cords and can, on their own, form a syllable, or *sílaba* (SEE-lah-bah). Spanish vowels, when not accompanied by another vowel, have only one characteristic pronunciation, whereas their English counterparts have in excess of three. If you've mastered the fifteen-plus vowel sounds in English, you'll have no trouble with the five vowel sounds in Spanish.

Each of the five vowels may be placed in one of two categories: *abierta* (ah-BYEHR-tah, "open") or *cerrada* (seh-RRAH-dah, "closed"). The "openness" or "closedness" of a vowel is determined by the extent to which you must open your mouth: *a*, *e*, and *o* are considered *vocales abiertas*, whereas *i* and *u* are described as *vocales cerradas*. A *vocal abierta* may also be described as *fuerte* (FWEHR-teh, "strong") and a *vocal cerrada* as *débil* (DEH-beel, "weak"). While you may think this information trivial or obscure, you will soon see that this is a detail that you will need to internalize with most words.

QUESTIONS?

What is a diphthong?
A diphthong is a complex vowel formed by two vowels that essentially become one sound, because both are pronounced within the same syllable.

The Vowel A

The first *letra* (letter) of *el abecedario* is a *vocal abierta*. When saying it, your mouth is widely open and the distance between the palate and the tongue is at its greatest. You use the sound of *a* every day: What do you say when after a long day's work you can finally sit down and put up your feet? Or when you go to the doctor and he asks you to open your mouth as he peers inside? Exactly! You say "ahhhhhhh." Now just skip the six extra h's and you have the Spanish letter *a*.

Spanish *a* always sounds like "ah" in the English word "father," NOT as in "back," "agree," "dare," "talk," or "tame." If you ever read a textbook that tells you to pronounce the Spanish *a* as "a" in "back," it refers to the British or "the Queen's English" pronunciation, not the American English.

Try saying the words in **TABLE 2-2** out loud.

TABLE 2-2

PRONUNCIATIONS OF *A*		
SPANISH	PRONUNCIATION	ENGLISH
ajo	AH-hhoh	garlic
altar	ahl-TAHR	altar
América	ah-MEH-ree-cah	America
árbol	AHR-bohl	tree
clavo	CLAH-voh	nail
fruta	FROO-tah	fruit
gata	GAH-tah	cat (female)
mano	MAH-noh	hand
naranja	nah-RAHN-hhah	orange
santo	SAHN-toh	saint

True to its *abierta* vowel category, *a* does not combine to form diphthongs with its companion letters *e* and *o*, but it does combine with *las vocales cerradas*. That is, when *a* is immediately in front of an unaccented *i* or a *u*, the sound that is produced is neither a pure *a*, the dominant vowel in this case, nor a pure *i* or *u*, the subordinate vowels within the combination. As a result, the *ai* sound is not "ah-ee" but rather "i" as in "tie." The *au* resembles the "ahw" combination in "ouch."

What happens if the unaccented *i* or *u* precedes the *a*? See for yourself in **TABLE 2-3** and try saying the words out loud.

TABLE 2-3

PRONUNCIATIONS OF DIPHTHONGS WITH *A*		
SPANISH	PRONUNCIATION	ENGLISH
aduana	ah-DWAH-nah	customs
ahuyentar	ahw-yehn-TAHR	to drive away
aire	i-reh	air
aislar	is-LAHR	to isolate
audaz	ahw-DAHS	bold
auto	AHW-toh	automobile
baile	BI-leh	dance
desahucio	deh-SAHW-syoh	eviction
dialecto	dyah-LEHK-toh	dialect
haitiano	i-TYAH-noh	Haitian
piano	PYAH-noh	piano

You've just seen how the *i* and the *u* kowtow to the stronger *a*, but what if *otra* (another) *vocal fuerte* challenges *a*? Well nothing really. Each vowel keeps its own sound and is pronounced. Try saying the words in **TABLE 2-4** out loud.

TABLE 2-4

PRONUNCIATIONS OF *A* WITH STRONGER VOWELS		
SPANISH	PRONUNCIATION	ENGLISH
aéreo	ah-EH-reh-oh	aerial
atraer	ah-trah-EHR	to attract
caer	kah-EHR	to fall
caos	KAH-ohs	chaos
maestro	mah-EHS-troh	teacher
paella	pah-EH-yah	Spanish rice dish
traer	trah-EHR	to bring

The Vowel E

E is the fifth letter of the alphabet, also a *vocal fuerte*. Pronounce it between the palate and the tongue by opening your mouth halfway.

The letter *e* alone has the sound "eh" as in "get," and does not sound at all like the "ay" in "say," or "e" in "hyphen," "gene," "been," and "terse." To practice pronouncing your *e*s, try saying the words in **TABLE 2-5** out loud.

TABLE 2-5

PRONUNCIATIONS OF *E*		
SPANISH	PRONUNCIATION	ENGLISH
crecer	creh-EHR	to grow
estar	ehs-TAHR	to be (located)
hacer	ah-SEHR	to do
joven	HHOH-vehn	young
nacer	nah-SEHR	to be born
necesito	neh-seh-SEE-toh	I need
ser	sehr	to be
tener	teh-NEHR	to have

As a *vocal fuerte*, *e* keeps its own sound when combining with other *vocales fuertes*. Practice pronouncing words with *ea*, *ee*, and *eo* in **TABLE 2-6**.

TABLE 2-6

PRONUNCIATIONS OF *E* WITH OTHER VOWELS		
SPANISH	PRONUNCIATION	ENGLISH
crear	creh-AHR	to create
creer	creh-HER	to believe
deseo	deh-SEH-oh	desire, wish
peaje	peh-AH-hheh	toll
peor	peh-OHR	worse
reaccionar	rreh-ahk-SYOH-nahr	to react
reanudar	rreh-ah-noo-DAHR	to renew
reembolsar	rreh-ehm-bohl-SAHR	to reimburse
reexaminar	reh-ehks-ah-mee-NAHR	to re-examine
reo	RREH-oh	criminal

FACTS

The combinations *sa*, *se*, *si*, *so*, and *su* at the beginning of a word are not native to Spanish. When a word that begins with one of these combinations makes a transition to Spanish, an *e* is added to the beginning (and, vice versa, the initial *e* is deleted when the word moves from Spanish to English). For example: Spain/*España*, to study/*estudiar*, snob/*esnob*, and special/*especial*.

TABLE 2-7

PRONUNCIATIONS OF WORDS THAT BEGIN WITH *ES–*		
SPANISH	PRONUNCIATION	ENGLISH
esbelto	ehs-BEHL-toh	proportioned
esbozo	ehs-BOH-soh	first draft
escala	ehs-CAH-lah	scale
escultura	ehs-cool-TOO-rah	sculpture
especial	ehs-peh-SYAHL	special
estilo	ehs-TEE-loh	style

A *vocal fuerte* forms diphthongs only with *vocales débiles*. When *e* is immediately followed by an unaccented *i* or *u*, the sound produced is a blend—the *ei* sound becomes "ey" as in "haystack"; the *eu* generally resembles "ehw" (unless the *u* is accented or naturally stressed within the word). To practice diphthongs *eu* and *ei*, review the words in **TABLE 2-8**.

TABLE 2-8

PRONUNCIATIONS OF *EU* AND *EI*		
SPANISH	PRONUNCIATION	ENGLISH
afeitar	ah-fey-TAHR	to shave
euforia	ehw-FOH-rya	euphoria
europeo	ehw-roh-PEH-oh	European
neumático	nehw-MAH-tee-koh	tire
reino	RREY-noh	kingdom
treinta	TREYN-tah	thirty

When the positions are reversed, that is, when an unaccented *i* or *u* is immediately followed by an *e*, the sounds that are produced are both expected and surprising. As with the letter *a*, the *i* takes on a "y" sound within the *ie* combination, like in the English word "yet." The *ue* combination is a little trickier to get right away because it can have two possible, mutually exclusive pronunciations. In many words, *ue* will have the "weh" sound as in the English word "wet." To practice *ie* and *ue*, see **TABLE 2-9**.

TABLE 2-9

PRONUNCIATIONS OF *IE* AND *UE*		
SPANISH	PRONUNCIATION	ENGLISH
cuento	KWEHN-toh	story
duelo	DWEH-loh	sorrow
mientras	MYEHN-trahs	while
muebles	MWEH-blehs	furniture
pueblo	PWEH-bloh	town, village
riesgo	RRYEHS-goh	risk
sediento	seh-DYEHN-toh	thirsty
siempre	SYEHM-preh	always

In some cases, the *u* in the *ue* combination is *muda* (mute), and the diphthong is pronounced as *e*. The *u* becomes silent when *ue* is preceded by a *g* or a *q* (see **TABLE 2-10**).

TABLE 2-10

PRONUNCIATIONS OF *UE* PRECEDED BY *G* OR *Q*		
SPANISH	PRONUNCIATION	ENGLISH
descargue	dehs-KAHR-gheh	an unloading
guedeja	gheh-DEH-hhah	lion's mane
guerra	GHEH-rrah	war
pagué	pah-GHEH	I paid
parque	PAHR-keh	a park
quemar	keh-MAHR	to burn
queso	KEH-soh	cheese
relampagueo	rreh-lahm-pah-GHEH-oh	lightning flash

The Vowel *I*

The tenth letter of the Spanish alphabet is a *vocal cerrada* and is spoken through the smallest opening between the palate and the tongue. When unaccompanied by other *vocales*, *i* most resembles the "ee" sound in the word "machine" (see **TABLE 2-11**). It is never pronounced as the English letter "i" in "mint," "edible," and "site."

TABLE 2-11

PRONUNCIATIONS OF *I*		
SPANISH	PRONUNCIATION	ENGLISH
avenida	ah-veh-NEE-dah	avenue
bistec	bees-TEHK	(beef) steak
cita	SEE-tah	appointment
fácil	FAH-seel	easy
gentil	hhehn-TEEL	courteous
marido	mah-REE-doh	husband
piso	PEE-soh	floor
rincón	rreen-KOHN	corner
simple	SEEM-pleh	simple

Remember that when followed by other *vocales*, the *i* is usually best represented by the letter "y." To practice the combinations *ia, ie, io,* and *iu*, see **TABLE 2-12**.

TABLE 2-12

PRONUNCIATIONS OF *I* FOLLOWED BY OTHER VOWELS		
SPANISH	PRONUNCIATION	ENGLISH
ciego	SYEH-goh	blind
cielo	SYEH-loh	sky
desperdiciar	dehs-pehr-dee-SYAHR	to waste
diario	DYAH-ryoh	daily
fierro	FYEH-rroh	iron
idioma	ee-DYOH-mah	language
pianista	pyah-NEES-tah	pianist
pie	pyeh	foot
piedad	pyeh-DAHD	pity, mercy
viuda	VYOO-dah	widow

If the *i* is accented (*í*), it is pronounced as "ee" even though it may precede or follow another vowel. Practice saying *ai, ei, ii, oi, ui, ia, ie,* and *io* combinations in the words listed in **TABLE 2-13**.

TABLE 2-13

PRONUNCIATIONS OF ACCENTED *I* FOLLOWING ANOTHER VOWEL		
SPANISH	PRONUNCIATION	ENGLISH
caída	kah-EE-dah	fall
día	DEE-ah	day
freír	freh-EER	to fry
friísimo	free-EE-see-moh	most cold
frío	FREE-oh	cold
(la) huida	(lah) oo-EE-dah	(the) escape
líe	LEE-eh	he deceives
lío	LEE-oh	mess
maíz	mah-EES	corn
oír	oh-EER	to hear
país	pah-EES	country
panadería	pah-nah-deh-REE-ah	bakery
reír	rreh-EER	to laugh
roí	rroh-EE	I gnawed

In *ui* combinations, as in the *ue* combinations, the *u* is silent when it is preceded by a *g* or a *q*. That is, the *ui* combination sounds like *i*. See **TABLE 2-14** for examples.

TABLE 2-14

PRONUNCIATIONS OF *UI* PRECEDED BY *G* OR *Q*		
SPANISH	PRONUNCIATION	ENGLISH
Arequipa	ah-reh-KEE-pah	a city in Peru
guiñar	ghee-NYAHR	to wink
guisado	ghee-SAH-doh	stew
guitarra	ghee-TAH-rrah	guitar
quiero	KYEH-roh	I want
quitar	KEE-tahr	to take away
siguiente	see-GYEHN-teh	following
siquiera	see-KYEH-rah	at least

The Vowel *O*

The sixteenth letter of the Spanish alphabet is a *vocal fuerte* and is spoken through a medium-sized opening between the palate and the tongue. The letter o has the sound "oh" similar to, but actually shorter than, the "o" in the English word "toll." To practice your pronunciation, repeat out loud the words listed in **TABLE 2-15**.

TABLE 2-15

PRONUNCIATIONS OF *O*		
SPANISH	**PRONUNCIATION**	**ENGLISH**
olor	oh-LOHR	smell
olvidar	ohl-vee-DAHR	to forget
oreja	oh-REH-hhah	exterior ear
oro	OH-roh	gold
operar	oh-peh-RAH	to operate
ojo	OH-hhoh	eye
oler	oh-LEHR	to smell
golpe	GOHL-peh	blow, hit
mozo	MOH-soh	waiter
mortal	mohr-TAHL	fatal

Combinations with o follow the same rules as other *vocales abiertas* and *vocales cerradas* with an accent, with the one exception being the *ou* combination. To practice saying *oa, oe, oí, oi, oo,* and *ou* combinations, see **TABLE 2-16**.

TABLE 2-16

PRONUNCIATIONS OF *O* WITH OTHER VOWELS		
SPANISH	**PRONUNCIATION**	**ENGLISH**
alcohol	ahl-KOH-ohl	alcohol
bou	BOH-oo	two-boat net fishing
cohibir	koy-BEER	to inhibit
coincidir	koyn-SEE-deer	to coincide
oasis	oh-AH-sees	oasis

oído	oh-EE-doh	internal ear
oigo	OY-goh	I hear
poema	poh-EH-mah	poem
roedor	roh-eh-DOHR	rodent
toalla	toh-AH-yah	towel
zoológico	soh-oh-LOH-hhi-koh	zoo

The Vowel *U*

The twenty-third letter of the *abecedario* is *vocal débil* and is spoken through a small-to-medium opening between the palate and the tongue. The letter *u* often adopts the "oo" sound as is found in "too." See **TABLE 2-17** to practice with some examples.

TABLE 2-17

PRONUNCIATIONS OF *U*		
SPANISH	**PRONUNCIATION**	**ENGLISH**
blusa	BLOO-sah	blouse
crudo	KROO-doh	raw
curso	KOOR-soh	course
dulce	DOOL-seh	sweet
luna	LOO-nah	moon
menú	meh-NOO	menu
nube	NOO-beh	cloud
turco	TOOR-koh	Turk
unir	oo-NEER	to unite
uña	OO-nyah	fingernail
usar	oo-SAHR	to use
útil	OO-teel	useful

You've already seen many different *u* combinations. In general, an unaccented *u* in combination with other *vocales* takes on a *sonido* (soh-NEE-doh, "sound") similar to the English "w." The exceptions to this rule involve the position of the *u*. The *u* is mute in the following combinations: *gue, gui, que,* and *qui* (**TABLE 2-18**).

TABLE 2-18

PRONUNCIATIONS WHEN *U* IS MUTE

SPANISH	PRONUNCIATION	ENGLISH
antiguo	ahn-TEE-gwoh	old
averiguar	ah-veh-ree-GWAHR	to inquire
cuidar	cwee-DAHR	to care for
deuda	DEHW-dah	debt
huevo	WEH-voh	egg
huir	weer	to flee
máquina	MAH-kee-nah	machine
rueda	RWEH-dah	wheel

However, there are a few words where the *u* in the diphthong is NOT mute. To indicate that the *u* should be pronounced, a *diéresis* (¨) is added over it (*ü*). **TABLE 2-19** illustrates examples of words with *güe* and *güi*. Note that *qüe* and *qüi* do not exist in Spanish.

TABLE 2-19

PRONUNCIATIONS OF *GÜE* AND *GÜI*

SPANISH	PRONUNCIATION	ENGLISH
bilingüe	bee-LEEN-gweh	bilingual
cigüeña	see-GWEH-nyah	stork
desagüe	dehs-AH-gweh	drain
pingüino	peen-GWEE-noh	penguin
yegüita	yeh-GWEE-tah	small mare

If naturally stressed or accented within a word, *u* keeps its "oo" sound (see **TABLE 2-20**).

TABLE 2-20

PRONUNCIATIONS OF ACCENTED *U*

SPANISH	PRONUNCIATION	ENGLISH
ataúd	ah-tah-OOD	coffin
baúl	bah-OOL	chest or trunk
grúa	GROO-ah	crane
laúd	lah-OOD	lute

CHAPTER 3

Pronunciation II: Consonants and Accents

Spanish consonants are a little tougher than Spanish vowels— Spanish has a few more consonants than English, and when combined with other letters, some consonants take on different pronunciations. Take your time; if you feel that this chapter has too much information to learn at one sitting, take breaks and go back occasionally to review what you've learned.

Introducing the Consonants

Las consonantes (the consonants) are those letters that produce sounds with the help of *las vocales* (the vowels). Many Spanish consonants are very similar to their English counterparts. There are twenty-three consonants: *b, c, d, f, g, h, j, k, l, m, n, ñ, p, q, r, rr, s, t, v, w, x, y,* and **z**, as well as *ch* and *ll* (though they are no longer considered separate letters). This chapter will examine the Spanish consonants by breaking them down into smaller groups, as follows:

- *b* and *v*
- *c, k,* and *q*
- *c, s,* and *z*
- *d* and *f*
- *g* and *j*
- *h*
- *k* and *w*

- *l* and *ll*
- *m, n,* and *ñ*
- *p*
- *r* and *rr*
- *t*
- *x* and *y*

Pronunciation of Spanish Consonants
The Consonants B and V

Nowadays Spanish *b* and *v* are widely considered identical in sound. When spoken by native speakers, the brevity of the sound attributed to these letters may give this impression. This book forsakes this modern simplification of their pronunciations for that of the older, more correct, standard.

B is a *consonante labial* ("labial consonant," or consonant formed by the lips). It is formed at the union of one's upper and lower lips and is a clipped version of the American English "b." *M* and *p* also belong to the *labial* category. *V,* on the other hand, is a *consonante dentolabial* ("dentolabial consonant," formed by the lips and the teeth). It is formed at the union of one's upper front teeth and lower lip and is similar to, though softer than, the American English "v." *F* also belongs to the *dentolabial* category. **TABLE 3-1** gives examples of pronunciations for both *b* and *v.*

TABLE 3-1

PRONUNCIATIONS OF *B* AND *V*		
SPANISH	PRONUNCIATION	ENGLISH
barón	bah-ROHN	baron
baso	BAH-soh	I base
devolver	deh-vohl-VEHR	to return
tubo	TOO-boh	tube
tuvo	TOO-voh	(s)he had
vaca	VAH-cah	cow

Here's a *trabalenguas* ("tongue twister") for you to practice pronouncing *b* and *v*:

Pablito clavó un clavito. (Little Pablo nailed a little nail.)
Un clavito clavó Pablito. (A little nail was nailed by little Pablo.)
¿Qué clavó Pablito? (What did little Pablo nail?)
Un clavito clavó Pablito. (A little nail was nailed by little Pablo.)

The Consonants *C*, *K*, and *Q*

C (except in combinations *ce, ci,* and *ch*), *q,* and *k* share the American English "k" sound. Try saying the words in **TABLE 3-2** out loud.

TABLE 3-2

PRONOUNCIATIONS OF *CA, CO, CU, Q,* AND *K*					
coser	to sew/stitch	*blanco*	white	*acabar*	to finish
mecánico	mechanic(al)	*placa*	license plate	*sacar*	to draw out
kilo	kilogram	*kilómetro*	kilometer	*kilovatio*	kilowatt
quebrar	to break	*quedar*	to remain	*quejarse*	to complain
quizás	perhaps	*quijada*	jaw	*aquel*	that

Here's a *trabalenguas* to practice your *c*s:

Compadre, cómprame un coco. (Friend, buy me a coconut.)
Compadre, yo no compro coco. (Friend, I don't buy coconuts.)

Porque como poco coco, (Because I eat so little coconut,)
poco coco compro. (I seldom buy coconuts.)

The Consonants *C, S,* and *Z*

The Spanish **s** is easy. It sounds the same as the American English "s." How you should pronounce **c** (in combinations *ce* and *ci*) and **z** will vary, depending on the dialect of Spanish you use. In Latin America and Andalusia (a region in southern Spain), they are also pronounced as "s." In most regions of Spain, **c** (when followed by *e* or *i*) and **z** sound like the American English "th" sound in "thin."

FACTS

You might have noticed that natives of Latin America who learn English have difficulty with the "th" sounds in words like "thin" or "thought." That is because this sound does not exist in Latin American Spanish.

As practice, try saying the words in **TABLE 3-3** out loud.

TABLE 3-3

PRONUNCIATIONS OF *CE, CI, S,* AND *Z*					
accidente	accident	*acecinar*	to dry-cure	*aceituna*	olive
centeno	rye	*cerca*	near	*lucir*	to shine
cintura	waist	*ciruela*	plum	*posible*	possible
asesinar	to murder	*esbozo*	outline	*salpicar*	to sprinkle
tasa	measure	*taza*	cup/bowl	*omisión*	omission

Here's a *trabalenguas* to practice your **s** sounds:

Solo sé una cosa, y eso es que solo sé
(I only know one thing, and that is the only thing I know)
que no sé nada, y si sé que no sé nada
(that I know nothing, and if I know that I know nothing)
algo sé, porque entonces sé una cosa
(I know something, because then I know one thing,)

siquiera sea una sola, esto es:
(though it be only one, this is:)
sé que no sé nada.
(I know that I know nothing.)

The Combination *Ch*

Ch (cheh) sounds like the American English "ch" in "church." Dictionaries published before 1994 listed *ch* as a separate letter after *c*. Now words that begin with a *ch* can be found under the letter *c*, between *ce* and *ci*. Use **TABLE 3-4** to practice words with *ch*.

TABLE 3-4

PRONUNCIATIONS OF *CH*					
cheque	check	*chuleta*	(pork chop)	*chanclas*	slippers
cuchillo	knife	*chicle*	chewing gum	*choclo*	overshoe, corn
chocolate	chocolate	*poncho*	poncho, cape	*ancho*	wide, broad
colchón	mattress	*echar*	to throw out	*hecho*	fact, deed

The Consonants *D* and *F*

The Spanish *d* is another dentolingual consonant. As such, it is pronounced a little more like "th" in the English words "the" or "this" or "that" than like the "d" in "dad" (with clenched teeth). Try to practice this by placing the very tip of your tongue between your teeth and saying English words that begin with "d." Use **TABLE 3-5** to practice your pronunciation of the Spanish *d*.

TABLE 3-5

PRONUNCIATIONS OF *D*					
docto	learned/expert	*debajo*	under(neath)	*ceder*	surrender
madrina	godmother	*madrugar*	to rise early	*pedazo*	piece
sudar	to sweat	*dependiente*	clerk	*tenedor*	fork
redactar	to compose	*redondo*	round	*perder*	to lose

F belongs to *las consonantes dentolabiales* and is pronounced as the English "f" in "food." The peculiarities associated with this letter are that no other letter, or combination of letters, produces this sound. This means that English cognates using "ph" and "ff" are transformed to employ a single *f*: for example, the English word "telephone" becomes *teléfono* in Spanish. Try saying the words in **TABLE 3-6** out loud to practice pronouncing the Spanish *f*.

TABLE 3-6

PRONUNCIATIONS OF F					
fácil	easy	*ferocidad*	fierceness	*fijar*	to fasten
febril	feverish	*elefante*	elephant	*diferente*	different
fachada	façade	*fiar*	to trust, lend	*difícil*	difficult

The Consonants G and J

When *g* is followed by any consonant or *a, o,* or *u,* it sounds like the American English "g" in "golf." **TABLE 3-7** has some examples for you to practice with.

TABLE 3-7

PRONUNCIATIONS OF G BEFORE A, O, AND U					
gordo	fat	*bolígrafo*	pen	*halagüeño*	attractive
rogar	to plead	*entregar*	to hand over	*vergüenza*	shame, shyness
gusto	pleasure	*guardar*	to store	*gusano*	worm, caterpillar
gozar	to enjoy	*gloria*	glory	*grueso*	thick, stout

G (in combinations *ge* and *gi*) and *j* share a sound not found in American English—an overemphasized "hh" that starts at the back of the throat. Try saying the words listed in **TABLE 3-8** out loud, emphasizing your *g*s and *j*s:

TABLE 3-8

PRONUNCIATIONS OF GE, GI, AND J					
escoger	to choose	*genial*	pleasant	*gesto*	facial gesture
contagioso	contagious	*exigir*	to demand, require	*lógico*	logical
ejemplo	example	*joya*	jewel	*juez*	judge
masaje	massage	*paisaje*	landscape	*reloj*	watch

The Consonant *H*

H in Spanish is a relic—once upon a time, it was used to designate an aspirated sound that no longer exists. Today, it is silent, unless coupled with the letter *c* to denote "ch." Note the pronunciations of the words containing *h* in **TABLE 3-9**, and practice saying them out loud.

TABLE 3-9

PRONUNCIATIONS WITH *H*		
SPANISH	**PRONUNCIATION**	**ENGLISH**
desahogo	dehs-ah-OH-goh	emotional relief
exhalar	ex-ah-LAHR	to exhale
hábil	AH-beel	skillful
hábito	AH-bee-toh	habit
hablar	ah-BLAHR	to speak
rehusar	reh-oo-SAHR	to refuse

The Consonants *K* and *W*

These letters are not native to Spanish but exist to spell a limited number of foreign terms. They are pronounced the same as in English—take a look at **TABLE 3-10** to review some words containing letter *k* or *w*.

TABLE 3-10

PRONUNCIATIONS WITH *K* OR *W*			
káiser	*kinesiologia*	*kilogramo*	*kiwi*
wagneriano	*Walkman*	*Washington*	*wIndsur fIslu*

The Consonant *L* and Combination *Ll*

The single *l* is among the few letters that consistently has the same exact pronunciation in Spanish as in English. Keep in mind, however, that unlike the English, where the *ll* is virtually indistinguishable from *l*, in Spanish their sounds are quite different. To practice a few words with *l*, try saying the words in **TABLE 3-11** out loud.

TABLE 3-11

PRONUNCIATIONS OF THE SINGLE L		
SPANISH	PRONUNCIATION	ENGLISH
ladrón	lah-THROHN	thief
lechuga	leh-CHOO-gah	lettuce
lujo	LOO-hhoh	luxury
perla	PEHR-lah	pearl
sal	sahl	salt

Ll has many pronunciations, depending on where the speaker is from. Pronunciations differ even within regions of the same country. The most common *ll* equivalent is y (see below).

ESSENTIALS

Other pronunciations of *ll* employed in Latin America include: the "ly" sound in "million"; the "j" sound in "treasure"; or the "sh" sound in "she."

Try saying the words in **TABLE 3-12** out loud.

TABLE 3-12

PRONUNCIATIONS OF THE COMBINATION LL		
SPANISH	PRONUNCIATION	ENGLISH
caballo	kah-BAH-yoh	horse
cabello	kah-BEH-yoh	hair
hallar	ah-YAHR	to find
millón	mee-YOHN	million

The Consonants M, N, and Ñ

M and *n* have the same sounds as their respective English counterparts. Unlike in English, however, the "mm" combination does not exist in Spanish. Some English words employing "nn" are translated with this combination intact, but most use a single "n." Take a look at **TABLE 3-13** for examples.

TABLE 3-13

PRONUNCIATIONS OF *M* AND *N*		
SPANISH	PRONUNCIATION	ENGLISH
anual	ah-NWAHL	annual
anunciar	ah-noon-SYAHR	to announce
comercial	coh-mehr-SYAHL	commercial
innovar	een-noh-VAHR	to innovate
inocente	ee-noh-SEHN-teh	innocent
recomendar	reh-coh-mehn-DAHR	to recommend

M and *n* are fairly easy to understand—they are very similar to their English counterparts. However, what about that ñ? The closest American English approximation to ñ, pronounced "EH-nyeh," is the "ni" sound in "onion." Try practicing this sound with the words listed in **TABLE 3-14**.

TABLE 3-14

PRONUNCIATIONS OF Ñ		
SPANISH	PRONUNCIATION	ENGLISH
acompañar	ah-kohm-PAH-nyahr	to accompany
año	AH-nyoh	year
compañero	cohm-pah-NYEH-roh	companion
niñez	nee-NYEHS	childhood
puño	POO-nyoh	fist
reñir	REH-nyeer	to quarrel

The Consonant P

P is very similar to the American English "p," minus the trailing breath. The clipped nature of both *b* and *p* often leads to confusion between the two. Again, as with other letters that are doubled in English, *p* is never combined with itself. Practice saying the words in **TABLE 3-15** out loud.

TABLE 3-15	PRONUNCIATIONS OF *P*				
poesía	poetry	*aplicar*	to apply	*papel*	paper, role
platicar	to chat	*pelea*	fight	*aparecer*	to appear
episodio	episode	*hipo*	hiccup	*oponer*	to oppose

The Consonant R and Combination Rr

The Spanish *r* is the letter that gives people the most trouble, because it must be trilled. Remember that all *rr*s and the *r*s at the beginning of a word are generally held longer than other *r*s. Begin practicing your trilled *r*s with the words listed in **TABLE 3-16**.

TABLE 3-16	PRONUNCIATIONS OF *R*	
SPANISH	**PRONUNCIATION**	**ENGLISH**
bucear	boo-seh-AHR	to scuba-dive
raíz	rrah-EES	root, origin
reto	RREH-toh	challenge
sierra	SYEH-rrah	mountain range
terreno	teh-RREH-noh	land, field

Here's a *trabalenguas* with *r*s:

El perro de San Roque no tiene rabo (The dog from San Roque
   doesn't have a tail)
porque Ramón Ramírez se lo ha robado. (because Ramon Ramirez
   has stolen it.)

The Consonant T

The Spanish *T* is a *consonante dentolingual*, and is similar to the "t" in "total." *T*, however, is pronounced with a short burst and the tip of the tongue positioned between both sets of teeth. The difference in these sounds is very subtle. Keep in mind also that Spanish does not have the "th" or "tt" combinations. As a result, when translating English words that employ these combinations, Spanish simply replaces them with a single *t*. Use **TABLE 3-17** to practice your pronunciation of the Spanish *t*.

TABLE 3-17

PRONUNCIATIONS OF *T*					
atención	attention	*atraer*	to attract	*autor*	author
catedral	cathedral	*techo*	roof	*tela*	fabric
tinto	tinged, red (wine)	*tocar*	to touch, play	*tomar*	to take
tomate	tomato	*tos*	a cough	*triste*	sad

The Consonants X and Y

The letter *x* has different pronunciations depending on its position within the *palabra* (word). Between vowels, within *exce-* and *exci-* combinations, and at the end of the word, it sounds like "ks" or "gs." In some regions, when an *x* begins a word or is situated between a vowel and a consonant, it has an "s" sound. In some words, it sounds the same as the Spanish *ge* or *j* (that is, like an overemphasized American English "h"). It also takes on a "sh" sound in some words that originate from indigenous Latin American languages. Fortunately, you won't encounter this letter very often. Take a look at **TABLE 3-18** for some examples.

TABLE 3-18

PRONUNCIATIONS OF *X*		
SPANISH	**PRONUNCIATION**	**ENGLISH**
examen	ehk-SAH-mehn	exam
excelente	ehk-seh-LEHN-teh	excellent
excitante	ehk-see-TAHN-teh	exciting
exhibir	ehk-see-BEER	to exhibit
extranjero	es-trahn-HHEH-roh	foreigner
Ixtapa	eesh-TAH-pah	a town in Mexico
mexicano	meh-hhee-KAH-noh	Mexican
texano	teh-HHAH-noh	Texan
Tuxtla	TOOSH-tlah	a volcano; various towns in Mexico
xilófono	see-LOH-foh-noh	xylophone

You might have learned a long time ago that the American English vowels included "a," "e," "i," "o," "u," and sometimes "y." Though not considered *una vocal* in the strictest sense, the Spanish y usually acts like the *vocal i* when it sounds like the "y" in "yam." *Ay, ey,* and *oy* share their pronunciations with *ai, ei,* and *oi,* respectively; *uy* sounds like "oo-y." On its own, y sounds like "ee." Practice pronouncing y with the words listed in **TABLE 3-19**.

TABLE 3-19

PRONUNCIATIONS OF Y		
SPANISH	PRONUNCIATION	ENGLISH
apoyo	ah-POH-yoh	support
hay	ai	there is, there are
hoy	oi	today
muy	mooy	very
raya	RRah-yah	line
rey	rrei	king
suyo	SOO-yoh	yours
yerno	YEHR-noh	son-in-law

You've done it! You've just completed the Spanish alphabet! Take this time to pat yourself on the back—you deserve it. If you liked practicing Spanish pronunciations by doing tongue twisters, search for more online—just enter *trabalenguas* into a search engine, and see where it takes you.

Introducing Accent Marks

Now that you know how to read each Spanish letter, you need to learn something else that will help you put letters together into syllables and words—the rules for choosing which syllable in a word should be stressed, and the purpose of accent marks.

If you've ever tried your hand at French, you know that accent marks are often arbitrary—and there are four different ones to choose from! In Spanish, you only have one accent mark (*el acento agudo,* an acute accent mark), denoted as (´) and placed over the vowel to indicate that the syllable should be stressed. Only the words that do not follow the normal rules of Spanish actually have accent marks. These rules are:

1. If a word ends with an *n*, an *s*, or a vowel, the emphasis is placed on the second-to-last syllable within that word. These words are known as *palabras llanas*.
2. If a word ends in a consonant other than *n* or *s*, the emphasis is placed on the last syllable within that word. These words are known as *palabras agudas*.

If a word is not accented according to these simple rules, the accented syllable is denoted with an accent mark. Every Spanish word is classified in terms of where the word is accented, implicitly or explicitly. In addition to *llanas* and *agudas*, words are also categorized as *esdrújulas* (accented on the third-to-last syllable) and *sobresdrújulas* (accented on the fourth-to-last syllable and beyond).

Accents provide you with more than a pronunciation guide. In English, some words require a context to know their pronunciation and meaning. Compare "The project is due tomorrow" and "He wanted to project an air of confidence." In Spanish, accent marks are sometimes used to help distinguish words. Take a look at a few examples in **TABLE 3-20**. Note that the only difference between these pairs is the accent mark—their pronunciations are exactly the same.

TABLE 3-20

EXAMPLES OF USING ACCENT MARKS TO DISTINGUISH WORDS					
SPANISH	PRONUNCIATION	ENGLISH	SPANISH	PRONUNCIATION	ENGLISH
él	ehl	he	*el*	ehl	the*
qué	keh	what	*que*	keh	that
sólo	SOH-loh	only	*solo*	SOH-loh	alone

* (definite article used with male nouns)

Practice Your Accent Marks

Figure out whether each of the following words is *aguda*, *llana*, *esdrújula*, or *sobresdrújula*. Check your answers in the back of the book.

revista	magazine
voluntad	will
fácilmente	easily
ferrocarril	railway
huésped	guest
espíritu	spirit
pásasela	pass it to him
tráigamelos	bring them to me
mínimo	minimum

Use the following pronunciations to try spelling each Spanish word. Remember to use accent marks where appropriate. Check your answers in the back of the book.

ah-TRAHS

dehs-PWEHS

CAHR-sehl

TEE-ah

hhoh-SEH

leh-HHEE-tee-moh

pah-GAHR

hhoo-vehn-TOOD

AHL-hheh-brah

CHAPTER 4

Subjects:
Who Are You?

A s you might remember from grade school, every sentence has at least one subject—the thing or person who performs the action indicated by the verb. This chapter has all you need to know about the subject of a Spanish sentence to get you on your way to start putting together complete sentences.

Determining the Gender

Most of the time, the subject of your sentence will be a noun. Nouns work the same way in Spanish as they do in English—with one major exception. In Spanish, all nouns have an assigned gender, whether the noun represents a person, place, or thing. The sex of a noun is either natural, referring to people who do have an established gender, or grammatical, where gender has been arbitrarily assigned to things or concepts.

Natural Gender

Most nouns in this category come in two versions: masculine and feminine. Take a look at **TABLE 4-1**.

TABLE 4-1

NATURAL GENDER NOUNS	
MASCULINE	FEMININE
muchacho (boy)	*muchacha* (girl)
perro (male dog)	*perra* (female dog)
doctor (male doctor, professor)	*doctora* (female doctor, professor)
inglés (Englishman)	*inglesa* (Englishwoman)
hombre (man)	*mujer* (woman)
toro (bull)	*vaca* (cow)

Did you notice any trends? Actually, there are four basic rules for dealing with natural gender nouns:

1. When a masculine noun ends in –o, substitute an –a to make it feminine. For example, *muchacho* becomes *muchacha*, and *perro* becomes *perra*.
2. When a masculine noun ends in a consonant, add an –a at the end to make it feminine. For example, *doctor* becomes *doctora*, and *inglés* becomes *inglesa*.
3. Sometimes nouns have only one gender. For example, there is no corresponding feminine noun for *hombre*, so use *mujer*; *toro* becomes *vaca*.

4. Sometimes the same word may be used for both genders; in these cases, the gender is specified by articles or adjectives. This rule includes (but is not limited to) words that end in —ista or —e For example, *el periodista* becomes *la periodista*, *el estudiante* becomes *la estudiante*, and *el modelo* becomes *la modelo*. (You will learn all about articles later in this chapter.)

Grammatical (Assigned) Gender

Grammatical gender does not follow a logical pattern and must be memorized. You can, however, identify some cases of grammatical gender by looking at the endings (see **TABLES 4-2** and **4-3**).

ESSENTIALS

Keep in mind that islands, letters of the alphabet, cars, and firms are generally expressed with feminine nouns. Rivers, ships, months, mountains, volcanoes, watches, planes, languages, and metals tend to be expressed with masculine nouns.

TABLE 4-2

	MASCULINE ENDINGS		
ENDING	EXAMPLE	ENGLISH	FEMININE EXCEPTIONS
-aje	*viaje*	journey	n/a
-men	*examen*	exam	n/a
-gen	*origen*	origin	*imagen* (image), *margen* (margin)
-or	*doctor*	male doctor	*labor* (work)
-o	*libro*	book	*mano* (hand)

TABLE 4-3

	FEMININE ENDINGS		
ENDING	EXAMPLE	ENGLISH	MASCULINE EXCEPTIONS
-dad	*verdad*	truth	n/a
-ud	*salud*	health	*ataúd* (coffin)
-ed	*merced*	mercy	n/a
-ión	*religión*	religion	concrete nouns like *gorrión* (sparrow)
-umbre	*costumbre*	custom	n/a

FEMININE ENDINGS *(continued)*			
ENDING	EXAMPLE	ENGLISH	MASCULINE EXCEPTIONS
-ie	*serie*	series	n/a
-sis	*síntesis*	synthesis	*analysis, énfasis, éxtasis* (ecstasy)
-a	*libra*	pound, lb.	*mapa* (map); abstract nouns like *problema*

Some nouns are feminine even though they end with an -o because they are really abbreviations. For example, *foto* (photo) is a feminine noun because it is really *fotografía* (photograph), and ends with an -a.

An "S" for Plural

Making nouns plural is easy, because in most cases the concept is the same as in English—just add an -s or an -es. Well, there are some variations, so take a look at the following rules:

1. When the noun ends with an unstressed vowel, just add an –s. For example, *playa* (beach) becomes *playas* in plural.
2. When the noun ends with a consonant other than -s, add an –es. For example, *flor* (flower) becomes *flores* in plural.
3. When the noun ends with a stressed vowel, add an –es. For example, *iraní* (Iranian) becomes *iraníes*; *inglés* (Englishman) becomes *ingleses* in plural.
4. When the noun ends with an unstressed vowel and -s, don't add anything. For example, *crisis* remains *crisis* in the plural.

FACTS

In Spanish, adjectives and articles (both definite and indefinite) are also conjugated by gender and number, to match their respective nouns. You will learn more details in the following sections.

How Articles Can Help

So far, all these rules may have left you dismayed. Do you really have to keep all those noun endings in mind just to establish the gender? Well, here is where the articles can help. Once you know the article, you can figure out whether the noun is feminine or masculine, singular or plural. Just as in English, they may be divided into definite and indefinite.

Definite Articles

With the exception of proper names, Spanish articles are employed liberally with most nouns. Keep in mind that articles must agree with the nouns they modify in gender and number—that is, they may be feminine or masculine, singular or plural (take a look at **TABLE 4-4**).

TABLE 4-4

	DEFINITE ARTICLE (THE)	
	MASCULINE	FEMININE
Singular	*el*	*la*
Plural	*los*	*las*

Exceptions to the Rule

How a word is stressed plays a significant role in determining the article used with it, so the exception rule goes as follows: A masculine article is always used before the singular form of a word beginning with a stressed *a* or *ha*. Take a look at some examples in **TABLE 4-5**.

TABLE 4-5

	EXCEPTIONS		
SINGULAR	PRONUNCIATION	PLURAL	ENGLISH
el agua	(AH-gwah)	*las aguas*	the water(s)
el águila	(AH-gee-lah)	*las águilas*	the eagle(s)
el alma	(AHL-mah)	*las almas*	the soul(s)
el ave	(AH-veh)	*las aves*	the bird(s)

**E**SSENTIALS   When you learn a new noun, rather than making up mnemonic devices or memorizing complicated rules, memorize nouns with *la* or *el* before them—it's much easier. For example, "the house" is *la casa*, so you know that this noun is feminine.

An Aside on Prepositions

Here is another important point to remember—when the masculine definite article follows prepositions *a* or *de*, they form a contraction: *a* + *el* = *al*; *de* + *el* = *del*. Try pronouncing *a el* quickly and then switch to *al*; you'll quickly see why Spanish speakers formed this contraction: It's a lot easier and faster to pronounce. And the same goes for the transformation from *de el* to *del*.

QUESTIONS?

What is a contraction?
When two words combine to form one, they form a contraction. Contractions in English are very common: "isn't," "can't," and "don't" are just a few examples.

The Preposition *A*

En español, a is a preposition that expresses movement toward something, be it physical or conceptual, within space or time. *A* often acts as an equivalent of "to" or "at" in English. If someone were to ask, "Where are you going?" you might reply, "to the store" or *a la tienda*. Similarly, if you were asked, "At what time is your meeting" you could say "at three" or *a las tres*.

Certain verbs always appear with the preposition *a*. Some of these include verbs listed in **TABLE 4-6**.

TABLE 4-6

VERBS WITH PREPOSITION *A*			
ascender a	to ascend toward	*bajar a*	to go down to
ir a	to go to	*necesitar a*	to need (somebody)
subir a	to go up toward	*venir a*	to come to

FACTS

Spanish also uses a "personal" *a* that has no English translation. Whenever the verb is directed to a person or persons, the *a* is inserted to precede the word that refers to the person or persons. For example: "I see Juan" becomes *yo veo a Juan*, but "I see the dog" would translate to *yo veo el perro*.

A may also be employed to express proximity of position. Refer to **TABLE 4-7** for some examples.

TABLE 4-7

USE OF PREPOSITION *A TO* EXPRESS PROXIMITY	
a cien metros de altura	at one hundred meters of height (from the ground)
a diez manzanas de la casa	(at) ten blocks from the house
a la puerta	at the door
al habla	(at) currently speaking (usually on the telephone)
al quite	at the ready to help someone

Here are some more examples of how *a* may be used in a Spanish sentence:

Susana quiere ir a casa. (Susana wants to go home.)

La escuela está a dos manzanas de la estación de trenes. (The school is two blocks from the train station.)

La vecina viene a conversar. (The neighbor is coming to talk.)

Henri está a la puerta. (Henry is at the door.)

El calor no sube al segundo piso. (The heat does not go up to the second floor.)

Una criatura necesita a su madre. (A young child needs its mother.)

La niña baja a la calle para saludar a su amiga. (The girl goes down to the street to greet her friend.)

El dependiente está al quite con los clientes. (The clerk is at the ready to help with the clients.)

The Preposition *De*

Though *en inglés* you would use two different prepositions, "of" and "from," *en español* you simply use *de*. *De* is often used to express a sense of belonging. In English, you have the construction "'s"—you can say, "Charlie's book," "kids' toys." In Spanish, however, you will need to rely on *de* to convey the same information: *el libro de Charlie* (the book of Charlie), *los juguetes de los niños* (the toys of the kids). Take a look at the following examples of how *de* is used in the Spanish sentence.

La mesa es de madera. (The table is made of wood.)
Jonathan es de Chicago. (Jonathan is from Chicago.)
La muñeca de Jenny es de Inglaterra. (Jenny's doll is from England.)
Yo soy la hija de Luis y Anna Moncayo. (I am the daughter of Luis and Anna Moncayo.)
El pan es de trigo. (The bread is made of wheat.)
Yo estoy en clase de dos a tres. (I am in class from two to three.)

Article's Role in the Meaning of the Noun

Some grammatically gendered nouns may appear as either masculine or feminine, but their meanings are often unrelated and depend on the gender. Some of these nouns are listed in **TABLE 4-8**.

TABLE 4-8

NOUNS THAT RELY ON ARTICLES FOR MEANING			
MASCULINE NOUN	**ENGLISH**	**FEMININE NOUN**	**ENGLISH**
el capital	the sum of money (business)	*la capital*	the capital of a city
el cólera	the cholera	*la cólera*	the anger
el coma	the coma	*la coma*	the comma
el cometa	the comet	*la cometa*	the kite
el corte	the cut	*la corte*	the court
el cura	the priest	*la cura*	the cure
el frente	the front line in battle	*la frente*	forehead
el guía	the person who guides	*la guía*	the book, booklet
el orden	the opposite of chaos	*la orden*	the command
el pez	the fish	*la pez*	the tar

Indefinite Articles

In English, the indefinite articles include "a" or "an," which are used only with singular nouns. Spanish speakers use *un* or *una* (depending on the gender of the noun) as equivalents to "a" or "an," and also use the indefinite articles *unos* and *unas* when the nouns are plural—you might think of these articles as meaning "some" (see **TABLE 4-9**).

TABLE 4-9

INDEFINITE ARTICLES ("A," "AN," OR "SOME")		
	MASCULINE	**FEMININE**
Singular	*un*	*una*
Plural	*unos*	*unas*

For example:

un coche	a car	*unos coches*	some cars
una actriz	an actress	*unas actrices*	some actresses

Note that in Spanish, *uno* means "one," and *unos* and *unas* are the masculine and feminine versions of "some." When applying a Spanish "one" to a masculine noun, *uno* loses its final vowel. For example, *un libro* could be translated as "one book" or "a book," depending on context.

From Nouns to Pronouns

A subject may be a noun or a pronoun; basically, pronouns are words that are used to substitute for nouns: "you" can replace "the reader," "his" may be used instead of "John Smith's," and "them" might refer to "the students." In English, "I," "we," "you," "he," "she," "it," and "they" are known as subject pronouns (see **TABLE 4-10**). In Spanish, subject pronouns are organized in the same way—see **TABLE 4-11**.

TABLE 4-10

PERSONAL PRONOUNS IN ENGLISH		
	SINGULAR	PLURAL
First Person	I	we
Second Person	you	you (or y'all)
Third Person	he, she, it	they

TABLE 4-11

PERSONAL PRONOUNS IN SPANISH		
	SINGULAR	PLURAL
First Person	yo	*nosotros* (m), *nosotras* (f)
Second Person	*tú, usted*	*ustedes*
Third Person	*él* (m), *ella* (f)	*ellos* (m), *ellas* (f)

Subject pronouns in Spanish and English are organized by person (first, second, or third) and number (singular or plural), but if you compare the two tables, you may notice two differences. In Spanish, *nosotros* is the equivalent of "we" when referring to males or mixed groups, while *nosotras* refers to females only. Furthermore, *tú, usted*, and *ustedes* all translate as different forms of "you," depending on the number of people and the degree of politeness.

FACTS

Latin American Spanish does not offer a specifically familiar second-person plural form—the plural equivalent of *tú*. *Ustedes* is used to address people both formally and informally. However, the Spanish of some regions in Spain does retain a word for the familiar second-person plural: *vosotros*. This book does not provide the endings for verb forms conjugated for *vosotros*.

Tú Versus Usted

Have you noticed that the pronoun chart above lists three forms of "you"—*tú, usted*, and *ustedes*? *Ustedes* is the easiest one to explain.

You've noticed that all pronouns are divided into singular and plural ones. But in English, "you" is the same, whether you address one person or a group of people (unless you use the term "y'all"). Well, in Spanish, the plural "you" is *ustedes*—use it to address more than one person. And what's the difference between *tú* and *usted*? Both translate to the singular "you"; *usted* is a polite term, while *tú* is more informal.

ESSENTIALS   If you read in Spanish, you will soon encounter *Ud.* and *Uds.*, which are simply contractions of *usted* and *ustedes*, much like the contraction of "Mister" to "Mr." (When they appear as contractions, *Ud.* and *Uds.* are always capitalized.)

Use the following rule of thumb when debating whether to choose *tú* or *usted*: *tú* should be used to address your friends, or by permission only. When in doubt, it's always best to be polite. The verb for using the *tú* form is *tutear*. *Me puede tutear* means "you can use the *tú* form with me." For a more detailed list of guidelines you may want to keep in mind, refer to **TABLE 4-12**.

TABLE 4-12

USTED VERSUS *TÚ*	
USTED (FORMAL ADDRESS)	*TÚ* (INFORMAL ADDRESS)
Demonstrates respect	Demonstrates acceptance
Used with elders (including your parents)	Used with friends and people your age, as well as with younger people and children
Used with persons of rank or nobility	Used with colleagues (informality pre-established)
Used with strangers	Used with friendly acquaintances
Used to maintain social distance	Used to reduce social distance

It's All About Good Manners

What if you are introduced to your daughter's new friend Carlos, and right away he calls you by your first name, John, or maybe even addresses you as "Jocko" and slaps you on the back? At a certain point, he may seem more disrespectful than friendly. His manners, or lack thereof, may reflect not only poor social skills but a wanting upbringing. This situation is akin to using *tú* inappropriately.

What if the opposite happens? Say your name is Tricia Guzzetta. Every time you see Carlos Verdaguer, the new employee, he addresses you as "Ms. Guzzetta," even though you are two coworkers working in a laid back environment, and you have repeatedly asked Carlos to call you "Trish." Soon, you might begin to think that Carlos is somewhat aloof. After you have tried being appropriately friendly, his use of the polite form may be interpreted as his being an unfriendly person or even a little full of himself.

The person who wants to avoid any conflict might think that simply choosing the polite form of address all the time will help avoid misunderstandings. While this may be true when meeting someone for the first time, it is less so as a relationship develops. Eventually, this person may feel offended. The extended use of *usted* past a socially acceptable point within a relationship is akin to a limp handshake and wandering eyes.

So how do you guide yourself through this potential social minefield? First, unless you are attending an event where informality is actually encouraged, remember that any initial meeting should begin with each party's using the formal form of address, *usted*. An exception might be when you are being introduced to a friend's social circle. Try to pick up on social cues as offered by the people you are meeting. If the situation is social and the party you meet treats you informally, try to determine why they are being familiar. Is it because that person wants you to feel relaxed and within an accepting environment? Or is it that the person is much older than you are and has the social option of being familiar?

If the situation warrants it and you want to break the ice, encourage the person you meet to treat you informally—if this person requests that you do likewise, go ahead. If the person does not reciprocate this request, be straightforward and ask how the person prefers to be treated.

Ask if you may address the person informally, and be prepared for any answer. There is nothing wrong with requesting familiarity as long as you do it formally and don't respond negatively to either answer. Here's what you might say:

> ¿Me permite tratarlo/tratarla a usted de tú?
>> (Do you permit me to treat you in the familiar?)
> ¿Me permite tutearlo/tutearla?
>> (May I use the familiar form of address with you?)
> ¿Lo/La puedo tutear?
>> (Can I use the familiar form of address with you?)

FACTS

"Familiarity breeds contempt" takes on special significance when viewed in light of Spanish history—where centuries ago, noblemen had been known to assault each other with knives when not addressed formally. Fortunately, all you have to worry about now are raised eyebrows.

Common Courtesy

Respect or courtesy (*la cortesía*) may be expressed in a variety of ways. In addition to the formality within verbs, you will find courteous titles similar to the ones used *en ingles* (in English):

señor García	Mr. Garcia
señora Robles	Mrs. Robles
señorita Sánchez	Miss Sanchez

As *en inglés*, Spanish uses *abreviaturas de cortesía*—notice that these abbreviations are capitalized, whereas the full words are capitalized only at the beginning of a sentence:

Sr.	Mr.
Sra.	Mrs.
Srta.	Miss

When addressing a person directly, it is customary to simply say the appropriate title followed by the person's last name:

¿Cómo está (usted), señor Smith?
(How are you, Mr. Smith?)
Señora Sandoval, ¿cómo desea su café?
(Mrs. Sandoval, how do you want your coffee?)
Buenos días, señorita Delgado.
(Good morning Miss Delgado.)

However, when speaking about someone or when identifying yourself and others by title, the definite article is used appropriate to the person's gender:

El Sr. Smith es bombero. (Mr. Smith is a fireman.)
La Sra. Menendez vive en Lima. (Mrs. Menendez lives in Lima.)
Yo soy el Sr. Gómez. (I am Mr. Gomez).
¿Es usted la Srta. Salgado? (Are you Miss Salgado?)

There are two other forms of address that you may come across: *don* and *doña*. Though once used as a title for nobility and land ownership, in many regions *don* and *doña* have simply replaced *señor* and *señora*. In some regions, the term *doña* has evolved into a criticism of sorts, equivalent to a "gossip" or a "busybody."

Politeness in Conversation

By its very nature, polite speech is very structured and almost formulaic. In addition to a universal greeting, a typical encounter will likely include the following query and response:

¿Cómo está (usted)?　　How are you?
Bién, gracias. ¿Y usted?　(I am) well, thank you. And yourself?

The following is a simple dialogue to help you practice what you have learned so far. The conversation is taking place at a conference; Linda Rodriguez and Alonso Calderón have never met before:

Linda: Buenos días, señor. (Good morning, sir.)
Alonso: Buenos días. Yo soy el Sr. Calderón, Alfonso Calderón.
    (Good morning. I am Mr. Calderon—Alfonso Calderon.)
Linda: Linda Rodriguez, con mucho gusto. Me permite tutearlo?
    (Linda Rodriguez, nice to meet you. May I address you
    informally?)
Alonso: Sí. Y la puedo tutearla también? (Yes, and may I address you
    informally too?)
Linda: Sí. ¿Cómo estás? (Yes. How are you?)
Alonso: Muy bien, gracias. ¿Y tú? (Very well, thanks. And you?)
Linda: Muy bien. (Very well.)

Tú or *Usted*?

Write the correct form of address, *tú* or *usted*, that should be used for the following. Refer to the answer key in the Appendix D.

1. Grandmother
2. Younger brother
3. Your local bank's president
4. The family pet
5. A deacon
6. Your best friend
7. Your spouse

It is worth remembering that rules for formal and informal address may vary slightly by country, region, and even socioeconomic status. And sometimes, some people are just more polite than others.

Conjunctions

You can string nouns together with conjunctions—those little words "and," "or," "but," . . . well, you get the point. In Spanish, as in English, conjunctions are the connectors of words, phrases, and complete sentences. They may be divided into two broad forms:

- Those words that relate two or more items of equal function.
- Those words that mark a dependence of one item on another.

The two most basic conjunctions to learn are *y,* which usually translates to "and," and *o,* usually translated as "or" in English. As one-vowel words, these two conjunctions are vulnerable to a particular spelling change that is done to avoid colliding two vowels and losing the sound of *y* and *o.* When *y* precedes a word that begins with *i* or *hi,* it changes to *e.* For example, compare the following two sentences:

Yo soy inteligente y honesto.   (I am intelligent and honest.)
Yo soy honesto e inteligente. (I am honest and intelligent.)

See, to avoid the "*y inteligente*" collision (if you were to pronounce this phrase correctly, you would have to drop one of the ee's because the *y* and the *i* sound exactly the same), the *y* transforms to *e,* which is pronounced "ey."

A similar spelling and pronunciation change occurs with *o.* When it precedes a word that begins with *o* or *ho,* this conjunction will change to *u.* For example:

Quiero seis o siete chocolates.   "I want six or seven chocolates."
Quiero siete u ocho chocolates. "I want seven or eight chocolates."

Again, to avoid the collision of the two "oh" sounds in *o* and *ocho,* the conjunction *o* changes to *u* (pronounced "oo").

Chapter 5

Verbs: What Do You Do?

In this chapter you will continue your development of self-expression by learning about the basic Spanish verbs. Your prior experience will provide you the conceptual tools for successfully completing this material. As with the previous chapters, *relájate, y ¡adelante!* ("relax and forward!")—at your own pace, of course.

Working with the Verbs

El verbo (the verb) is one of the most fundamental building blocks for Spanish expression. With it, you can often describe an action and who is performing that action. The simplest sentence *en inglés* (in English) requires a separate subject and predicate: "I am." *En español* (in Spanish), that sentence becomes simpler still, *Soy.* Because each verb is conjugated according to its subject, its ending will indicate who is doing the action—in this case, the *yo* is optional, and may be dropped.

QUESTIONS?

What does "conjugating" mean?
"Conjugating" refers to modifying a verb based on such factors as number, person, tense, or mood. In Spanish, all verbs must be conjugated according to their subjects for number and person, and also according to the tense and mood that they convey. (To find out what is meant by "mood," refer to the next section.)

A Spanish verb is made up of two parts: the base and the ending. Think of the base as the repository that holds the essence and definition of the verb, and the ending as the personal label indicating who owns the action and when it is occuring. For example: *Camino* (I walk) may be divided into *camin* (base) and *-o* (the ending that indicates a first-person singular subject "I" and the present tense). Furthermore, verbs are subdivided into regular and irregular. To say a verb is regular is to say that its base is unchanged regardless of the ending employed. An irregular verb's base might vary according to a specific conjugation.

The Verb's Mood

Any complete thought that you can convey possesses mood, whether it is by what you say, how you say it, or under what circumstances you say it. When talking about the mood of an expression, you are focusing on the speaker's motivation in stating something in a particular way. The moods that you will encounter in Spanish fall under three general categories.

Indicative

Also known as the active voice, the indicative is the mood with which you try to express "what is" in an objective manner—by using facts, observations, and narration. You can argue (and many would probably agree) that no observation can be objective. This poses no problem in using the indicative; the use of this mood does not depend on truth so much as it depends on the speaker's motivation to lend authority to his or her statements. In a sense, you can say that it is the truth as he, or she, sees it and/or wishes to convince others to see it.

Imperative

With the imperative, you express action as commands, warnings, and requests. Keep in mind that there are no imperious overtones with respect to a command. Also, *en español,* a command and a request are not opposites but actually equivalent. The same structure underlies both; the difference lies in the situation and the tone of voice that you employ. You've seen a form of this mood in the introduction to this chapter, with the command that asked you to relax.

Subjunctive

By using the subjunctive, you try to express "what might be" or "what ought to be." This mood is contrary to the indicative in that it allows expression that is more apparently subjective. As such, it may express doubt, desire, emotion, impersonal opinion, and uncertainty. Native Spanish speakers employ the subjunctive naturally. So much so, that it may become a holy grail of sorts for you to master after you become fairly proficient in the language. You will touch upon the subjunctive in Chapter 16.

The Most Basic Form: Infinitive

The infinitive allows you to speak of a verb without really needing to assign it as an action to anyone or anything. It allows you to speak of an action in the abstract, as a noun. In English, infinitives are verbs preceded by a "to": to be, to go, to stay, and so on. The Spanish infinitives do not have any function words equivalent to the English "to" that precedes them, but you can recognize them by one of three possible endings: *-ar, -er,* and *-ir*. These three groupings spell out general ending assignments that depend on person, number, and time frame.

SSENTIALS Spanish verbs have tenses that correspond loosely with the English present tense, past tense, future tense, and so on. You will start with the present tense, and then concentrate on other tenses as you go through the book.

There Is Nothing Like the Present

Most language books teach present-tense verbs first, since these are generally most straightforward, and also the most useful. You can employ the present tense verbs in situations that describe the following:

- An action that occurs now. For example: *Camino a la parada de bus.* (I walk/am walking to the bus stop.)
- An ongoing experience. For example: *Fumo demasiado.* (I smoke too much.)
- A future act that will occur soon within a specified time frame. For example: *Empiezo el trabajo dentro de un mes.* (I will start the job within a month.)
- An act that you wish to convince yourself, or others, will occur. For example: *Si encuentro un vestido rojo, lo compro.* (If I find a red dress, I will buy it.)

Conjugating Verbs in the Present Tense

Let's first take a look at conjugating regular verbs in the present. Remember: In order to conjugate a verb, you must first determine its infinitive form to figure out whether it belongs to the *-ar, -er,* or *-ir* category. Then, simply drop the infinitive ending, and add the appropriate one to indicate correct person and number (refer to **TABLES 5-1, 5-2,** and **5-3**).

TABLE 5-1

	–AR VERB ENDINGS	
-ar	cantar	to sing (infinitive)
-o	(yo) canto	I sing
-as	(tú) cantas	you sing (informal)
-a	(él, ella) canta	he, she, it sings
	(usted) canta	you sing (formal)
-amos	(nosotros) cantamos	we sing
-an	(ellos, ellas) cantan	they sing
	(ustedes) cantan	you (plural) sing

TABLE 5-2

	–ER VERB ENDINGS	
-er	aprender	to learn (infinitive)
-o	(yo) aprendo	I learn
-es	(tú) aprendes	you learn (informal)
-e	(él, ella) aprende	he, she, it learns
	(usted) aprende	you learn (formal)
-emos	(nosotros) aprendemos	we learn
-en	(ellos, ellas) aprenden	they learn
	(ustedes) aprenden	you (plural) learn

TABLE 5-3

	–IR VERB ENDINGS	
-ir	vivir	to live (infinitive)
-o	(yo) vivo	I live
-es	(tú) vives	you live (informal)
-e	(él, ella) vive	he, she, it lives
	(usted) vive	you live (formal)
-imos	(nosotros) vivimos	we live
-en	(ellos, ellas) viven	they live
	(ustedes) viven	you (plural) live

QUESTIONS?

Why do *usted* **and** *ustedes* **forms take on the verb forms of the third person?**

The explanation is simple: *Usted* is an abbreviation of *vuestra merced* (your mercy), which technically corresponds to "it," a third-person pronoun. Although this phrase was shortened to form the modern pronoun "you," it remained in the third person.

EXERCISE

Practicing Conjugations

The only way you can learn these conjugations is through practice. The list in **TABLE 5-4** contains regular *-ar*, *-er*, and *-ir* verbs. Use them to complete the exercises below. Refer to the answer key at the back of the book for answers.

TABLE 5-4

REGULAR VERBS	
acudir	to frequent (a place)
beber	to drink
buscar	to look for
caminar	to walk
comprar	to buy
cumplir	to carry out, keep
discutir	to discuss
estudiar	to study
hablar	to speak
recibir	to receive
trabajar	to work

Fill in the blanks with the correct form of the verb listed in parentheses.

1. *(Yo)* _____ *(abrir) la puerta para entrar.* (I open the door to come in.)
2. *Nosotros* _____ *(deber) estudiar mejor.* (We should study better.)

3. *Sandra y sus amigas* _____ *(caminar) hacia la parada de autobus.* (Sandra and her friends are walking to the bus stop.)

4. *¿Ustedes* _____ *(asistir) la universidad?* (Do you attend the university?)

5. *(Yo)* _____ *(estudiar) los fines de semana.* (I study on weekends.)

6. *Carlos, ¿por qué (tú)* _____ *(acudir) los restaurantes italianos?* (Carlos, why do you frequent Italian restaurants?)

7. *Juan* _____ *(prometer) hacer sus tareas.* (Juan promises to do his chores.)

8. *Mañana (nosotros)* _____ *(caminar) al trabajo.* (Tomorrow we will walk to work.)

9. *Usted siempre* _____ *(cumplir) con sus promesas.* (You always keep your promises.)

10. *(Yo)* _____ *(aprender) la lección.* (I am learning the lesson.)

11. *(Tú)* _____ *(beber) demasiado.* (You drink too much.)

12. *(Ellas)* _____ *(buscar) a la calle Main.* (They are looking for Main Street.)

13. *¿Ustedes* _____ *(trabajar) en la ciudad?* (Do you work in the city?)

14. *Él* _____ *(recibir) cartas cada día.* (He receives letters every day.)

15. *(Yo)* _____ *(vivir) feliz si gano la lotería.* (I will live happily if I win the lottery.)

16. *Ellos* _____ *(comer) manzanas en el parque.* (They are eating apples in the park.)

17. *Él* _____ *(comprar) leche y galletas en el supermercado.* (He buys milk and cookies at the supermarket.)

18. *María y Luis* _____ *(hablar) por teléfono.* (Maria and Luis are talking on the telephone.)

19. *Mi marido y yo* _____ *(discutir) las noticias durante la cena.* (My husband and I discuss the news during dinner.)

20. *(Tú)* _____ *(temer) la verdad.* (You are afraid of the truth.)

21. *¿Usted* _____ *(comprender) mis instrucciones?* (Do you understand my instructions?)

How did you do? If you made mistakes, try to figure out why. To practice some more, try to put together your own sentences. Use the regular verbs in **TABLE 5-5** to describe things that you do or are planning to do.

TABLE 5-5

REGULAR VERBS			
aplaudir	to applaud, to approve	bienvivir	to live well
comprar	to purchase	confundir	to confuse
contestar	to repond (to)	cubrir	to cover
debatir	to debate, to argue	decidir	to decide
depender	to depend	entrar	to enter
hablar	to speak	interrumpir	to interrupt
llegar	to arrive	llevar	to carry, to wear
necesitar	to need	ofender	to offend
pagar	to pay	permitir	to permit
preguntar	to ask	preparar	to prepare
remitir	to send	resistir	to resist, to tolerate
sorprender	to surprise	subir	to ascend
tomar	to take	transcurrir	to pass, to elapse
unir	to unite	vender	to sell

CHAPTER 6

Who Are You? Introducing Ser

Now that regular verbs are a piece of cake, how about something a little more complex to spice up the mix? The Spanish verbs **ser** and **estar** both translate as "to be," but they cannot be used interchangeably. The next two chapters will show you how to distinguish between these two verbs, and the correct contexts for their usage.

Permanent States of Being: *Ser*

What if somebody were to ask you: "Who are you?" What would you say? How would you describe yourself?

¿Quién es usted? (Who are you?)
Yo soy María Fernanda. (I am Maria Fernanda.)
Soy profesora de matemáticas. (I am a math teacher.)
Soy alta y rubia. (I am tall and blonde.)
Soy de Chile. (I am from Chile.)

Maria's description of herself contains permanent facts: her name, her occupation, what she looks like, and where she is from. This is why she used **soy**, the **yo** form of the verb *ser*, to describe herself. To learn how to conjugate *ser* in the present tense, take a look at **TABLE 6-1**.

TABLE 6-1	CONJUGATING *SER* IN THE PRESENT TENSE
(yo) soy	I am
(tú) eres	you are (informal)
(él, ella, usted) es	he, she, it is; you are (formal)
(nosotros, nosotras) somos	we are
(ellos, ellas, ustedes) son	they are; you are (plural)

Place of Origin

Use *ser* when discussing place of origin and nationality. For example:

¿De dónde es usted? (Where are you from?)
Soy de Rusia. (I am from Russia.)
¿Es usted ruso? (Are you Russian?)
Sí, soy ruso. Sí, lo soy. (Yes, I am Russian. Yes, I am.)
No, no lo soy. (No, I'm not.)

TABLE 6-2 lists other countries and words for nationality (which can be used as either adjectives or nouns). Please remember to add the right endings to words of nationality, depending upon whether they describe males or females, and whether they refer to one or many. For example, "American" may be *americano, americana, americanos,* or *americanas.* Unless there are irregularities, generally only the male singular form is provided.

TABLE 6-2

VOCABULARY: COUNTRIES AND THEIR CITIZENS	
PAÍS (COUNTRY)	CIUDADANO (CITIZEN)
Afganistán	afgano
África del Sur (South Africa)	sudafricano
Alemania	alemán, alemana
Argentina	argentino
Australia	australiano
Austria	austriaco
Bélgica	belga (masculine and feminine)
Brasil	brasileño
Canadá	canadiense (masculine and feminine)
Chile	chileno
China	chino
Colombia	colombiano
Costa Rica	costarriqueño
Ecuador	ecuatoriano
Egipto	egipcio
Francia	francés, francesa
Gran Bretaña	británico
Grecia	griego
Guatemala	guatemalteco
Haití	haitiano
Holanda	holandés, holandesa
India	indio
Inglaterra	ingles, inglesa
Irán	iraní (masculine and feminine)
Iraq	iraquí (masculine and feminine)

Irlanda	irlandés, irlandesa
Israel	israelí (masculine and feminine)
Italia	italiano
Jamaica	jamaicano
Japón	japonés, japonesa
México	mexicano
Nicaragua	nicaragüense
Panamá	panameño
Perú	peruano
Polonia (Poland)	polaco
República Checa (Czech Republic)	checo
El Salvador	salvadoreño
Suecia (Sweden)	sueco
Suiza (Switzerland)	suizo
Tailandia	tailandés, tailandesa
Turquía	turco
Venezuela	venezolano
Yugoslavia	yugoslavo

Notice that in Spanish you don't need to capitalize adjectives of nationality as you would in English, so "American" becomes *americano*, and so on. However, names of countries are capitalized in both languages.

Points of Culture and Geography

There is no doubt that U.S. citizens are known as "Americans" throughout the world. In many Latin American countries, however, *americanos* are people who live in the western hemisphere. U.S. citizens are termed *estadounidenses*, from the words *Estados Unidos* (United States). More colloquially, Spanish speakers refer to Americans as *norteamericanos, yanquis,* or *gringos*.

FACTS

People who live in Latin America do not identify themselves as *hispanos*. Being "hispanic" is a political identity that diverse immigrant groups use to participate in the greater society within the United States. As such, it does little to actually describe the white, indigenous, black, Asian, and multiracial people that may comprise the category.

Physical Characteristics

The adjectives appearing in **TABLE 6-3** are permanent, and don't change from day to day. They go with the verb *ser*.

TABLE 6-3

ADJECTIVES DESCRIBING PHYSICAL CHARACTERISTICS			
alto	tall	*anciano*	elderly
bajo	short	*bello*	beautiful
bonito	pretty	*calvo*	bald
delgado	thin	*elegante* *	elegant
feo	ugly	*fuerte* *	strong
gordo	fat	*grande* *	big, large
grueso	stocky	*guapo*	handsome
hermoso	beautiful	*joven* *	young
mayor *	older	*moreno*	dark-haired
pelirrojo	redheaded	*pobre* *	poor
rubio	blond(e)	*viejo*	old

* (masculine and feminine)

Ser and the Preposition *De*

You will often find yourself using *de* when describing personal characteristics with the verb *ser*. (To review the basics on this preposition, refer back to Chapter 4.) **TABLE 6-4** illustrates how *de* might be used in Spanish.

TABLE 6-4

USES OF *DE*	
Soy de buena familia.	I am of good family stock.
Ella es de Chicago.	She is from Chicago.
Somos de la asociación de personas retiradas.	We are from the association of retired persons.
Soy de estatura mediana.	I am of medium height.
Eres de ojos claros.	You are of light eyes. (You have light eyes.)

Occupation

Think of occupation as a permanent characteristic. To describe your occupation, you should use the verb *ser*. Consider the following:

¿Cuál es su profesión?	What is your profession?
¿Qué hace usted?	What do you do?
Soy una actriz.	I am an actress.

For related vocabulary, refer to **TABLE 6-5**.

TABLE 6-5

PROFESIONES (OCCUPATIONS)			
actor, actriz	actor, actress	*amo (de casa)*	homeowner
analista de inventario	inventory analyst	*arquitecto*	architect
asistente ejecutivo, asistente ejecutiva	executive assistant	*banquero*	banker
camarero	waiter	*consejero de inversiones*	investment advisor
consultor	consultant	*contador*	accountant
director	director	*diseñador*	designer
diseñador de software	software developer	*estudiante* *	student
gerente *	manager	*hipotecario*	pharmacist
ingeniero químico	chemical engineer	*juez* *	judge
maestro	teacher	*médico*	doctor
mercader	merchant	*modista* *	dressmaker

músico *	musician	*pediatra* *	pediatrician
periodista *	journalist	*piloto* *	pilot
profesor de música	music teacher	*repostero*	pastry maker
sastre	tailor for men	*supervisor*	supervisor
tabernero	barkeeper	*vendedor*	salesperson

* (masculine and feminine)

Unless noted otherwise, please remember to add feminine ending *-a* when referring to female workers, and plural ending *-s* if you are referring to more than one person.

Personal Relationships

The verb *ser* is used for describing personal relationships for the same reason that it is used to describe occupations—relationship roles are considered to be permanent characteristics. You will always be your parents' daughter or son, and they will always be your parents. While some relationships might not last quite as long, they are still considered permanent in the grammatical sense. Take a look at these sentences as examples.

Carolina es la amiga de Estefi. (Carolina is Estefi's friend.)
Las dos estudiantes son grandes enemigas. (The two students are great enemies.)
Marco y Juan son socios. (Marco and Juan are friends/associates.)
Ellos son competidores. (They are rivals.)
Elena es la hija de Sandra. (Elena is the daughter of Sandra.)

ESSENTIALS

Note that relationships that go with *ser* need not be family relationships. For the vocabulary on the relationships between family members, go to Chapter 14, "Family and Friends."

Counting on *Ser*

Ser is also used in the language of numbers and counting. Think about it this way: The fact that two plus two is four is a permanent characteristic, not a temporary state, so you would say *dos más dos son cuatro*. Take a look at the following simple math steps and how to say them in Spanish. (For a complete overview of Spanish numerals, refer to Chapter 9, "The Vocabulary of Time.")

$2 \times 2 = 4$	*dos por dos son cuatro*
$10 + 10 = 20$	*diez más diez son veinte*
$9 - 2 = 7$	*nueve menos dos son siete*
$8 \div 8 = 1$	*ocho dividido por ocho es uno*

Ser can also be used in discussing prices, where it can substitute *costar* (to cost). For instance, compare the two sentences below:

El kilo (gramo) de manzanas es doscientos pesetas. (The kilogram of apples is 200 pesetas.)
La copa de vino tinto cuesta siete dólares. (The glass of red wine costs seven dollars.)

FACTS

A useful phrase to know is how to ask for the bill at a restaurant in Spanish: *¿Cuánto es la cuenta?* (How much is the bill?) The answer (if you've been frugal in your menu options) might be something like the following phrase: *La cuenta es doce dólares.* (The bill is $12.00.)

CHAPTER 7

How Are You? Introducing Estar

Now that you understand the verb *ser* and how it is used in Spanish, you can go on to examine the other "to be" verb—*estar*. Whereas *ser* is a verb of permanence, *estar* is much more fluid. It will help you discuss such "temporary" points as the weather, your mood, and physical location.

Location and Temporary State: *Estar*

Estar can help you answer the questions "Where are you?" and "How are you?" This verb refers to a person's physical location or temporary state of being.

¿Cómo está usted? (How are you?)
Estoy muy bien, gracias. (I'm very well, thanks.)
¿Dónde está usted? (Where are you located?)
Estoy en mi casa. (I'm at home.)

For the other forms of the verb *estar* in the present tense, refer to **TABLE 7-1**.

TABLE 7-1

CONJUGATING *ESTAR* IN PRESENT TENSE	
(yo) estoy	I am
(tú) estás	you are (informal)
(él, ella, usted) está	he, she, it is; you are (formal)
(nosotros, nosotras) estamos	we are
(ellos, ellas, ustedes) están	they are; you are (plural)

Estar is often used when dealing within a time frame—the how, when, where, and who at a particular point in time. *¿Cómo está usted?* is a common social inquiry—part courtesy, part small talk, generally a way to catch up on current physical, mental/emotional, positional, and professional condition.

Physical State

Use the verb *estar* and the adjectives and adverbs in **TABLE 7-2** to describe how you might feel. Keep in mind that adjectives and adverbs need to agree in person and number with their respective subjects. For example: *Él está cansado. Ella está cansada. Ellos están cansados. Ellas están cansadas.*

TABLE 7-2

VOCABULARY: DESCRIBING HOW YOU FEEL			
así así	so-so	*cansado*	tired
débil	weak	*despierto*	awake
dolorido	in pain	*dormido*	asleep
ebrio	drunk	*enfermo*	sick
ileso	unharmed	*limpio*	clean
mareado	dizzy	*ocupado*	busy
palido	pale	*sobrio*	sober

Mental State

In addition to physical conditions, *estar* is also used to describe mental and emotional conditions. **TABLE 7-3** contains some vocabulary you will need to help you describe your state of being.

TABLE 7-3

VOCABULARY: MENTAL AND EMOTIONAL CONDITIONS			
aburrido	bored	*afectuoso*	affectionate
amable *	kind, amiable	*ambicioso*	ambitious
amistoso	friendly	*ansioso*	anxious
antipático	unpleasant	*apacible* *	pleasant, gentle
atontado	stunned	*avergonzado*	embarrassed
bondadoso	good, kind	*cariñoso*	loving
celoso	jealous	*cómico*	funny
contento	satisfied, happy	*difícil* *	difficult
enfadado	disgusted	*enojado*	angry
feliz *	happy	*generoso*	generous
lleno (a) de vida	full of life	*loco*	crazy, outgoing
maduro	mature, wise	*molesto*	annoyed
nervioso	nervous	*preocupado*	worried
sosegado	calmed	*temeroso*	fearful

* (masculine and feminine)

Point of Location

Estar also expresses a "positional" situation—where you are at a particular time, answering the question *¿Dónde está usted?* (Where are you?) Physical location may include an actual place (country, town, street, building, and so on), or a reference to a place in relation to a person's environment:

¿Dónde está usted? Estoy . . .

• *en México*	in Mexico
• *en Nueva York*	in New York
• *en la calle Sucre*	on Sucre Street
• *en la calle Sucre, número 1551*	at 1551 Sucre Street
• *en el edificio de la O.N.U.*	in the U.N. building
• *en casa*	at home
• *aquí*	here
• *acá*	over here (in this general area)
• *más allá de . . .*	beyond . . .

Refer to **TABLE 7-4** for a list of prepositions you can use to indicate the location of an object or person.

TABLE 7-4

PREPOSITIONS			
a mano derecha	on the right side	*a la derecha de*	to the right of
a mano izquierda	on the left side	*a la izquierda de*	to the left of
al fondo de	at/in the back of	*al lado de*	to the side of, next to
abajo	downstairs	*arriba*	upstairs
adentro	inside	*afuera*	outside
cerca de	close to	*lejos de*	far from
debajo de	under	*sobre*	over, on top of
atrás	in the back	*delante de*	in front of
detrás de	behind	*enfrente*	in front (facing)

FACTS

In English, "where you are" isn't necessarily tied to a physical position, but can also point to a position within a process. This also holds true for Spanish:

¿En qué día está en su dieta?   In what day are you on your diet?
Estoy en mi tercer día.   I am in my third day.

Here are some examples of sentences with prepositions you have just learned:

Los niños están afuera. (The children are outside.)
La gasolinera está a mano derecha. (The gas station is on the right hand side.)
Celso está detrás de su amigo en la fila. (Celso is behind his friend in the line.)
Yo vivo enfrente de una iglesia. (I live in front of/facing a church.)
Ricardo camina delante de mi. (Ricardo walks in front of me.)
La tienda está lejos del banco. (The store is far from the bank.)
El coche está atrás. (The car is in the back.)
Las llaves están sobre la mesa. (The keys are on top of the table.)
Cesar trabaja cerca de su casa. (Cesar works close to his home.)
El regalo está debajo del árbol. (The present is beneath the tree.)

Situational Prepositions

The "situational" aspect of *estar* is brought out by the prepositions that frequently follow it immediately. It is this aspect that makes it so flexible and as a result more widely used than *ser*.

Con

The preposition *con* (with) may be used to express physical proximity:

Estoy con el teléfono inalámbrico. (I am with the wireless phone.)
Estoy con mis padres. (I am with my parents.)

It may also be used to express religious or ideological proximity:

Está con Dios. (He is with God.)
Está con los demócratas. (She is with the Democrats.)

Con is also used to express physical, mental, or emotional experiences (primarily used with nouns that describe a physical state):

Estoy con calor. (I am hot.)
Estoy con fiebre. (I am feverish.)
Están con gripe. (They have the flu.)
Estamos con hambre. (We are hungry.)
¿Estás con sed? (Are you thirsty?)
Estoy con vergüenza. (I am embarrassed.)

Contra

The preposition *contra* (against) may be used to express physical contact or opposition to ideology or circumstances:

Estoy contra la pared. (I am leaning against the wall.)
Están contra la guerra. (They are against the war.)
Estamos en contra del socialismo. (We are in opposition to socialism.)

De

The preposition *de* (of, from) may be used to express physical position, mental position, a change in position, or a momentary condition. Here are some examples with the phrase *estar de*:

Estoy de espaldas. (I am lying on my back.)
Está de moda. (It's in fashion.)
Estamos de pie. (We are standing; literally, on our feet.)
Están de vacaciones. (They are on vacation.)
Estamos de acuerdo. (We are in agreement.)
Estoy de regreso. (I am on my way back.)
¿Estás de paso? (Are you here for a short time?)
Estoy de profesor. (I am currently acting as the professor.)
Está usted de suerte. (You are in luck.)

Entre

The preposition *entre* (between) may be used to express physical position or mental or emotional condition (usually idiomatic).

Estoy entre dos personas. (I am between two people.)

Estás entre amigos. (You are among friends.)

Están entre la espada y la pared. (They are trapped; literally, they are between a sword and a wall.)

Estoy entre sí y no. (I am undecided; literally, between yes and no.)

Para

The preposition *para* in combination with *estar* may be used to express a prepared condition, mood, or inclination to act for someone or something. Take a look at the following examples:

Estoy para llegar a casa. (I am about to arrive at home.)

Estamos para ir a la tienda. (We are about to go to the store.)

Está para fiestas. (He is generally open to parties.)

Por

The preposition *por* (for), in combination with *estar*, may be used to express a reasoned or emotional preference for a person and ideology, or as a reasoned preference or contemplation of an act.

Estoy por el presidente. (I am in favor of the president.)

Estamos por los derechos humanos. (We are for human rights.)

Estoy por ir al cine. (I am in favor of going to the movies.)

Está por salir de la casa. (He is about to leave the house.)

Están por ir a la tienda. (They are going to go to the store.)

Sin

The preposition *sin* (without) may be used to express a lacking condition:

Estoy sin dinero. (I am without money.)

Estamos sin dormir. (We are without sleep.)

Prepositions and *Estar*

Translate the following sentences to Spanish, using *con, contra, de,* or *sin.* For additional vocabulary, refer to **TABLE 7-5**.

1. I am here with a friend.

2. We are returning with Rita.

3. You (plural) are against government waste.

4. Today I am not having luck.

5. She is cold.

6. I am a lawyer, but today I am a professor.

7. They don't have even a penny.

8. I am in a hurry.

9. Today I am without problems.

10. We are standing outside.

TABLE 7-5

VOCABULARY			
abogado	lawyer	afuera	outside
amigo	friend	aquí	here
profesor	professor	centavo	penny
desperdicio gubernativo	government waste	frío	cold
hoy	today	ni	not even
prisa	hurry	(el) problema	problem

Estar and the Present Progressive Tense

Often when translating the present tense of verbs, you will find some reference to the action as it progresses. It's not unusual to see **yo camino** translated as "I am walking." While the Spanish present tense does capture an action in the moment, it is more like a simple snapshot than a video. The present progressive is the tense that allows you to "see" the action as it is "occurring."

The present progressive actually combines two different parts of speech, *estar* (conjugated according to the subject) and the present participle of the verb that shows action in progress, to realize a description of an action in movement. Think of the present progressive as the equivalent of the English construction "is –ing." To look at how *cantar* (to sing), *aprender* (to learn), and *vivir* (to live) are conjugated in the present progressives, refer to **TABLE 7-6**.

TABLE 7-6

PRESENT PROGRESSIVE TENSE	
yo	estoy cantando, aprendiendo, viviendo
tú	estás cantando, aprendiendo, viviendo
él, ella, usted	está cantando, aprendiendo, viviendo
nosotros	estamos cantando, aprendiendo, viviendo
ellos, ellas, ustedes	están cantando, aprendiendo, viviendo

ESSENTIALS
To make a present participle, add -*ando* to the bases of -*ar* verbs, and —*iendo* to the bases of -*er* and -*ir* verbs. The English equivalent of these endings is "–ing," as in "speaking," "drinking," and "living."

Here are some more examples of how to use the present progressive tense:

Michelle está escribiendo la novela. (Michelle is writing a novel—right now, not in general.)
Jonathan está corriendo en el parque. (Jonathan is running at the park.)
Gertrudes y Júlio están jugando al ajedrez. (Gertrude and Julio are playing chess.)
¿Estás hablando por teléfono? (Are you talking on the phone?)
Mis padres están viviendo en Madrid ahora. (My parents are living in Madrid now.)

ESSENTIALS
As you will learn other verb tenses, you will also discover that the construction of *estar + verbo* that forms the present progressive tense, which you have just learned, also exists in other tenses with the following forms of *estar*: *yo estaba* (I used to be), *estuve* (I was), *he estado* (I have been), *yo estaré* (I will be).

Which Is Which?

To a native English speaker, it might not always be obvious when to use *ser* and when to use *estar*—in English, we have only one "to be" verb. If you need the most basic guideline, memorize the following rule of thumb:

Ser corresponds to expressions of permanent characteristics.
Estar corresponds to description of situation.

For instance, compare the following pairs:

Soy aburrida. (I'm boring.) *Estoy aburrida.* (I'm bored.)
Ella es de Florida. (She's from Florida.) *Ella está en la Florida.*
(She is in Florida.)
Ellos son contentos. (They are happy people.) *Ellos están contentos.* (They are happy.)

For a detailed list of rules on how to choose between *ser* and *estar*, refer to **TABLE 7-7**.

TABLE 7-7

RULES FOR USING *SER* AND *ESTAR*	
Se Usa Estar Para Expresar: *(Estar* Is Used to Express:)	*Se Usa Ser Para Expresar:* *(Ser* Is Used to Express:)
situación física (a physical situation)	*professión, oficio, y actividad* (profession, occupation, and activity)
estado físico (physical state)	*parentesco y relaciones* (familial and other relationships)
estado mental (mental state)	*personalidad* (personality)
apariencia temporal (temporary appearance)	*apariencia característica* (characteristic appearance)
los resultados de una acción (results of an action)	*posesión* (possession)
el progreso de una acción (progress of an action)	*acción, con occurir o tener lugar* (action, when something occurs or takes place)
	materia y origen (essence and origin)
	tiempo, cantidad, precio, y numero (time, quantity, price, and number)
	construcciones de impersonalidad (impersonal constructions)

Ser and Estar

Translate the following sentences using the appropriate form of *estar* and *ser*. Use the vocabulary words provided in Chapter 6 and 7, as well as in **TABLE 7-8**. (Answers are provided in the back of the book.)

1. We are sick.
2. Miguel's friend is French.
3. He is boring.
4. I am very tired.
5. He is eating in the Italian restaurant on the left-hand side.

6. You (formal) are sober.
7. I am (a) sober (person).
8. Venezuelans are friendly.
9. They are always happy.
10. You (informal) are embarrassed.
11. The building is on Main Street, close to Grove Street.

12. I am crazy today.
13. The car is a block from here.
14. You (plural) are never here.

TABLE 7-8

VOCABULARY WORDS			
amigo	friend	amistoso	friendly
aquí	here	(el) coche	car
comer	to eat	edificio	building
(la) gente	people	hoy	today
manzana	block	muy	very
nunca	never	restaurante	restaurant
siempre	always		

CHAPTER 8

As Time Goes By: Other Verb Tenses

So far, the discussion of verbs has been centered on the present. But at any given moment, you might be remembering the past or looking toward the future. Just as verbs are conjugated according to person and number, they are also conjugated according to their point in time—their tense.

Conjugating Regular Verbs

For most Spanish regular verbs that you come across, their use will be as simple as "plug and play." If you know who is acting and when the action is occurring in relation to you, simply attach the appropriate ending to the verb base and, like magic, you've expressed a complete thought in Spanish. It really is that easy. With respect to regular verbs, the key lies in knowing the tenses to the extent that you can decide in a split second what tense to use. As you practice memorizing the tenses and their endings, apply verbs immediately to yourself and your situation and then extend your situation to others. Repetition will help you focus in on, and eventually internalize, the base of a few model verbs. At some point, probably when you least expect it, you'll start "sensing" how the thousands of regular verbs relate to these models, and you will have begun to conquer Spanish.

Preterite Tense

The preterite tense refers to the simple past and often to a single occurrence within one instance or recurring more specific instances. It is important to understand that the action is rooted in the past and physically and psychologically cut off from the present; the past action has terminated and is in effect complete (or perfect). The action may be tied to the past in terms of any of the following:

- A particular moment or date. For example: *Nací el 12 de junio de 1966.* (I was born on June 12, 1966.)
- Several isolated instances. For example: *Llamé cinco veces.* (I called five times.)
- Its duration. For example: *En aquel año trabajé en el Cuerpo de Paz.* (In that year, I worked in the Peace Corps.)

Conjugating Verbs in the Preterite Tense

As you remember, regular verbs may fall into the *-ar, -er,* or *-ir* category. **TABLE 8-1** provides you with the endings that you will need to learn in order to be able to conjugate verbs in the preterite tense. The regular verbs used as examples are the same as in Chapter 5, where you were first introduced to these verbs: *cantar* (to sing), *aprender* (to learn), and *vivir* (to live).

TABLE 8-1	VERB ENDINGS IN THE PRETERITE TENSE	
	—AR VERBS	—ER AND —IR VERBS
yo	-é (canté)	-í (aprendí, viví)
tú	-aste (cantaste)	-iste (aprendiste, viviste)
él, ella, usted	-ó (cantó)	-ió (aprendió, vivió)
nosotros	-amos (cantamos)	-imos (aprendimos, vivimos)
ellos, ellas, ustedes	-aron (cantaron)	-ieron (aprendieron, vivieron)

Imperfect Tense

The companion to the preterite, the imperfect (or copreterite) tense, also refers to the simple past. However, whereas the preterite is enclosed by time, the copreterite is not. An action can have occurred over a span of time with no clear beginning or ending point. There may or may not be a connection with the present; it may or may not still be happening. This vagueness regarding the end to an action, or this developing and lasting quality of past action, is the reason for this tense's being named the "imperfect" tense. The action of the imperfect tense may be tied to the following:

- An unspecified amount of time. For example: *De niño, quería un caballo.* (As a boy, I wanted a horse.)
- An indefinite number of occurrences, such as a habit or custom. For example: *Cada vez que la veía, me sentía feliz.* (Each time I saw her, I felt happy.)

Conjugating Verbs in the Imperfect Tense

TABLE 8-2 includes the verb endings for verbs in the imperfect tense. Notice that the yo form and *él, ella, usted* form of these verbs is the same. To avoid confusion, simply add the relevant pronoun to identify the correct person.

TABLE 8-2

	VERB ENDINGS IN THE IMPERFECT TENSE	
	–AR VERBS	**–ER AND –IR VERBS**
yo	-aba (cantaba)	-ía (aprendía, vivía)
tú	-abas (cantabas)	-ías (aprendías, vivías)
él, ella, usted	-aba (cantaba)	-ía (aprendía, vivía)
nosotros	-ábamos (cantábamos)	-íamos (aprendíamos, vivíamos)
ellos, ellas, ustedes	-aban (cantaban)	-ían (aprendían, vivían)

It's common to combine the preterite and the imperfect verbs in the same sentence. Take a look at the examples below:

A la vez que hacía la broma, sonrió. (As he was telling the joke, he laughed.)

Ayer cuando caminaba al trabajo, vió un accidente. (Yesterday when he was walking to work, he saw an accident.)

Nunca hablaba mal de otros, pero lo hizo hoy. (He never used to speak badly of others, but today he did.)

For the list of words that will help you form sentences in the imperfect tense, refer to **TABLE 8-3**.

TABLE 8-3

	WORDS USED WITH THE IMPERFECT TENSE		
a la vez	at the same time	algunas veces	sometimes
a menudo	often	a veces	at times
cada día	each day, every day	contadas veces	seldom
de vez en cuando	once in a while	esta vez	this time
frecuentemente	frequently	muchas veces	many times
nunca	never	repetidas veces	repeatedly
siempre	always	tantas veces	so many times
toda la semana	all week long	toda la vida	whole life

Take a look at the following two phrases: *cada mes* (each month) and *cada semana* (each week). Though *mes* is a masculine noun and *semana* is a feminine noun, the word *cada* does not change its ending. And, of course, it does not exist in the plural—"each" is always a singular idea.

Preterite Versus Imperfect

Native English speakers often have trouble differentiating between the preterite and the imperfect. Though verbs in these two tenses may be translated as the same verb tense in English, differences do exist.

The preterite is a precise and limiting tense. The imperfect, on the other hand, is less restricted; it represents the vagueness of time with respect to the action. For a detailed review of when to use the preterite and the imperfect, refer to **TABLE 8-4**.

TABLE 8-4

PRETERITE VERSUS IMPERFECT	
PRETERITE	IMPERFECT
An act that occurs as a single event.	An act that was customary in the past.
An act limited in the times it is performed.	An act that may be ongoing indefinitely.
An act that is defined within specified time frames.	An act that is defined within broad frames.

Here are some examples to help you differentiate between the imperfect and the preterite:

Ella fue al cine ayer. (She went to the movies yesterday.)
Ella iba al cine cada sábado. (She used to go to the movies every Saturday.)
Me gustó la película. (I liked the movie.)
A Jonathan le gustaba mucho el programa de televisión de Los Tres Chiflados. (Jonathan liked *The Three Stooges* television program very much.)

La cita comenzó a las diez de la mañana. (The meeting began at ten in the morning.)

De niños, comenzaban llorar cada vez que oyeron el trueno. (As children they used to begin to cry every time they heard thunder.)

Present Perfect Tense

The present perfect tense is constructed by using a form of the auxiliary verb, *haber* (to have), with the past participle form of the primary verb. It characterizes a past connected to a now-expanded present. It is used to describe the following:

- An immediate past. For example: *No he comido porque acabo de llegar.* (I've not eaten because I have just arrived.)
- A past inhabited by the speaker. For example: *Últimamente he tenido mucho sueño.* (Lately, I have been very sleepy.)
- Information independent of time. For example: *No he hablado con María.* (I haven't talked to Maria.)
- A psychologically or emotionally linked past. For example: *He perdido a mi abuelita hace diez años.* (I lost my grandmother ten years ago.)

Conjugating Verbs in Present Perfect Tense

Because present perfect is a composite tense—that is, the main verb is set as a past participle of the verb *haber* (in this case the Spanish equivalent of the English verb "to have")—conjugating verbs in this tense is really easy: All you need to know is how to conjugate *haber* and set the main verb as a past participle (see the following E-Alert). See **TABLE 8-5** for how to conjugate *haber*.

To use the present perfect tense, remember that most verbs follow a common formula to benefit from the description afforded by the past participle. If a verb ends in *ar*, its corresponding past participle substitutes -*ar* with -*ado*. If it ends with -*er* or -*ir*, its corresponding past participle substitutes -*er* or -*ir* with -*ido*.

TABLE 8-5	CONJUGATING VERBS IN PRESENT PERFECT		
	−AR VERB	**−ER VERB**	**−IR VERB**
yo	he cantado	he aprendido	he vivido
tú	has cantado	has aprendido	has vivido
él, ella, usted	ha cantado	ha aprendido	ha vivido
nosotros	hemos cantado	hemos aprendido	habemos vivido
ellos, ellas, ustedes	han cantado	han aprendido	han vivido

Future Tense

What the future tense describes should seem fairly straightforward. The following types of actions are treated in the future tense:

- Actions asserted as certain to occur within a period following the present. For example: *Viajaré a Londres en septiembre.* (I will travel to London in September.)
- A probable action given uncertain but possible circumstances. For example: *Comeré almuerzo si tengo tiempo.* (I will eat lunch if I have time.)

Conjugating Verbs in the Future Tense

The endings for verbs in the future tense are the same for *-ar, -er,* and *-ir* verbs. However, you add the ending to the infinitive form without dropping the infinitive ending. **TABLE 8-6** lists the conjugation endings, as well as examples.

TABLE 8-6	CONJUGATING VERBS IN FUTURE TENSE			
		−AR VERBS	**−ER VERBS**	**−IR VERBS**
yo	-é	cantaré	aprenderé	viviré
tú	-ás	cantarás	aprenderás	vivirás
él, ella, usted	-á	cantará	aprenderá	vivirá
nosotros	-emos	cantaremos	aprenderemos	viviremos
ellos, ellas, ustedes	-án	cantarán	aprenderán	vivirán

Conditional Tense

The conditional tense in Spanish is generally equivalent to the English construction "would + verb." In Spanish, the conditional has five basic uses:

1. It roots a future action to the past. For example:

   Manuel me dijo que llegaría antes de las tres. (Manuel told me that he would arrive before three.)

   Pensaban que sus hijos no crecerían tan rápido. (They were thinking that their kids would not grow up so quickly.)

2. It allows for the hypothetical—with the implication that the conditional statement is unlikely. For example:

   Te compraría un pasaje a Europa, pero perdí todo el dinero en Las Vegas. (I would buy you a trip to Europe, but I lost all my money in Las Vegas.)

   Te ayudaría mover el sofá, pero desgraciadamente me lesioné la espalda hoy por la mañana. (I would help you move the sofa, but unfortunately I hurt my back this morning.)

3. It gives room for a probability that is more expansive and may include conjecture or approximation. For example:

   ¿Con quién hablaría Juan a esas horas de la noche? (With whom would Juan speak at that hour of night?)

   Serían las diez cuando la vi. (It might have been ten when I saw her.)

4. It allows for a concession in light of a contrary view or experience introduced by *pero* (but). For example:

   Sería tacaño pero nunca me negó su ayuda. (He might have been stingy but he never refused me his help.)

   Ella tendría poca instrucción formal pero es una persona brillante. (She might have had little formal education but she is a brilliant person.)

5. It provides an alternative to the copreterite in expressing a courteous request. For example:

   ¿Podría decirme donde está la parada de autobús? (Could you tell me where the bus stop is?)

   ¿Me dejarías usar tu teléfono? (Would you allow me to use your phone?)

The underlying idea to remember about the conditional is that the future is not so certain because what it depends on is either unlikely or too expensive to pin down and know readily.

ESSENTIALS   The conditional tense also appears in "if/then" constructions that are posed in the past tense. For instance, in English you would say, "If I had a dog, I would take care of it well." In Spanish, you would use the conditional for the "then" clause: *Si tuviera un perro, lo cuidaría bien.*

Conditional-Tense Conjugations

Conjugating verbs in the conditional tense is very easy, as long as you know the future-tense base. For regular verbs, that's simply the infinitive form, which you will use without dropping the *-ar*, *-er*, or *-ir* ending. (Irregular verbs will have the same base in the conditional tense as they do in the future tense. You will learn the irregular future conjugations in Chapter 15.)

The conditional endings are the same for all verbs. For some examples, take a look at **TABLE 8-7**.

TABLE 8-7

		–AR VERBS	*–ER* VERBS	*–IR* VERBS
		CONJUGATING VERBS IN CONDITIONAL TENSE		
yo	-ía	*cantaría*	*aprendería*	*viviría*
tú	-ías	*cantarías*	*aprenderías*	*vivirías*
él, ella, usted	-ía	*cantaría*	*aprendería*	*viviría*
nosotros	-íamos	*cantaríamos*	*aprenderíamos*	*viviríamos*
ellos, ellas, ustedes	-ían	*cantarían*	*aprenderían*	*vivirían*

Reviewing What You've Learned

To review the tenses you have learned so far, take a look at the following list. The examples of verbs in each verb tense should help you distinguish various tenses and apply them correctly.

Aprender (To Learn)

- *Aprendí los buenos modales en casa.* I learned good manners at home. (Although the time frame is vague, the act of learning good manners is definitely over, accomplished, and locked in the past—hence the use of preterite tense.)
- *Aprendía como nadar cada Sábado.* I used to learn how to swim every Saturday. (The act of learning was a customary occurrence over time—every Saturday—which is why the imperfect tense is used.)
- *He aprendido a cocinar pollo guisado.* I have learned to cook stewed chicken. (It has happened recently—so present perfect is used.)
- *Algún día aprenderé a esquiar.* Someday I will learn (how) to ski. (When it happens is uncertain, but I am planning on doing it at some point in the future; future tense is used.)

Caminar (To Walk)

- *Anoche caminé por tres horas.* Last night I walked for three hours. (It was a single event that was over after a specific time frame, three hours; the verb is conjugated in preterite tense.)
- *Caminaba por el lago.* Last night I was walking along the lake. (The time frame is set up by the walk, a continuous event with no clear end; this action is described in the imperfect tense.)
- *He caminado seis manzanas.* I have walked six city blocks. (It just happened and/or is affecting me now; present perfect tense.)
- *Si no hay bus, caminaré al trabajo.* If there is no bus, I will walk to work. (Because the bus is unreliable, I am planning to walk in case it is late or does not appear; the future tense is used.)

Vivir (To Live)

- *Viví allí por mucho tiempo.* I lived there for a long time. (Although "a long time" is again vague, the act of living specifically in that place is clearly over and separate from today; this sentence is in the preterite tense.)
- *Vivía en un apartamento pésimo.* I used to live in an apartment that was as bad as can be. (The act of living is a snapshot of an

occurrence over a vague period—no end is implied; this is an example of the imperfect tense.)

- *Siempre he vivido de mis propios esfuerzos.* I have always lived off my own efforts. (My assertion is independent of a specific time; present perfect tense is used.)
- *Viviré en España si consigo el puesto.* If I get the position, I will live in Spain. (It is uncertain that I will be hired. But if I am, I will live in Spain because it is that office that is seeking to fill the position—the future tense conjugation is used.)

Conjugating *Ser* and *Estar*

You already know how to conjugate regular verbs, but unfortunately not all Spanish verbs are regular. You already know that the conjugation forms for *ser* and *estar* in the present tense do not follow regular rules for *-er* and *-ar* verbs, respectively. Now let's see how these verbs conjugate in preterite, imperfect, present perfect, and future tense.

The Preterite Tense

In the preterite, *ser* is used on "permanent" characteristics that nevertheless had a definite ending point—think of them as life-altering changes. *Estar*'s focus on the situational goes along better in describing a simple past that is at odds with the present. After all, a lot of things do in fact change, particularly situations. The action is still rooted in the past and cut off from the present, but the changes that may occur in the movement toward the present are more easily assigned to a discrete point in time, rather than a continuum as is the case with the imperfect tense.

> *Ser: Fui bajo.* I was short. (But now I'm tall.)
> *Estar: Ayer estuve cansado.* I was tired yesterday. (At that point in time.)

Take a look at **TABLE 8-8** on how to conjugate *ser* and *estar* in the preterite tense.

TABLE 8-8	SER AND ESTAR IN THE PRETERITE TENSE	
	SER	ESTAR
yo	fui	estuve
tú	fuiste	estuviste
él, ella, usted	fue	estuve
nosotros	fuimos	estuvimos
ellos, ellas, ustedes	fueron	estuvieron

Note: In the preterite, the conjugations for *ser* are irregular. Moreover, the verb *ir* (to go) looks exactly the same in the preterite (to be discussed later). And if you compare the preterite forms of *estar* to regular *-ar* verbs, you'll find them to be irregular as well.

Imperfect Tense

Estar, in the copreterite, describes continuous, habitual, or customary acts of "being" that coincide with the English "I used to be" or "I was (being)." For example: *Estaba en el jardín cuando llegó el sol.* (I was in the garden when the sun came.) The preterite and the copreterite can actually coincide. That is, the preterite can be contained within a time frame established by the copreterite as in: *Ayer mientras estaba en el trabajo, estuve de mal humor.* (Yesterday while I was at work, I was in a bad mood.)

With regard to *ser*, the imperfect tense may describe habitual or customary acts of "being" that coincide with the English "used to be" during a fairly vague period of time. It is often employed to complete the phrase "When I was . . ."

Cuando era niño, era travieso. (When I was a boy, I was mischievous.)

Cuando era adolescente, era buena estudiante. (When she was an adolescent, she was a good student.)

Notice that these time frames are common to everyone. You've also been a child and an adolescent at one time or another. Because the imperfect makes no reference to something having ended, it is often used to render descriptions of personal characteristics by relying on the preposition *de*. You can say:

De joven, era audaz. (When I "belonged to the young group," I was bold.)
De soltera, era demasiado seria. (When I "belonged to the single group," I was too serious.)
De casado, era tranquilo. (When I "belonged to the married group," I was at peace.)

For conjugated forms of *ser* and *estar* in the imperfect, refer to **TABLE 8-9**.

TABLE 8-9	*SER* AND *ESTAR* IN THE IMPERFECT TENSE	
	SER	**ESTAR**
yo	era	estaba
tú	eras	estabas
él, ella, usted	era	estaba
nosotros	éramos	estábamos
ellos, ellas, ustedes	eran	estaban

The Present Perfect Tense

In this tense, *ser* and *estar* both translate to "have been." As you might remember, the conjugations are constructed by using a form of the auxiliary verb *haber* ("to have") with the past participle (or *-do*) form of the primary verb: in this case, *sido* and *estado*. For example:

Durante mi vida he sido estudiante, marinero, y vendedor de zapatos.
During my life I've been a student, sailor, and shoe seller.
He estado (aquí) por dos horas. I have been here for two hours.
He estado con gripe desde ayer. I have had a cold since yesterday.

The Future Tense

Despite offering the present tense to describe future events, Spanish also has its own strictly future-focused tense.

La semana próxima estaré en Buenos Aires. Next week I will be in Buenos Aires.

Qué será, será. What will be, will be.

TABLE 8-10 contains the conjugations of *ser* and *estar* in the future tense.

TABLE 8-10

SER AND ESTAR IN THE FUTURE TENSE		
	SER	ESTAR
yo	seré	estaré
tú	serás	estarás
él, ella, usted	será	estará
nosotros	seremos	estaremos
ellos, ellas, ustedes	serán	estarán

CHAPTER 9

The Vocabulary of Time

Despite the many tenses that you have just covered and the many you have yet to discover, the Spanish language allows only three basic frames of reference—past, present, and future—by which to witness daily life. Measuring and telling time is an important part of learning a language—and a good way for you to practice your verb tenses!

Cardinal Numbers

Spanish employs cardinal and ordinal numerals (as does English). You are probably more familiar with the cardinals—numerals that express quantity and are used for counting: one, two, three, and so on. In fact, Spanish often uses cardinal numerals even when American English would choose ordinals—numerals that show the order of an item in a given series: first, second, third, and so on.

The Basics: 1–15

The numbers 1–9 are the most utilized in Spanish because they are employed alone or within larger numbers. All you need to do is memorize the numbers up to *quince* (fifteen); the rest is a matter of combining what you already know. When simply counting, numerals stand alone. Treat them as you would pronouns:

0	*cero*	SEH-roh	8	*ocho*	OH-choh
1	*uno*	OO-noh	9	*nueve*	NWEH-veh
2	*dos*	dohs	10	*diez*	dyehs
3	*tres*	trehs	11	*once*	OHN-seh
4	*cuatro*	KWAH-troh	12	*doce*	DOH-seh
5	*cinco*	SEEN-koh	13	*trece*	TREH-seh
6	*seis*	sehys	14	*catorce*	kah-TOHR-seh
7	*siete*	SYEH-teh	15	*quince*	KEEN-seh

When enumerating items, however, the numeral is an adjective and precedes the items enumerated. Any number above *uno* requires the use of the plural form of the item (see Chapter 4 for rules on how to add plural endings to nouns). Keep in mind that the actual numeral employed will not be in the plural form for quantities less than 200. For example:

un sacerdote	one priest
una bebida	one drink
cinco dedos	five fingers
cinco quejas	five complaints

ocho vestidos	eight dresses
ocho cortinas	eight curtains

FACTS

The cardinal number as a preceding adjective often enumerates the quantity of items. When the cardinal number follows the item(s), it is limiting the discussion to the item in the position described by the number. For example: *cinco volúmenes* (five volumes), as opposed to *volumen cinco* (volume five).

Moving On: 16–99

Double-digit numbers are formed similarly to the way they are formed in English. For example, "21" is "twenty-one." If you know the words for "twenty," "thirty," "forty," and so on, as well as how to count from 1 to 9, you will be able to come up with any number from 1 to 100. It is pretty much the same in Spanish. Take a look at the list of the numbers divisible by 10:

10	*diez*	60	*sesenta*
20	*veinte*	70	*setenta*
30	*treinta*	80	*ochenta*
40	*cuarenta*	90	*noventa*
50	*cincuenta*		

The numbers 16 through 29 are special because they may be represented in two different ways—as three distinct words or as a single word.

16	*diez y seis → dieciséis*	24	*veinte y cuatro → veinticuatro*
17	*diez y siete → diecisiete*	25	*veinte y cinco → veinticinco*
18	*diez y ocho → dieciocho*	26	*veinte y seis → veintiséis*
19	*diez y nueve → diecinueve*	27	*veinte y siete → veintisiete*
20	*veinte*	28	*veinte y ocho → veintiocho*
21	*veinte y uno → veintiuno*	29	*veinte y nueve → veintinueve*
22	*veinte y dos → veintidós*		
23	*veinte y tres → veintitrés*		

The numbers 30 through 99 can only be expressed as three separate words, with the conjunction y (and) in between the tens place and the units place. Here are a few examples:

36 30 + 6 → *treinta y seis*
48 40 + 8 → *cuarenta y ocho*
59 50 + 9 → *cincuenta y nueve*
81 80 + 1 → *ochenta y uno*

Hundreds

In Spanish, you rarely if ever say "one hundred"—instead, you simply say *cien* (hundred). Any number between 101 and 199 uses the term *ciento* in combination with the numerals specified in the previous section. Notice that a conjunction is not used between the "hundred" and "ten" words:

116 100 + 10 + 6 → *ciento dieciséis*
131 100 + 30 + 1 → *ciento treinta y uno*
177 100 + 70 + 7 → *ciento setenta y siete*

Multiples of 100 are *cientos*. To create a specific number of "hundred" units, all you really need to do is combine the number of 100s with *cientos*:

200 *dos + cientos → doscientos*
300 *tres + cientos → trescientos*
400 *cuatro + cientos → cuatrocientos*
500 *cinco + cientos → quinientos*
600 *seis + cientos → seiscientos*
700 *siete + cientos → setecientos*
800 *ocho + cientos → ochocientos*
900 *nueve + cientos → novecientos*

It follows, then, that for numbers 201 to 999, the process for putting together the numbers goes like this:

206   200 + 6 → *doscientos seis*
331   300 + 30 + 1 → *trescientos treinta y uno*
447   400 + 40 + 7 → *cuatrocientos cuarenta y siete*
650   600 + 50 → *seiscientos cincuenta*
809   800 + 9 → *ochocientos nueve*

Use *y* only between the "tens" and the "units" values. Otherwise, the *y* is omitted. Also, the numbers containing "hundreds" parts do conform to the gender of the nouns they modify. For example: *trescientas casas* (300 homes), *quinientas veintiuna quejas* (521 complaints).

Notice that the words for 500, 700, and 900 do not follow the regular *numeral + cientos* pattern. To review, they are: *quinientos* (500), *setecientos* (700), and *novecientos* (900).

When you use the term "hundreds" in English, you are using it as a noun rather than an adjective describing the quantity of a noun. Spanish provides you with the construction *centares de* + noun to express the same idea. For example: *En el concierto, Samantha vió a centares de admiradores de Donna Adler.* (At the concert, Samantha saw hundreds of Donna Adler fans.)

Thousands

Like *cien, mil* (thousand) generally exists without a preceding article. Unlike *ciento*, however, *mil* does not take on any endings when it is part of a number. For any number of thousands above 1,000, simply place the number of thousands before *mil (dos mil, tres mil,* and so on). For example:

1,216   1,000 + 200 + 10 + 6 → *mil doscientos dieciséis*
2,331   2 + 1000 + 300 + 30 + 1 → *dos mil trescientos treinta y uno*
3,477   3 + 1000 + 400 + 70 + 7 → *tres mil cuatrocientos setenta y siete*
5,000   5 + 1000 → *cinco mil*
45,783   40 + 5 + 1000 + 700 + 80 + 3 → *cuarenta y cinco mil setecientos ochenta y tres*

ESSENTIALS

Spanish provides two equivalent constructions to express the collective noun "thousands"—*miles de* + noun or *millares de* + noun. For example: *Miles de personas votan. Millares de personas votan.* (Thousands of people vote.) Preference for one over the other is largely a regional issue.

Note that when you write in Spanish, you use a period instead of a comma to separate the digits in numbers greater than 1,000, and vice versa for the sign used to denote decimal points (see **TABLE 9-1**).

TABLE 9-1

PERIOD AND COMMA IN SPANISH NUMBERS	
SPANISH	ENGLISH
3.000	3,000 (three thousand)
4,7	4.7 (four and seven tenths)

Millions and Beyond

This is a time to recall the warning on misleading cognates from the first chapter. Though some Spanish and American-English numbers do coincide (like million and *millón*), larger numbers do not. Compare:

millón (million)
mil millones (one billion)
billón (one trillion)

Use the following examples to practice what you have just learned.

1.000.001	*un millón uno*
2.000.002	*dos millones dos*
1.000.000.345	*mil millones, trescientos cuarenta y cinco*
14.500.900.005	*catorce mil quinientos millones, novecientos mil, cinco*
1.000.100.700.000	*un billón, cien millones, setecientos mil*

A subtle change in meaning occurs when you begin using numbers in the millions and larger. You already know that "hundreds" and "thousands" no longer describe the quantity of things, but that they themselves become the objects of discussion. This is generally true of one million and beyond. Whereas you can say *cien mujeres* (100 women), you cannot say *un millón mujeres*—the correct phrase would be *un millón de mujeres* (one million women), where *de mujeres* describes the million. If you are talking of an unspecified number of books ranging in the millions, then you would say *millones de libros*.

Practice Counting

1. The interrogative pronoun *¿cuántos?* asks the question "how many?"—*¿Cuantos tiene usted?* (How many do you have?) Answer the following questions:

¿Cuántos automóviles tiene usted? (How many cars do you have?)

- -

¿Cuántas hijas tiene usted? (How many daughters do you have?)

- -

¿Cuántas monedas tiene usted? (How many coins do you have?)

- -

¿Cuántos sombreros tiene usted? (How many hats do you have?)

- -

2. Write out the following numbers in Spanish:

eighteen -
ninety-nine -
three hundred and forty-five -

ten thousand five hundred and eighty-seven

twenty-two thousand seven hundred and thirteen

three million and eighty thousand

Ordinal Numbers

When ordinal numbers describe a noun's position in a series, they act as adjectives and generally come before the noun they are modifying. Unlike cardinal numbers, ordinal numbers correspond in gender and number with the noun they describe. For example:

el primer día (the first day)
la primera semana (the first week)
los primeros días (the first days)
las primeras semanas (the first weeks)

On its own, an ordinal may express a "position" as a place, rather than a description, as in this sentence: **Yo salí de la casa primero.** (I left the house first.)

The following list presents ordinal numbers. Unless otherwise noted, this general form is the same as the masculine singular form.

primer, primero (first)   *octavo* (eighth)
segundo (second)   *noveno* (ninth)
tercer, tercero (third)   *décimo* (tenth)
cuarto (fourth)   *undécimo* (eleventh)
quinto (fifth)   *duodécimo* (twelfth)
sexto (sixth)   *decimotercero* (thirteenth)
séptimo (seventh)   *decimocuarto* (fourteenth)

Recall what happens to *uno* when used to describe quantity with respect to a masculine noun. As you might remember, "one car" in Spanish would be translated as **un coche**. That is, **uno** loses the final

-o before a masculine noun. The same is true with the ordinals *primero* and *tercero* when they precede the noun they modify. For example: *el primer coche* (the first car), but *el decimotercer coche* (the thirteenth car).

Before you go on to the next section, take a look at the following sentences that contain ordinal or cardinal numbers. These sentences should help you review what you have just learned and clarify any questions you might still have about using numerals correctly.

> *De joven, Eliza ganó dos trofeos de fútbol.* (When she was young, Eliza won two soccer trophies.)
>
> *Él salió en primer puesto en la competencia.* (He came out in first place in the competition.)
>
> *María vive en el apartamento ocho.* (María lives in apartment eight.)
>
> *Los políticos asignan miles de millones de dolares cada año.* (Politicians allocate thousands of millions of dollars each year.)
>
> *Nací en el año mil novecientos cincuenta y seis.* (I was born in the year 1956.)
>
> *Treinta y siete más diez son cuarenta y siete.* (Thirty-seven plus ten is forty-seven.)
>
> *Patricio es el décimo hijo de Roberta y Alicia.* (Patrick is Robert and Alicia's tenth child.)
>
> *Millares de televidentes vieron la boda de Carlos y Diana.* (Thousands of television viewers saw the wedding of Charles and Diana.)

Days of the Week

To help you review the ordinal numbers, how about learning the days of the week? The following list answers the question *¿Cuáles son los días de la semana?* (What are the days of the week?)

> *El lunes es el primer día de la semana.* (Monday is the first day of the week.)
>
> *El martes es el segundo día de la semana.* (Tuesday is the second day of the week.)

El miércoles es el tercer día de la semana. (Wednesday is the third day of the week.)

El jueves es el cuarto día de la semana. (Thursday is the fourth day of the week.)

El viernes es el quinto día de la semana. (Friday is the fifth day of the week.)

El sábado es el sexto día de la semana. (Saturday is the sixth day of the week.)

El domingo es el séptimo día de la semana. (Sunday is the seventh day of the week.)

For a list of the days of the week, refer to **TABLE 9-2**.

TABLE 9-2

DAYS OF THE WEEK		
lunes	LOO-nehs	Monday
martes	MAHR-tehs	Tuesday
miércoles	MYEHR-koh-lehs	Wednesday
jueves	HHWEH-vehs	Thursday
viernes	VYEHR-nehs	Friday
sábado	SAH-bah-doh	Saturday
domingo	doh-MEEN-goh	Sunday

Other words that will help you set the sentence in the correct time frame include the following (listed in chronological order):

el año pasado (last year)

la semana pasada (last week)

anteayer (day before yesterday)

ayer (yesterday)

este año (this year)

esta semana (this week)

hoy (today)

mañana (tomorrow)

el día pasado mañana (day after tomorrow)

la semana próxima (next week)
el año próximo (next year)

The following set of examples illustrates how these vocabulary words work within the Spanish sentence:

Esta semana he estado con resfrío. (This week I have been sick with a head cold.)
Toda la semana pasada, estuve de vacaciones. (I was on vacation all last week.)
Estaré en las Islas Galápagos la semana próxima. (I will be in the Galápagos Islands next week.)
Este año estaré en un nueve empleo. (This year I will be in a new job.)
El año pasado, estaba en Santo Domingo. (Last year I was in Santo Domingo.)
El año próximo, estoy en Madrid. (Next year, I will be in Madrid.)

SSENTIALS

To use *ser* in expressing time and days of the week, follow the format of the following question and answer: *¿Qué día es hoy?* (What day is it today?) *Hoy es lunes.* (Today is Monday.) Consequently, you would say *mañana es martes, en dos días es miércoles, en tres días es jueves,* and so on.

You know how to say what day it is, but what about the date? In Spanish, the date is known as *la fecha*:

¿Cuál es la fecha de hoy? (Which is the date today?)
Hoy es lunes, el catorce de junio. (Today is Monday, June 14.)
De hoy en ocho es martes, el veintidos de junio. (Eight days from today, it is Tuesday, June 22.)

Days of the Week

Translate the following sentences to Spanish. Remember to use the appropriate articles. For additional vocabulary, refer to **TABLE 9-3**.

1. Yesterday I was in a hurry. (all day, but not today)

2. Saturday, I was with Elena.

3. Sunday I will be in Florida.

4. I am better since last week.

5. I work Tuesdays.

6. The birthday party is on the twenty-fifth.

7. We traveled more this year.

8. I will begin the diet the day after tomorrow.

TABLE 9-3

VOCABULARY			
comenzar	to begin	con	with
de prisa	in a hurry	dieta	diet
en la Florida	in Florida	este año	this year
fiesta de cumpleaños	birthday party	más	more
mejor	better	trabajar	to work
viajar	to travel		

The Months and Seasons

Moving on from days of the week, let's look at the months of the year and the four seasons. The list of *los meses* (the months) in Spanish appears in **TABLE 9-4**.

TABLE 9-4

MONTHS OF THE YEAR		
enero	eh-NEH-roh	January
febrero	feh-BREH-roh	February
marzo	MAHR-soh	March
abril	ah-BREEL	April
mayo	MAY-oh	May
junio	HHOO-nyoh	June
julio	HHOO-lyoh	July
agosto	ah-GOHS-toh	August
septiembre	sehp-TYEHM-breh	September
octubre	ohk-TOO-breh	October
noviembre	noh-VYEHM-breh	November
diciembre	dee-SYEHM-breh	December

There is a slight difference in handling days, seasons, and months. Unless replaced by other modifiers such as "each," the masculine article, *el,* precedes days and seasons. However, months are only specified by *el* when speaking about a specific time when an event occurred or will occur.

In Spanish, the four seasons of the year correspond to the English winter, spring, summer, and fall. The seasons are listed in **TABLE 9-5**.

TABLE 9-5

SEASONS OF THE YEAR		
invierno	een-VYEHR-noh	winter
primavera	pree-mah-VEH-rah	spring
verano	veh-RAH-noh	summer
otoño	oh-TOH-nyoh	autumn, fall

Asking and Telling the Time

What time is it? It's a common enough question. In Spanish, *tiempo* refers to the general concept of "time." Curiously enough, however, it also means "weather." If you ask someone about *el tiempo*, the person will probably give you a weather report, rather than the time. You will be better served by thinking in terms of *la hora* ("the hour"). The most common ways to ask the time include: *¿Qué hora es?* and *¿Qué horas son?*

FACTS

In Spain and Latin American countries, time is generally noted with respect to a twenty-four-hour clock (particularly in written form). Depending on the country, you may see 2 P.M. written as 1400, 14h00m, 14:00, or 14'00; and 2:30 A.M. may be written as 02.30, 02h30m, 02:30, or 02'30.

Before going any farther, keep in mind that both phrases are referring to a particular time. Though essentially employing the same words, each phrase is relying on a different number of *la hora*. *En ingles* (in English), the questions are translated exactly the same, "What time is it?" Depending on the region, native speakers may be inclined to prefer one phrase to the other. Many speakers may even employ both. The possible responses may be:

> *Es la una.* (It's one o'clock.)
> *Son las once.* (It's eleven o'clock.)
> *Son las doce en punto.* (It's twelve o'clock on the dot.)

Did you notice that only one response employed the present tense singular form of *ser*? That's because whenever you speak of any full hour other than *la una*, you are talking about more than one *hora* and, as a consequence, must use the plural form of *ser*. So *¿Qué hora es?* can be taken to mean that the person asking the question assumes it to be approximately 1:00. On the other hand, *¿Qué horas son?* may refer to the assumption that it is not 1:00. Many people choose *¿Qué horas son?* as their standard time-asking question, since the probability of it not being between 1:00 and 1:59 is one in twelve, or maybe even one in twenty-four!

In actual conversation, however, the hour is treated much as in English—it is differentiated by the part of the day:

> *de la madrugada* (of the early morning, until dawn)
> *de la mañana* (of the morning, until noon)
> *de la tarde* (of the afternoon/of the evening, before sunset)
> *de la noche* (of night, after sunset until midnight)

For example: *Son las dos de la madrugada* (it's two in the early morning); *son las seis de la mañana* (it's six in the morning); *son las dos de la tarde* (it's two in the afternoon); *son las diez de la noche* (it's ten at night). But what are the chances that the time will be exactly six or two or ten? Generally, these rules would apply:

1. Minutes 1 through 30 are "added" to *la hora*. For example:
   13:23 —*la una y veintitrés de la tarde* (one twenty-three in the afternoon)
2. Minutes 31 through 59 are "subtracted" from *la hora* with *menos* (minus). For example:
   5:49 —*las seis menos once de la mañana* (eleven before six in the morning)
3. You can also tell time by dividing the hour in half *(media)* and in quarters *(cuartos)*. For example:
   13:15 —*la una y cuarto de la tarde* (quarter past one in the afternoon)
   1:30 —*la una y media de la madrugada* (one-thirty in the early morning)
   13:45 —*las dos menos cuarto de la tarde* (quarter to two in the afternoon)

ALERT

To avoid confusing *mañana* (tomorrow) with *mañana* (morning), keep this in mind—references to "morning" are generally preceded by a definite article; references to "tomorrow" are not.

What Time Is It?

Try your hand at these times:

1. It's a quarter to three in the afternoon.

2. It's seven-thirty in the morning.

3. It's a quarter after eleven at night.

4. It's midnight.

5. 14:36

6. 8:23

7. 13:28

8. 4:42

9. 23:08

10. 12:00 noon

CHAPTER 10

Important Verbs to Know

The Spanish language has a plethora of verbs—some are regular in all their conjugations, and others have various irregularities. This chapter will examine a few irregular verbs that are often found in the Spanish sentence. These verbs are connected with concepts that are important to learn, and will help you master other areas of the Spanish language.

To Have and To Have To: *Tener*

So far you've looked in detail at two Spanish words used to describe yourself and your existence—*ser* and *estar*. Now it's time to meet *tener*, one of those verbs it's hard to get along without. *Tener* corresponds to descriptions of experience. In its simplest form, it means "to have." To conjugate *tener* in the present tense, refer to **TABLE 10-1**.

TABLE 10-1

CONJUGATING *TENER* IN PRESENT TENSE		
yo	tengo	I have
tú	tienes	you have (informal)
él, ella, usted	tiene	he, she, it has; you have (formal)
nosotros	tenemos	we have
ellos, ellas, ustedes	tienen	they have, you have (plural)

Tengo un coche rojo. (I have a red car.)
Marisela tiene un paraguas azul. (Marisela has a blue umbrella.)
¿Cuántos años tiene usted? (How old are you?)

Take another look at the question *¿Cuántos años tiene usted?* (How old are you?) As you can see, the concept of age in Spanish is expressed with the verb *tener*. To answer, you would say *Tengo ___ años.* (I am ___ years old.)

Experience with *Tener*

Tener may also be used as "being with," physically, mentally, or emotionally. Oddly enough, *tener* is used in many of the same situations as the *estar con* combination. Take a look at **TABLE 10-2**.

TABLE 10-2

TENER USED AS "TO BE"		
SPANISH	LITERALLY	ENGLISH
tengo calor	I am (experiencing) heat	I am hot
tengo celos	I am (experiencing) jealousy	I am jealous
tengo fiebre	I am (experiencing) fever	I am feverish

tengo frío	I am (experiencing) cold	I am cold
tengo gripe	I am (experiencing) influenza	I have the flu
tengo hambre	I am (experiencing) hunger	I am hungry
tengo miedo	I am (experiencing) fear	I am afraid
tengo pena	I am (experiencing) sorrow, discomfort	I am sad, embarrassed
tengo sed	I am (experiencing) thirst	I am thirsty
tengo sueño	I am (experiencing) sleepiness	I am sleepy
tengo vergüenza	I am (experiencing) shame	I am embarrassed

To be more specific, you can then add modifiers to clarify what you are experiencing. Pick one of two modifiers—*mucho* (much, many) or *poco* (few, little). Remember: The modifiers must adopt the gender and number of the condition. For examples, see **TABLE 10-3**.

TABLE 10-3

MUCHO O POCO? (MANY OR FEW?)		
Tengo miedo.	*Tengo mucho miedo.*	*Tengo poco miedo.*
Tengo sed.	*Tengo mucha sed.*	*Tengo poca sed.*
Tengo celos.	*Tengo muchos celos.*	*Tengo pocos celos.*

Other situations where you would use *tener* include:

Tengo cuidado. (I am careful.)
Tengo la culpa. (I am at fault.)
Tengo éxito. (I am successful; I have success.)
Tengo quince años. (I am fifteen years old; I have reached fifteen years.)
Tengo razón. (I am in the right; I am right.)
Tengo suerte. (I am lucky; I have luck.)

An Infinitive Construction: *Tener Que*

Up to this point you've seen the infinitive only as a point of reference to determine meaning and conjugation. You may recall that the infinitive also allows you to speak of an action without really needing to make it active, or attribute it to an actor. For example: *Aprendí a nadar.* (I learned to swim.)

An interesting manifestation of this use of the infinitive can be seen in the expression of obligation that is created when *tener* combines with *que* ("what/that" though not translated in this situation) and the infinitive. In this case, the *tener que* construction may be translated as "have to" or "has to":

Tengo que ir a casa. (I have to go home.)
Ellos tienen que practicar cada día. (They have to practice each day.)
¿Cuándo tienes que comer? (When do you have to eat?)

Conjugating *Tener* Through the Spanish Tenses

In the preterite tense, *tener* describes an experience, or sensation, that is known to have ended and, as a result, is tied only to the past, often as a single event. For example:

Anoche tuve poca hambre. (I was not very hungry last night.)
Anoche Miguel tuvo mucho de comer. (Miguel had a lot to eat last night.)

Notice that the conjugations do not follow the regular *-er* verb rules. The base changes to *tuv-*, and the endings are slightly different as well. Refer to **TABLE 10-4** for how to conjugate *tener* in the preterite.

TABLE 10-4

CONJUGATING *TENER* IN PRETERITE TENSE		
yo	tuve	I had
tú	tuviste	you had (informal)
él, ella, usted	tuvo	he, she, it had; you had (formal)
nosotros	tuvimos	we had
ellos, ellas, ustedes	tuvieron	they had, you had (plural)

Luckily, *tener* follows regular verb rules in the imperfect tense. The imperfect is characterized by its ongoing development in the past, rather than by its termination, which is vague. Here are a few examples with respect to the imperfect form of *tener*:

De joven, tenía mucha suerte. (Throughout my youth, I was very lucky.)
Hace muchos años, tenía un mascota. (Several years ago, I had a pet.)

ESSENTIALS

Compare how *tener que* is used in the preterite and the imperfect:
Tuve que ir a casa. I had to go home (and did).
Tenía que ir a casa. I had to go home (but may or may not have).

As you remember, the present perfect tense characterizes an experience as having occurred in the recent past:

He tenido sueño todo el día. (I have been sleepy all day.)
He tenido varios empleos. (I have had many jobs.)

Finally, in the the future tense, *tener* describes a future state, bounded or unbounded by reference to time. Note that while the endings for conjugating *tener* in the future tense are regular, the base is not *tener-* but *tendr-*. For example:

Tendré treinta y seis años en julio. (I will be thirty-six years old in July.)
Marina tendrá un coche para su cumpleaños. (Marina will have a car by her birthday.)

Working with *Tener*

1. Translate the following sentences into Spanish; use the vocabulary provided in **TABLE 10-5**. If you need further help, refer to the answer key.

1. I have to drive the car.

2. You (formal) will have to go at four.

3. They had to read the book (and did).

4. I have to dance with Fabian.

5. You (informal) have to attend the wedding.

TABLE 10-5

VOCABULARY			
asistir	attend	*bailar*	to dance
la boda	wedding	*con*	with
conducir	to drive	*ir*	to go
leer	to read	*libro*	book

2. Now it's your turn. Write down in complete sentences some of your obligations. If you like, use the vocabulary listed in **TABLE 10-6**.

TABLE 10-6

VOCABULARY			
acompañar	to accompany	*ahorrar*	to save
aprender a	to learn (to)	*ayudar con*	to help with
comer mejor	to eat better	*comprar*	to purchase
cuidarme mejor	to take better care of myself	*devolver*	to return (something)
estudiar	to study	*hacer arreglar*	to have fixed
hacer más ejercicio	to exercise more	*hacer un pago*	to make a payment
lavar	to wash (something)	*limpiar*	to clean (something)
llegar a tiempo	to arrive on time	*llevar*	to carry
resolver	to resolve	*traer*	to bring

Haber: To Have or To Be?

This verb should be familiar to you—it is the auxiliary verb "to have" that appears in the present perfect tense.

> *He sido plomero.* (I have been a plumber.)
> *Has estado en Nicaragua recientemente.* (You have been in Nicaragua recently.)
> *Han tenido sueño todo el día.* (They have been sleepy all day.)

However, *haber* can be found in other types of constructions, as well as alone. One of the most common usages for this verb is in the "impersonal third-person" present-tense form *hay*. Because it is used as both singular and plural, it may be translated as either "there is" or "there are," depending on the context. As such, it may be used to:

1. Ask questions characterized by existence:
   ¿Hay alguién aquí? (Is there someone here?)
   ¿Hay papel higiénico? (Is there toilet paper?)
   ¿Hay mucha gente en la entrada? (Are there many people at the door?)
   ¿Hay naranjas en casa? (Are there oranges at home?)
   ¿Qué hay allí? (What is there over there?)
2. State the existence of something:
   Hay pan fresco en la cocina. (There is fresh bread in the kitchen.)
   Hay un televisor en el cuarto de estar. (There is a television set in the living room.)
   Hay buenas escuelas públicas. (There are good public schools.)
   Hay ocho maravillas en el mundo. (There are eight wonders of the world.)
3. State a broad "impersonal" obligation (lacking a specific subject, sometimes translated into English as "one") in the form of *hay* + *que* + infinitive:
   Hay que luchar por la vida. (One must fight for one's life.)
   Hay que cortar el césped. (The lawn needs cutting; there is lawn to be cut.)
   Hay que ahorar siquiera un poco. (One must save at least a little.)

There are two important distinctions to be made regarding *hay* and other verbs with similar uses. First, there is a tendency to confuse *hay* with forms of *estar*. It is best to distinguish them by noting that whereas *estar* expresses the position or location of someone or something, *hay* refers to that someone's or something's very existence. Compare:

Está en casa. (He is at home.)
Hay alguien en casa. (There is someone at home.)

Second, there is also a tendency to confuse *hay* with *tener* within a *tener que* + infinitive phrase. Remember that while both expressions express an obligation, *tener que* ... has a specific subject (and *tener* is conjugated according to that subject), whereas the *hay que* ... construction expresses an obligation not specifically assigned to a particular individual. Compare:

Hay que comprarlo. (Someone should buy it.)
Tengo que comprarlo. (I have to buy it.)

Other Uses and Applications of *Haber*

The uses you have seen for *haber* are just the tip of the proverbial iceberg. As an auxiliary verb, it plays an important role in forming compound tenses. Though these tenses are really beyond the scope of this book, here's a short preview of what to expect.

When it comes to verb tenses, recall that a completed action is described as being "perfect." This being the case, you will often find a form of *haber* helping the past participle of a verb achieve this completion. You've already seen this occur in the present perfect, where *haber* is conjugated in the present tense to bring the completed action of a recent past into closer focus by means of the present. For example:

Yo he terminado el trabajo. (I have finished the work.)
¿Te has bañado ya? (Have you already showered?)

In the past perfect (or pluperfect) tense, the past participle remains, but *haber* is conjugated in the imperfect (see **TABLE 10-7**).

TABLE 10-7	*HABER* CONJUGATED IN THE IMPERFECT TENSE	
	yo	había
	tú	habías
	él, ella, usted	había
	nosotros	habíamos
	ellos, ellas, ustedes	habían

The key to understanding this tense is the use of "had" in its translation. The focus on completed action is now shifted from the present back to the past. For example:

Yo había terminado el trabajo antes que salimos. (I had finished the work before we went out.)
¿Te habías bañado ya? (Had you already showered?)

Similarly, *haber* also appears in the future perfect tense (see **TABLE 10-8**).

TABLE 10-8	HABER IN THE FUTURE PERFECT TENSE	
	yo	habré
	tú	habrás
	él, ella, usted	habrá
	nosotros	habremos
	ellos, ellas, ustedes	habrán

This compound tense is used in two situations:

1. To describe an action as something that "will have" occurred by a deadline of sorts. For example:
   Yo habré terminado el trabajo para las dos. (I will have finished the work by two.)
   ¿Te habrás bañado antes de yo llegaré? (Will you have showered before I arrive?)

2. To describe an action as something that "must have" occurred, though there is a very slight chance that it hasn't. For example:
Me habré equivocado. (I must have been mistaken.)
Se habrán olvidado la dirección, porque ya debían estar aquí. (They must have forgotten the address, because they should have been here already.)

The last compound tense in the indicative mood is the conditional perfect. This tense is the hardest to grasp because the focus of the completed action is not a single point in time but a continuum, where something may occur after one event but before another. See **TABLE 10-9** for conditional-tense conjugations of *haber*.

TABLE 10-9

HABER CONJUGATED IN CONDITIONAL PERFECT TENSE	
	HABER
yo	*habría*
tú	*habrías*
él, ella, usted	*habría*
nosotros	*habríamos*
ellos, ellas, ustedes	*habrían*

There are three uses for the conditional perfect. They include:

1. Expressing a future action sandwiched between two events. For example:
Usted me aseguró que habría pintado la casa antes de entregármela. (You assured me that you would have painted the house before giving it to me.)
2. Expressing an action that failed because of some hindrance:
Yo habría terminado el trabajo, pero no tenía las herramientas adequadas.
(I would have finished the work, but I did not have the appropriate tools.)
3. Expressing an expansive past probability, allowing for conjecture or approximation. Looking at a situation may assist in getting a better

handle on this use. If someone were to ask, "Why is Tom not in his office?" one possible response is, "He must have become ill" (the future perfect). But if the question was posed as a past event, "Why was Tom not in his office?" a possible response to this query is, "He must have been ill." (Conditional perfect: *Se habría enfermado*.) Remember: Both responses express probabilities, but the former forms a conjecture that begins in the future, and the latter forms one rooted in the past.

To Finish: *Acabar*

You will discover that in addition to *tener* and *haber*, there are a multitude of expressions that can be gotten from only a few simple words. And, as you have seen with *estar*, prepositions can make quite a significant addition to a verb. Take the word *acabar* (to finish). In its most basic form, it conjugates as a regular *-ar* verb (see **TABLE 10-10**).

TABLE 10-10

CONJUGATING *ACABAR* IN THE PRESENT TENSE		
(yo)	*acabo*	I finish
(tú)	*acabas*	you finish (informal)
(él, ella, usted)	*acaba*	he, she finishes; you finish (formal)
(nosotros, nosotras)	*acabamos*	we finish
(ellos, ellas, ustedes)	*acaban*	they finish; you finish (plural)

By itself, *acabar* is used exactly as you would expect:

Hoy acabo la tarea. (Today I finish the homework.)
¿Cuándo acabas el óleo? (When will you finish the oil painting?)

It also conjugates as a regular *-ar* verb in other tenses, such as the imperfect and the future (see the following examples):

De niños, acabábamos las peleas con un abrazo. (As children, we used to end fights with a hug.)
Raúl acabará sus vacaciones la semana próxima. (Raul will be finishing his vacation next week.)

When combined with the preposition *con* (with), *acabar* is used in the sense of "to destroy," "finish off," or "to break."

Mañana acabo con todo.
> (Tomorrow I will finish off everything.)

La revolución acabó con la opresión.
> (The revolution destroyed the oppression.)

In Conversation

In conversation, *acabar* often appears in combination with *de +* infinitive. Notice that this construction requires you to use the present tense to consider a recent action performed to its end. Though you will find the *acabar de + infinitivo* in other tenses, the immediacy related to a completed act is only apparent within the present and imperfect tenses, where the conjugated action itself is considered in midstate.

Acabo de terminar la tarea.
> (I have just finished the homework.)

Acabamos de nadar.
> (We have just finished swimming.)

Acababa de terminar la tarea.
> (I have just finished the homework.)

Acabábamos de nadar.
> (We have just finished swimming.)

Hugo y Marlene acababan de llegar.
> (Hugo and Marlene have just arrived.)

To Go: *Ir*

Ir is among the most useful, most versatile, and most difficult verbs to master, but your command of this verb will serve you well. Its meaning is simple, "to go," but as in English, its reach is farther than the two letters would suggest.

Ir is one of the few "innately" irregular verbs—its irregularities are specific to itself and have simply evolved without pronunciation concerns. Take a look at its different tenses and see how the verb changes across time (see **TABLE 10-11**).

TABLE 10-11

CONJUGATING *IR*				
	PRESENT	**PRETERITE**	**IMPERFECT**	**FUTURE**
(yo)	voy	fui	iba	iré
(tú)	vas	fuiste	ibas	irás
(él, ella, usted)	va	fue	iba	irá
(nosotros, nosotras)	vamos	fuimos	íbamos	iremos
(ellos, ellas, ustedes)	van	fueron	iban	irán

A significant step in understanding how *ir* is used involves coming to the realization that "to go" requires direction. Take a look at the following sentences:

> *¿Vas a la carnicería?* (Are you going to the butcher shop?)
> *Mauricio fue a la boda de su mejor amigo.* (Mauricio went to his best friend's wedding.)
> *De niños, íbamos a la casa de mi abuelita.* (When we were children, we used to go to Grandma's house.)
> *He ido a varios conciertos.* (I have gone to various concerts.)
> *Mañana iré al banco.* (Tomorrow I will go to the bank.)
> *Van a ser las dos de la tarde.* (It is going on two in the afternoon.)

FACTS

As you might remember, the present perfect tense is formed with the conjugation of the verb *haber* and the past participle form of the main verb. The past participle of *ir* is *ido*. You will see examples of *ir* in the present perfect tense among the sample sentences that follow.

Exercise: Using *Ir*

Translate the following sentences into Spanish; use the vocabulary provided in **TABLE 10-12**. If you need further help, refer to the answer key in the back of the book.

1. We intend to wait for them in the store.

2. I am going to listen to the music.

3. She is going to go to the concert today.

4. They were going to swim, but it did not happen.

5. We are going to leave on vacation.

TABLE 10-12

VOCABULARY			
concierto	concert	*tienda*	store
escuchar	to listen to	*de vacaciones*	on vacation
hoy	today	*esperar*	to wait
música	music	*nadar*	to swim
ocurrir	to occur, happen	*salir*	to leave

An important construction to keep in mind is that of the *ir a + infinitivo*. With it you can describe an immediate future (the beginning of an action) or an intention. In English, the equivalent construction is "to be going to." For example:

Voy a comprar una bicicleta. (I am going to buy a bicycle.)

Voy a comer un bistec. (I am going to eat a steak.)

Iba a tocar el piano cuando se lastimó la mano derecha. (He was about to play the piano when he hurt his right hand.)

Iban a visitar el museo. (They were going to visit the museum.)

Iré a ver los planes mañana. (I intend on going to see the plans tomorrow.)

To Know: *Saber* Versus *Conocer*

The idea of knowledge in Spanish is divided between two words—*saber* and *conocer*. Take a look at their present tense conjugations in **TABLE 10-13**.

TABLE 10-13

CONJUGATING *SABER* AND *CONOCER* IN THE PRESENT TENSE		
	SABER	*CONOCER*
yo	sé	conozco
tú	sabes	conoces
él, ella, usted	sabe	conoce
nosotros, nosotras	sabemos	conocemos
ellos, ellas, ustedes	saben	conocen

Although both *saber* and *conocer* may be translated as "to know," they deal with different concepts. *Saber* conveys knowledge of a fact or a skill, and *conocer* with familiarity, be it with people, places, or things. These differences are outlined in **TABLE 10-14**.

TABLE 10-14

SABER VERSUS *CONOCER*	
SABER	*CONOCER*
to know that . . .	to be acquainted with, or well versed in . . .
to know facts	to know people (remember to include the personal *a*)
to know information	to be familiar with places and things

To review, compare the following pairs:

Yo sé como llegar a tu casa. (I know how to arrive at your house.)
Yo conozco la ruta. (I am familiar with the way.)
Ella no sabe quien llamó. (She doesn't know who called—she doesn't
  have that information.)
Ella no conoce a la persona que llamó. (She is not acquainted with
  the person who called—she has never met that person.)

Using *Saber* and *Conocer*

Translate the following sentences into Spanish; use the vocabulary
provided in **TABLE 10-15**. If you need further help, refer to the answer key
in the back of the book.

1. I know how old Antonio is.

   ----

2. María knows how to drive well.

   ----

3. I don't know his brother.

   ----

4. We know that respect and communication are essential in a
   relationship.

   ----

5. He knows Acapulco well because he travels there a lot.

TABLE 10-15

VOCABULARY			
allí	there	*conducir*	to drive
cuantos años tiene	how old he/she is	*esencial*	essential
hermano	brother	*mucho*	a lot
porque	because	*relación*	relationship
respeto	respect	*viajar*	to travel

CHAPTER 11

Irregular Verbs I (Present Tense)

Not all verbs fit the regular-verb molds you've learned so far (*ser, estar, tener,* and *haber* are among those you already know). When you conjugate irregular verbs, you need to know how their bases change in various conjugations. This chapter will introduce you to verbs that are irregular in the present tense.

What's the Explanation?

Irregular verbs do not keep their infinitive bases in some or all of their conjugated forms. What are the reasons behind these irregularities? Some irregularities are actually "regular"; that is, the changes that verbs undergo run consistently across verb groups. You will see that group irregularities also depend on similar letter substitutions.

Some irregularities result from spelling accommodations describing changes that occur to keep pronunciation consistent. A few verbs are "naturally" irregular (most often these are words that have been present in Spanish for a long time, and have changed radically over centuries; *ser* is a good example—it is irregular in most of its conjugated forms). Fortunately, only a small fraction of all Spanish verbs are irregular. (Refer to **TABLE 11-1** for a list of irregular verbs this chapter will concentrate on.)

TABLE 11-1

IRREGULAR VERBS			
andar	to walk	*asir*	to seize
caber	to fit (into)	*caer*	to fall
dar	to give	*saber*	to know
decir	to say	*salir*	to leave
haber	to have/be	*hacer*	to do, to make
ir	to go	*oír*	to hear
poder	to be able (to)	*poner*	to place, to put
producir	to produce	*querer*	to want
traer	to bring	*valer*	to be valued
venir	to come	*ver*	to see

ESSENTIALS

As you learn each verb, check to see whether it is regular or irregular. If it happens to be irregular, try to see if its irregularity is the same as that of another verb you are already familiar with—then, all you'll need to do is memorize how to conjugate one irregular verb instead of two. For example, did you know that *estar* and *tener* behave similarly in the preterite tense?

A Good Strategy

Keep a notebook of the irregular verbs you will more than likely need. At first, limit them to about ten verbs throughout all tenses, but keep adding another verb or two every week. The progress may seem slow, but all you really need to do is become aware of the potential irregularity of a verb. At that point you can do what native speakers do—consult a Spanish verb manual or an online verb-conjugation search engine.

Be warned: There is a lot to learn about irregular verbs, so don't expect to read this information once and never look at it again. More than likely you will need to refer to it frequently, even after you have finished working through this book.

Reviewing What You Already Know

Remember, the present tense verbs are formed by dropping their infinitive endings -*ar*, -*er*, or -*ir*, and adding appropriate endings based on the person and number of the verb's subject (refer to Chapter 5 for a better review). **TABLES 11-2**, **11-3**, and **11-4** list the present tense verb endings.

TABLE 11-2

	–AR VERBS	
	-ar	ganar (to win, earn)
yo	-o	gano
tú	-as	ganas
él, ella, usted	-a	gana
nosotros	-amos	ganamos
ellos, ellas, ustedes	-an	ganan

TABLE 11-3

	–ER VERBS	
	-er	beber (to drink)
yo	-o	bebo
tú	-es	bebes
él, ella, usted	-e	bebe
nosotros	-emos	bebemos
ellos, ellas, ustedes	-en	beben

TABLE 11-4

	–IR VERBS	
	-ir	recibir (to receive)
yo	-o	recibo
tú	-es	recibes
él, ella, usted	-e	recibe
nosotros	-imos	recibimos
ellos, ellas, ustedes	-en	reciben

Group Irregularities

Group irregularities generally result from vowel-focused modifications. Letter substitutions often occur across person and number, without affecting the employment of the regular verb endings.

A diphthong base change from *e* to *ie* occurs with many irregular verbs, across all three conjugations. As an example, take a look at how to conjugate *calentar* (to warm up, heat), in **TABLE 11-5**.

TABLE 11-5

	DIPHTHONG BASE CHANGE FROM *E* TO *IE*	
	-ar	calentar (to warm up, heat)
yo	-o	caliento
tú	-as	calientas
él, ella, usted	-a	calienta
nosotros	-amos	calentamos
ellos, ellas, ustedes	-an	calientan

Take a look at the *nosotros* form of *calentar*. As you can see, it is the only form that does not undergo a base change. Can you figure out why this might be? Here is a hint: Compare where the accent falls in each verb conjugation. (In the *nosotros* form, the accent falls on the *a* in -*amos*, not on the *e* that would otherwise turn into a diphthong.)

The group of verbs that act similarly to *calentar* is not small. Refer to **TABLE 11-6** for the infinitives and a sample conjugation (in the *yo* form).

TABLE 11-6   LIST OF VERBS WITH BASE CHANGE FROM *E* TO *IE*

VERB	*YO* FORM	*NOSOTROS* FORM	ENGLISH
advertir	advierto	advertimos	to warn
apretar	aprieto	apretamos	to tighten
arrendar	arriendo	arrendamos	to rent, lease
ascender	asciendo	ascendemos	to ascend
cerrar	cierro	cerramos	to close
comenzar	comienzo	comenzamos	to begin
confesar	confieso	confesamos	to confess
convertir	convierto	convertimos	to convert
defender	defiendo	defendemos	to defend
discernir	discierno	discernimos	to discern
empezar	empiezo	empezamos	to begin
encender	enciendo	encendemos	to light
entender	entiendo	entendemos	to understand
enterrar	entierro	enterramos	to bury
extender	extiendo	extendemos	to extend
herir	hiero	herimos	to injure
hervir	hiervo	hervimos	to boil
mentir	miento	mentimos	to lie, deceive
merendar	meriendo	merendamos	to eat a snack (before dinner)
negar	niego	negamos	to deny
pensar	pienso	pensamos	to think
perder	pierdo	perdemos	to lose
preferir	prefiero	preferimos	to prefer
quebrar	quiebro	quebramos	to break
querer	quiero	queremos	to want
recomendar	recomiendo	recomendamos	to recommend
sentir	siento	sentimos	to feel

Practice What You've Learned #1

Translate the following sentences using the appropriate verb forms. If you don't know a word, check the vocabulary in **TABLE 11-7**.

1. I rent my dwelling.

2. What (are) you (informal) think(ing)?

3. Today you (formal) start the new job.

4. On Fridays we scrub the floors.

5. They want to go out to eat.

6. We warn of the danger.

7. Tomorrow I snack with my brother.

8. I recommend the chicken.

9. You (plural) turn on your computers.

10. She (is) los(ing) her patience.

11. We prefer green vegetables.

TABLE 11-7

VOCABULARY			
comer	to eat	mañana	tomorrow
hermano	brother	peligro	danger
paciencia	patience	pollo	chicken
piso	floor	viernes	Friday
verduras	green vegetables	vivienda	dwelling
computadora	computer		

Diphthong Base Change from *O* to *Ue*

Another common diphthong base change among *-ar* and *-er* verbs (though not in *-ir* verbs) is when the base vowel *o* changes to *ue*. Just as with the previous group of verbs, the *nosotros* form retains the base as it appears in the infinitive form. **TABLE 11-8** provides a sample conjugation for the verb *mostrar* (to show). Notice that only the base of this verb is irregular—the endings remain the same as for any regular *-ar* verb.

TABLE 11-8

DIPHTHONG BASE CHANGE FROM *O* TO *UE*		
	-ar	mostrar (to show)
yo	-o	muestro
tú	-as	muestras
él, ella, usted	-a	muestra
nosotros	-amos	mostramos
ellos, ellas, ustedes	-an	muestran

TABLE 11-9 lists common verbs that belong to the same group as *mostrar* and behave in a similar way.

TABLE 11-9

LIST OF VERBS WITH BASE CHANGE FROM *O* TO *UE*			
VERB	*YO* FORM	*NOSOTROS* FORM	ENGLISH
absolver	absuelvo	absolvemos	to absolve
almorzar	almuerzo	almorzamos	to eat lunch
apostar	apuesto	apostamos	to bet
avergonzar	avergüenzo	avergonzamos	to embarrass
colgar	cuelgo	colgamos	to hang, suspend
comprobar	compruebo	comprobamos	to verify, check
demostrar	demuestro	demostramos	to demonstrate
devolver	devuelvo	devolvemos	to return
encontrar	encuentro	encontramos	to find, encounter
moler	muelo	molemos	to grind
morder	muerdo	mordemos	to bite
mover	muevo	movemos	to move
poder	puedo	podemos	to be able to
remover	remuevo	removemos	to remove, dig
rogar	ruego	rogamos	to beg
soltar	suelto	soltamos	to release, let go
soñar	sueño	soñamos	to dream
volar	vuelo	volamos	to fly
volver	vuelvo	volvemos	to return

Practice What You've Learned #2

Translate the following sentences using the appropriate verb forms.
If you don't know a word, check the vocabulary in **TABLE 11-10**.

1. I eat lunch at noon.

2. Tomorrow they fly to San Diego.

3. I hang the shirts.

4. You (informal) show houses.

5. She finds a coin on the floor.

6. I don't dream much.

7. We beg María for ice cream.

8. I (am) return(ing) the book.

9. Something smells bad.

10. You (formal) dig the earth.

11. He doesn't bite.

12. We can swim.

13. I will return Monday.

14. Can you (plural) help?

15. Priests absolve sins.

TABLE 11-10

VOCABULARY			
algo	something	ayudar	to help
camisa	shirt	casa	house
helado	ice cream	libro	book
lunes	Monday	mal	bad
mediodía	noon	moneda	coin
mucho	much	nadar	to swim
pecado	sin	piso	floor
sacerdote	priest	tierra	earth

There is a special case to the "o to *ue* group" irregularity. Fortunately, it is limited to one verb, *oler* (to smell). In addition to transforming the o to *ue*, as in other cases, there is an additional *h* added to the beginning of the word: *yo huelo, tú hueles, él huele, nosotros olemos, ellos huelen.*

Base Change from *E* to *I*

Another group of verbs, exclusively from the *-ir* category, undergoes a base change where the letter *e* changes to *i*. Once again, the *nosotros* form is the only one not subject to this change. An example of this group is the verb *repetir* (to repeat)—see **TABLE 11-11** on how it is conjugated.

TABLE 11-11

DIPHTHONG BASE CHANGE FROM *E* TO *I* IN *–IR* VERBS		
	-ir	repetir (to repeat)
yo	-o	repito
tú	-es	repites
él, ella, usted	-e	repite
nosotros	-imos	repetimos
ellos, ellas, ustedes	-en	repiten

TABLE 11-12 contains a list of verbs similar to *repetir* in their behavior in the present tense.

TABLE 11-12

LIST OF VERBS WITH BASE CHANGE FROM *O* TO *UE*			
VERB	YO FORM	NOSOTROS FORM	ENGLISH
competir	*compito*	*competimos*	to compete
despedir	*despido*	*despedimos*	to see off, fire
freír	*frío*	*freímos*	to fry
impedir	*impido*	*impedimos*	to impede
medir	*mido*	*medimos*	to measure
reír	*río*	*reímos*	to laugh
rendir	*rindo*	*rendimos*	to hand over
servir	*sirvo*	*servimos*	to serve
sonreír	*sonrío*	*sonreímos*	to smile
vestir	*visto*	*vestimos*	to dress

The following words also belong to the same group—in each one, the *e* changes to *i*. However, they are also irregular in other respects (described in the following sections of the chapter). For now, simply look at how they have been conjugated (**TABLE 11-13**).

TABLE 11-13

BASE CHANGE FROM *E* TO *I* AND ADDITIONAL IRREGULARITIES					
	−IR	CONSEGUIR (TO OBTAIN)	CORREGIR (TO CORRECT)	ELEGIR (TO ELECT)	SEGUIR (TO FOLLOW)
yo	-o	*consigo*	*corrijo*	*elijo*	*sigo*
tú	-es	*consigues*	*corriges*	*eliges*	*sigues*
él, ella, usted	-e	*consigue*	*corrige*	*elige*	*sigue*
nosotros	-imos	*conseguimos*	*corregimos*	*elegimos*	*seguimos*
ellos, ellas, ustedes	-en	*consiguen*	*corrigen*	*eligen*	*siguen*

Practice What You've Learned #3

Translate the following sentences using the appropriate verb forms. If you don't know a word, check the vocabulary in **TABLE 11-14**.

1. I (am) boil(ing) eggs.

   -

2. We elect the president.

   -

3. You (formal) always follow all the rules.

   -

4. They follow the soaps.

   -

5. I (am) dress(ing) a baby.

   -

6. How tall are you (informal)? (Literally: How much do you measure?)

   -

7. This restaurant serves Mexican food.

   -

TABLE 11-14

VOCABULARY			
bebé	baby	*comida*	food
huevo	egg	*mexicano*	Mexican
presidente	president	*regla*	rule
restaurante	restaurant	*siempre*	always
telenovela	soap opera	*todo*	all

CHAPTER 12

Irregular Verbs II (Present Tense)

Now that you have taken a break and have come back rested, you can learn the other types of irregular verbs: verbs that undergo spelling accommodation, verbs that gain or lose an accent mark in particular conjugations, and verbs that, for one reason or another, are innately irregular.

Spelling Accommodations

Refer back to the table of verbs with two irregularities in the previous chapter. Take *corregir*, for instance. You might have expected "I correct" to be translated as *corrigo*. Instead, you saw it listed as *corrijo*. The *j* is used in place of the *g* so as to maintain the hard "hh" sound that is in the original word, *corregir* (coh-rreh-HHEER). Without this modification you would have had to pronounce it "coh-RREH-goh"—as you remember, *g* is pronounced "hh" before *e* or *i*, and "gh" when it precedes any other letter (see **TABLE 12-1**). The rule, then, is that when a verb ends with a -*ger* or -*gir*, the *g* changes to *j* whenever the verb ending does not end in an *e* or *i*—that is, the change only occurs in the *yo* form.

TABLE 12-1

SPELLING ACCOMMODATION IN VERBS THAT END WITH –*GER* AND –*GIR*				
	–*ER*	COGER (TO GRAB, TAKE)	–*IR*	FINGIR (TO FAKE)
yo	-o	*cojo*	-o	*finjo*
tú	-es	*coges*	-es	*finges*
él, ella, usted	-e	*coge*	-e	*finge*
nosotros	-emos	*cogemos*	-imos	*fingimos*
ellos, ellas, ustedes	-en	*cogen*	-en	*fingen*

TABLE 12-2 contains other verbs that undergo a *g* to *j* change. Again, compare the *yo*, *nosotros*, and *ellos/ellas/ustedes* forms.

TABLE 12-2

–*GER* VERBS WITH SPELLING CHANGE FROM *G* TO *J*				
VERB	YO FORM	NOSOTROS FORM	ELLOS/ELLAS/ USTEDES FORM	ENGLISH
emerger	*emerjo*	*emergemos*	*emergen*	to emerge
escoger	*escojo*	*escogemos*	*escogen*	to choose
exigir	*exijo*	*exigimos*	*exigen*	to demand
proteger	*protejo*	*protegemos*	*protegen*	to protect
recoger	*recojo*	*recogemos*	*recogen*	to collect, gather
restringir	*restrinjo*	*restringimos*	*restringen*	to restrict
surgir	*surjo*	*surgimos*	*surgen*	to surge, appear

Practice What You've Learned #1

Translate the following sentences using the appropriate verb forms. If you don't know a word, check the vocabulary in **TABLE 12-3**.

1. I take the small piece.

2. I choose the yellow apple.

3. I protect the family.

4. I gather the clothes from the floor.

5. I demand attention.

TABLE 12-3

VOCABULARY			
amarillo	yellow	*(la) atención*	attention
familia	family	*manzana*	apple
pedazo	piece	*pequeño*	little
piso	floor	*ropa*	clothes

Verbs That End in –*guir*

For verbs that end in -*guir*, the *g* is pronounced as the "g" in "get"—the *u* is silent because it is there to keep the *g* hard (-*gir* would sound like "hheer"). As you conjugate these verbs, you are trying to maintain a consistency of sound, which is why you need a modification in the **yo** form. Take a look at **TABLE 12-4** to see if you can figure out what is going on.

TABLE 12-4

–*GUIR* VERBS THAT DROP THE *U* IN THE *YO* FORM				
VERB	YO FORM	NOSOTROS FORM	ELLOS/ELLAS/ USTEDES FORM	ENGLISH
conseguir	*consigo*	*conseguimos*	*consiguen*	to obtain
extinguir	*extingo*	*extinguimos*	*extinguen*	to extinguish
perseguir	*persigo*	*perseguimos*	*persiguen*	to pursue

As you can see, when you are conjugating verbs that end in -*guir*, you need to drop the *u* in the *yo* form. To do otherwise would be to change the hard *g* in -*guir* from "g" as in "get" to "gw" as in "Gwen." For example: *consigo* would be *consiguo*, which would be pronounced kohn-SEEH-gwoh.

EXERCISE

Practice What You've Learned #2

Translate the following sentences using the appropriate verb forms. If you don't know a word, check the vocabulary in **TABLE 12-5**.

1. I follow the news.

----

2. Tomorrow I obtain a ticket for the concert.

----

3. I pursue justice.

TABLE 12-5

VOCABULARY			
boleto	ticket	*concierto*	concert
justicia	justice	*noticias*	news

Other –*uir* Verbs

This spelling accommodation focuses on other verbs that end in -*uir*. The modification is again very straightforward. The *i* is simply replaced by a *y* and the standard personal endings follow. For example, take a look at **TABLE 12-6** for the conjugation of *huir* (to flee).

TABLE 12-6

SPELLING ACCOMMODATION IN OTHER *–UIR* VERBS		
	-ir	*huir* (to flee)
yo	*-o*	*huyo*
tú	*-es*	*huyes*
él, ella, usted	*-e*	*huye*
nosotros	*-imos*	*huimos*
ellos, ellas, ustedes	*-en*	*huyen*

For the other verbs that behave like *huir* in the present tense, refer to **TABLE 12-7**.

TABLE 12-7

OTHER *–UIR* VERBS THAT UNDERGO *I* TO *Y* CHANGE				
VERB	YO FORM	NOSOTROS FORM	ELLOS/ELLAS/ USTED FORM	ENGLISH
construir	*construyo*	*construimos*	*construye*	to construct
contribuir	*contribuyo*	*contribuimos*	*contribuye*	to contribute
destruir	*destruyo*	*destruimos*	*destruye*	to destroy

You may be wondering why the *i* needs to be replaced at all, and why it is kept in the *nosotros* form. Notice that in the infinitive and in the *nosotros* form, the weak vowels have only themselves to contend with. They share the same strength and are each given equal weight. You've seen before how one weak vowel reacts when it is adjacent to a strong one—the *i* tends to adopt a "y" sound and the *u* a "w" sound. In this case, the *u* must retain its own sound, and the only way to keep it independent is to convert the *i* to *y* and thus make the separation between *u* and a strong vowel clearer with a more explicit "y" sound.

Practice What You've Learned #3

Translate the following sentences using the appropriate verb forms. If you don't know a word, check the vocabulary in **TABLE 12-8**.

1. Intolerance destroys society.

---

2. You (plural) construct homes.

---

3. We flee from the police.

---

4. Michelle contributes to her church.

---

5. You (informal) flee from responsibility.

TABLE 12-8

VOCABULARY			
de	from	*iglesia*	church
intolerancia	intolerance	*policía*	police
responsabilidad	responsibility	*sociedad*	society

Verbs That End with *–cer*

Verbs that end in *-cer* undergo spelling-accommodation changes in the *yo* form for the same reason that the *-guir* verbs undergo a change from *g* to *j*—in order to keep the pronunciation consistent. There are two changes that may occur.

FACTS

-Cer verbs must undergo a change in the yo form because if the *-er* is simply replaced by an *o*, the "s" sound produced by the *ce* combination in *-cer* would be transformed to a hard "k" sound.

The first scenario is that the base's final *c* may change to *z*. This occurs with verbs where the *-cer* ending is preceded by a consonant. For example, take the word *convencer* (cohn-vehn-SEHR), meaning "to convince." If you want to ascribe that action to yourself, you would say, "cohn-VEHN-soh," so it should be spelled *convenzo*. If you followed the regular-verb rule, you would have ended up with *convenco* (cohn-VEHN-coh) and, as a result, confuse a whole bunch of people. Refer to **TABLE 12-9** for verbs that undergo this particular type of spelling accommodation.

TABLE 12-9

	SPELLING ACCOMMODATION FROM *C* TO *Z*			
	-ER	*CONVENCER* (TO CONVINCE)	*EJERCER* (TO PRACTICE)	*VENCER* (TO CONQUER)
yo	-o	*convenzo*	*ejerzo*	*venzo*
tú	-es	*convences*	*ejerces*	*vences*
él, ella, usted	-e	*convence*	*ejerce*	*vence*
nosotros	-emos	*convencemos*	*ejercemos*	*vencemos*
ellos, ellas, ustedes	-en	*convencen*	*ejercen*	*vencen*

EXERCISE

Practice What You've Learned #4

Translate the following sentences using the appropriate verb forms. If you don't know a word, check the vocabulary in **TABLE 12-10**.

1. Each morning I conquer laziness.

2. I practice my profession.

3. Elena is convincing Juan that tomorrow is Saturday.

-----

4. On Sundays I conquer the lawn.

TABLE 12-10

VOCABULARY			
cada	each	*(el) césped*	lawn
domingo	Sunday	*mañana*	morning, tomorrow
pereza	laziness	*profesión*	profession
que	that	*sábado*	Saturday

As you have already seen, a verb may undergo more than one change. In the first-person present-tense conjugation of *torcer* (to turn), for example, two changes occur: the o is replaced by **ue**, and the -rcer changes to -rzo as in *tuerzo* (I turn), *tuerces* (you turn), *tuerce* (he, she, it turns; you turn), *torcemos* (we turn), *tuercen* (they turn; you turn).

If the letter that precedes the -cer ending in a verb is a vowel, the verb undergoes a slightly different transformation in the **yo** form of the present tense: In this case, the -cer ending changes to -zco. (This transformation is one of the many remnants left over from Latin.) The reasoning behind this transformation is similar—it is done to keep the *ce* sound that is voiced by the **z** in -zco. For a conjugation of a verb that belongs to this group, see **TABLE 12-11**.

TABLE 12-11

EXAMPLE OF SPELLING ACCOMMODATION FROM C TO ZC		
	-er	ofrecer (to offer)
yo	-o	ofrezco
tú	-es	ofreces
él, ella, usted	-e	ofrece
nosotros	-emos	ofrecemos
ellos, ellas, ustedes	-en	ofrecen

There are quite a few other verbs in Spanish that undergo this transformation in the yo form of the present tense (refer to the list in **TABLE 12-12**).

TABLE 12-12

VERBS WITH SPELLING ACCOMMODATION FROM C TO ZC			
VERB	YO FORM	*ÉL/ELLA/USTED* FORM	ENGLISH
agradecer	agradezco	agradece	to thank (for), give thanks
aparecer	aparezco	aparece	to appear
crecer	crezco	crece	to grow
desaparecer	desaparezco	desaparece	to disappear
desobedecer	desobedezco	desobedece	to disobey
embellecer	embellezco	embellece	to embellish, beautify
empobrecer	empobrezco	empobrece	to impoverish
enriquecer	enriquezco	enriquece	to enrich
envejecer	envejezco	envejece	to grow old
establecer	establezco	establece	to establish
favorecer	favorezco	favorece	to favor
florecer	florezco	florece	to flower, flourish
merecer	merezco	merece	to deserve
nacer	nazco	nace	to be born
obedecer	obedezco	obedece	to obey
padecer	padezco	padece	to suffer
parecer	parezco	parece	to seem, appear

However, there are some exceptions to this general rule of thumb. Take a look at the verbs *hacer* (to do), *cocer* (to cook), and *mecer* (to sway, rock), conjugated in **TABLE 12-13**. Their yo-form conjugations do not follow the rule established for verbs that end in *-cer* preceded by a vowel.

TABLE 12-13

EXCEPTIONS TO VERBS WITH SPELLING CHANGE FROM C TO ZC				
	–ER	*HACER* (to do)	*COCER* (to cook)	*MECER* (to sway)
yo	-o	*hago*	*cuezo*	*mezo*
tú	-es	*haces*	*cueces*	*meces*
él, ella, usted	-e	*hace*	*cuece*	*mece*
nosotros	-emos	*hacemos*	*cocemos*	*mecemos*
ellos, ellas, ustedes	-en	*hacen*	*cuecen*	*mecen*

Practice What You've Learned #5

Translate the following sentences using the appropriate verb forms. If you don't know a word, check the vocabulary in **TABLE 12-14**.

1. I give thanks for the help.

2. I am acquainted (with) María.

3. I do exercises in the morning.

4. I grow older with each worry.

5. I obey the rules.

6. I cook rice, meat, and vegetables.

7. I deserve a good grade.

TABLE 12-14

VOCABULARY			
arroz	rice	*ayuda*	help
buena nota	good grade	*carne*	meat
ejercicio	exercise	*preocupación*	worry
regla	rule	*vegetales*	vegetables

Verbs That End in *-ucir*

Treat verbs that end in *-ucir* as verbs that end in *-cer* preceded by a vowel (see previous section). That is, the *c* is transformed to a *cz* in the yo form of these verbs following the same rule of spelling accommodation. Use the conjugation of *traducir* as an example (**TABLE 12-15**).

TABLE 12-15

EXAMPLE OF SPELLING ACCOMMODATION FROM C TO ZC		
	−IR	*TRADUCIR* (to translate)
yo	-o	*traduzco*
tú	-es	*traduces*
él, ella, usted	-e	*traduce*
nosotros	-imos	*traducimos*
ellos, ellas, ustedes	-en	*traducen*

For a list of other *-ucir* verbs that behave similarly to *traducir*, refer to **TABLE 12-16**.

TABLE 12-16

VERBS WITH SPELLING ACCOMMODATION FROM C TO ZC			
VERB	**YO FORM**	***ÉL/ELLA/USTED* FORM**	**ENGLISH**
conducir	*conduzco*	*conduce*	to drive (a car)
deducir	*deduzco*	*deduce*	to deduce
introducir	*introduzco*	*introduce*	to introduce
lucir	*luzco*	*luce*	to shine
producir	*produzco*	*produce*	to produce

Practice What You've Learned #6

Translate the following sentences using the appropriate verb forms. If you don't know a word, check the vocabulary in **TABLE 12-17**.

1. I drive a yellow car.

2. I am translating a story.

3. Maribel shines at gatherings.

4. The cow produces milk.

5. The radio program introduces new singers.

TABLE 12-17

VOCABULARY			
amarillo	yellow	*cantante*	singer
coche	car	*cuento*	story
(la) leche	milk	*nuevo*	new
(el) programa	program	la *reunión*	gathering

Adding Accent Marks to Weak Vowels

With Spanish verbs ending in *-uar*, some ending in *-iar*, and a few in *-ar*, the present tense conjugations might sometimes require that the ordinarily weak vowels hold their own with the strong ones. In spelling, such vowels must be denoted with an accent mark. Look at what happens to *aislar* (to isolate), *enviar* (to send), and *actuar* (to act) in **TABLE 12-18**.

TABLE 12-18

		–AR	AISLAR (to isolate)	ENVIAR (to send)	ACTUAR (to act)
	yo	-o	aíslo	envío	actúo
	tú	-as	aíslas	envías	actúas
	él, ella, usted	-a	aísla	envía	actúa
	nosotros	-amos	aislamos	enviamos	actuamos
	ellos, ellas, ustedes	-an	aíslan	envían	actúan

ADDING ACCENT MARKS

Other examples of verbs that require accent marks in present tense conjugations (except, of course, in the *nosotros* form) are included in **TABLE 12-19**.

TABLE 12-19

OTHER VERBS THAT REQUIRE ACCENT MARKS

VERB	YO FORM	ÉL/ELLA/USTED FORM	NOSOTROS FORM	ENGLISH
ahijar	ahíjo	ahíja	ahijamos	to adopt
aullar	aúllo	aúlla	aullamos	to howl, shriek
continuar	continúo	continúa	continuamos	to continue

Unfortunately, this rule does not hold up for every *-iar* verb. The only way to know whether the *i* is accented is to memorize the exceptions or consult a verb manual. Take a look at **TABLE 12-20**. Note that for each verb, the *i* is either accented in all the forms except *nosotros*, or is not accented in any of the present tense conjugations.

TABLE 12-20

ACCENT IRREGULARITIES IN –IAR VERBS

VERB	YO FORM (WITH I)	VERB	YO FORM (WITH I)
abreviar (to abbreviate)	abrevio	averiar (to damage)	averío
acariciar (to caress, pet)	acaricio	confiar (to confide in)	confío
copiar (to copy)	copio	desviar (to deviate)	desvío
estudiar (to study)	estudio	guiar (to guide)	guío
rumiar (to ruminate)	rumio	vaciar (to empty)	vacío

Practice What You've Learned #7

Translate the following sentences using the appropriate verb forms. If you don't know a word, check the vocabulary in **TABLE 12-21**.

1. I send Christmas cards.

2. Marcela adopts a kitten.

3. The story continues for another thirty pages.

4. Sandra pets the zoo animals.

5. Adam and Berta study medicine.

TABLE 12-21

VOCABULARY			
Adán	Adam	*animal*	animal
cuento	story	*estudiar*	to study
gatito	kitten	*enviar*	to send
medicina	medicine	*otro*	another
página	page	*por*	for
tarjeta de Navidad	Christmas card	*zoológico*	zoo

Innate Irregularities

Recall that innate irregularities are those specific to verbs rather than groups of verbs. That is, the irregularities are not shared by different verbs across the three conjugations and are not simply spelling accommodations made to maintain consistent pronunciation.

Some verbs ending in *-er* or *-ir* may undergo a change in the *yo* form, where the ending becomes *-go*. This group may be divided into two subcategories: Some remain regular verbs in other forms, while others undergo base changes in second-, third-, or first-person plural forms.

Verbs that remain regular in all but the *yo* form are listed in **TABLE 12-22**.

TABLE 12-22

VERBS THAT TAKE ON *–GO* IN THE *YO* FORM			
–ER/–IR VERB	*YO* FORM	*ÉL/ELLA/USTED* FORM	ENGLISH
caer	*caigo*	*cae*	to fall
hacer	*hago*	*hace*	to do
poner	*pongo*	*pone*	to put, place
salir	*salgo*	*sale*	to leave, go out

Other verbs, however, are irregular in more than one way. That is, in addition to the *-go* ending in the *yo* form, they undergo other irregularities in the base, such as an *i* to *ie* change (in *venir* and *tener*), an *i* to *y* change (see *oír*), or an *e* to *i* change (like in the verb *decir*). **TABLE 12-23** provides these verbs' conjugations in the present tense.

TABLE 12-23

	VENIR (to come)	*TENER* (to have)	*OÍR* (to hear)	*DECIR* (to say)
yo	*vengo*	*tengo*	*oigo*	*digo*
tú	*vienes*	*tienes*	*oyes*	*dices*
él, ella, usted	*viene*	*tiene*	*oye*	*dice*
nosotros	*venimos*	*tenemos*	*oímos*	*decimos*
ellos, ellas, ustedes	*vienen*	*tienen*	*oyen*	*dicen*

Practice What You've Learned #8

Translate the following sentences. Check the vocabulary in **TABLE 12-24**.

1. I hear noises at night.

_____

2. Do you (formal) hear her?

_____

3. I leave from work at five.

_____

4. Ricardo does exercises at night.

_____

5. I have two pets.

_____

6. They come to visit.

_____

7. You (informal) say the truth.

_____

8. She says the truth; she never lies.

_____

9. He hears the ice-cream truck.

_____

10. They come to visit their parents.

_____

TABLE 12-24

VOCABULARY			
camión del heladero	ice-cream truck	*de visita*	to visit
ejercicio	exercise	*mascota*	pet
mentir	to lie	*(la) noche*	night
nunca	never	*padres*	parents
ruido	noise	*sus*	their
trabajo	work	*verdad*	truth

CHAPTER 13

In Addition to the Verb: Direct and Indirect Objects

You've learned about the subject of the sentence, and you've already covered quite a lot of ground on verbs. So what's next? Well, most of the time the subject and verb need an object, the target of the action done by the actor, so to speak. This chapter will give you a solid overview of direct and indirect objects and object pronouns.

Direct Objects

Transitive verbs cannot stand alone and require a direct object; they are ones that build an expectation for more to follow. In fact, without an object to follow the transitive verb, the sentence cannot be complete. Take a look at **TABLE 13-1**.

TABLE 13-1

TRANSITIVE VERBS AND CORRESPONDING DIRECT OBJECTS		
TRANSITIVE VERB PHRASE	DIRECT OBJECT	QUESTION IT ANSWERS
I used to read . . .	newspapers.	(What did I used to read?)
I saw . . .	Roberto.	(Whom did I see?)
I drove . . .	a car.	(What did I drive?)
I should thank . . .	Marcos.	(Whom should I thank?)
I will search for . . .	the keys.	(What will I search for?)
I will search for . . .	María.	(Whom will I search for?)

Direct Object Pronouns

You have already learned about subject pronouns—pronouns that replace nouns to make the sentence shorter. For example, instead of saying "the girl from sixth grade, the one with short hair," you can simply say "she." Similarly, you can replace objects with object pronouns.

Let's say that you are talking about Maria. Maybe you searched for Maria at a party, smiled when you saw Maria, walked toward (*hacia*) Maria, or embraced Maria. In this example, "Maria" acts as a direct object. However, once you've mentioned "Maria" once, you can then switch to the direct-object pronoun, "her." **TABLE 13-2** lists the direct-object pronouns available to you in Spanish.

TABLE 13-2

	OBJECT PRONOUNS		
me	(me)	*nos*	(us)
te	(you informal)		
lo	(him, it, you formal masculine)	*los*	(them)
la	(her, it, you formal feminine)	*las*	(them, you feminine plural)
le	(him, you formal masculine)	*les*	(them, masculine you all plural)

You may be confused to see that "*lo*" and "*le*" seem equivalent. The difference lies only in the region in which each is employed. Whereas "*lo*" and "*les*" are generally considered correct, Spaniards tend to use "*le*" and "*les*" instead.

To make sense of all these pronouns, take a look at a set of examples that illustrates the use of each direct-object pronoun:

Tú me viste ayer.
   (You saw **me** yesterday.)
Hermanito, te ayudo mañana.
   (Little brother, I will help **you** tomorrow.)
No lo encontré en el parque.
   (I didn't find **him** at the park.)
La encontrarás mañana.
   (You will find **her** tomorrow.)
Señor, le visitaré en dos días.
   (Señor, I'll visit **you** in two days.)
Señora, la conozco.
   (Señora, I know **you**.)
El profesor nos alabó por el buen trabajo.
   (The professor praised **us** for good work.)
Carlos no los miró en el teatro.
   (Carlos did not look at **them** at the theater.)
Cuando vemos a las muchachas, las preguntamos sus nombres.
   (When we saw the girls, we asked **them** their names.)
Les saludaré en la reunión.
   (I will greet **you all** at the reunion.)
María y Teresita, las buscaré por la tarde.
   (Maria and Teresita, I will look for **you** in the afternoon.)

Are you beginning to see a pattern here? You probably noticed that in Spanish, the direct object is placed *before* and not *after* the verb. The following rules apply to using a direct object in Spanish:

- The direct-object pronoun is always placed before the verb that is acting upon it.
- The negation of a transitive verb requires that *no* be placed immediately before the direct object.
- Only transitive verbs require the use of a direct-object pronoun.

To Clarify the Direct-Object Pronoun

In addition to the direct object, a Spanish speaker may add an additional phrase to help clarify the meaning of the direct object. For instance, in the phrase *las buscaré,* you might not always know based on the context whether *las* refers to "you" (feminine, formal) or "them" (feminine). To clarify, you might say *las buscaré a ellas* (I'll look for them) or *las buscaré a ustedes* (I'll look for you). *Las* and *a ellas* refer to the same thing—the object "them." **TABLE 13-3** provides the relevant clarifying phrase for each object pronoun.

TABLE 13-3

OBJECT PRONOUNS AND PRONOUN PHRASES					
me	*a mí*	(me)	*nos*	*a nosotros*	(us)
te	*a ti*	(you, informal)			
lo	*a él*	(him, it)	*los*	*a ellos*	(them)
la	*a ella*	(her, it)	*las*	*a ellas*	(them)
le	*a usted*	(you, formal)	*les*	*a ustedes*	(you, plural)

Remember that *a* sometimes acts as a personal preposition that introduces nouns and pronouns that refer to people (in which case it does not mean "to"). For example: *Yo veo a Mónica* may be said as *yo la veo* or, to clarify, *yo la veo a ella* (I see Monica; I see her; I see her).

For examples of how to use these direct-object phrases to emphasize or clarify who is being acted upon, take a look at the following list of sentences:

Me veo a mí bronceado. (I see **me** tanned; I see that I'm tanned.)
Te llamaré a ti la semana próxima. (I will call **you** next week.)

No lo encontré a él en el parque. (I didn't find **him** at the park.)
No la encontré a ella en el parque. (I didn't find **her** at the park.)
Le vi a usted. (I saw **you**.)
La vi a usted. (I saw **you**.)
Nos alabé a nosotros por el buen trabajo. (I praised **us** for the good work.)
Los saludaré a ellos en la reunión. (I will greet **them** at the reunion.)
Las saludaré a ellas en la reunión. (I will greet **them** at the reunion.)
Les saludaré a ustedes en la reunión. (I will greet **you all** at the reunion.)
Las saludaré a ustedes en la reunión. (I will greet **you all** at the reunion.)

ESSENTIALS

In many regions, formal structures of courtesy are still relied on to facilitate social interaction. Spanish integrates these structures within its forms of address, even when it comes to the direct object and direct-object phrases. Remember that choosing the correct pronoun to address a particular person is a social obligation.

EXERCISE

Object Pronouns

Translate the following sentences (for vocabulary that you don't know, refer to **TABLE 13-4**), and then substitute each direct object with the appropriate object pronoun. For example: I know (am acquainted with) Miguel. *Conozco a Miguel. Yo lo conozco.* To check your answers, see the answer key at the back of the book.

1. You (formal) have two cars.

2. I am looking for the street.

3. He makes the beds.

4. I put the book on the shelf.

5. Mr. Muñoz, I will see you tomorrow.

6. She saw Alicia and me at the dentist's office.

7. Yesterday I repaired a computer.

8. Robert has two motorcycles.

9. She drives the car.

10. Mom buys milk every Monday.

TABLE 13-4	VOCABULARY		
ayer	yesterday	cada	each
la calle	street	cama	bed
coche	car	comprar	to buy
conducir	to drive	(el) dentista	dentist
hacer	to make, do	(la) leche	milk
libro	book	(el) lunes	Monday
mamá	mom	mañana	tomorrow
(la) motocicleta	motorcycle	oficina	office
poner	to put	reparar	to repair
repisa	shelf	ver	to see

Reviewing the Personal A

As you already know, *a* may be translated as "to" and is sometimes used as a preposition of direction. For example:

¿Adónde van? (Where are you all going?)
Vamos a la playa. (We are going to the beach.)

However, when discussing it with respect to persons as direct objects, *a* cannot be translated at all. It becomes simply a Spanish construction designed to indicate which person is the direct object. Take a look at how this plays out with the verb *mirar* (to look [at]): *miro a mi esposa, a mi hija, y a mi hijo*, which means, "I look (at) my wife, daughter, and son." Now, compare that to *miro la televisión*, which means, "I watch television."

The first sentence often leads to an incorrect assumption. You may have assumed that the "at" in the English translation corresponds to *a*. But recall that "at" is actually part of the definition of *mirar*. This is more obvious in the second sentence, where the direct object is not a person. Also, note that in the first sentence each personal direct object requires an *a* to precede it. Take a look at a few other examples:

Esperaba el bus. (I was waiting for the bus.)
Esperaba a Beti. (I was waiting for Betty.)

Visité el museo. (I visited the museum.)
Visité a mi mama. (I visited my mother.)

There are some exceptions to keep in mind for the use of the personal *a*. Take a look at the following list of points to keep in mind:

- Animals may take a personal *a* if they have some emotional tie or relationship to the speaker. For example: *Amo a mi perrito.* (I love my dear/little dog.) *Vi un perro.* (I saw a dog.)
- Direct objects used with *ser*, *tener*, and *hay* (there is/are) are not preceded by *a*. For example: *Soy Rodolfo* (I am Rodolfo). *Tengo tres primas.* (I have three cousins.)
- Only "concrete" personal direct objects are preceded by *a*; object abstracts of persons are not. For example: *Busco un hombre intelligente, fiel, y muy divertido.* (I am looking for an intelligent, faithful, and very funny man.)

Using the Personal A

Translate the following sentences (refer to **TABLE 13-5** for translations of words you don't know). Remember to add a personal *a* where it is appropriate. To check your answers, see the answer key at the back of the book.

1. I see Ignacio, Amanda, and Pedro.

2. Who(m) do you (informal) love?

3. They have a daughter.

4. I am a citizen of the United States.

5. I love my cat.

TABLE 13-5	VOCABULARY		
amar	to love	*ciudadano*	citizen
Estados Unidos	United States	*gato*	cat
hija	daughter	*quién*	who?
tener	to have	*ver*	to see

Indirect Objects

Just as there are nouns or pronouns that directly interact with and complete the action of the verb, there are those that are related to the verb indirectly—they receive the completed action. These receivers are called indirect objects.

Indirect objects represent the nouns and pronouns that answer the questions "to whom," "for whom," "for which," and "to which" the verb's actions are intended. Take a look at the following sentences and try to figure out which are the direct objects and which are the indirect objects: "I bought Laura a beverage," "I will send you a letter," "I brought my friends lunch," and "I recommend them Jonathan."

The direct objects in the previous examples are "beverage," "letter," "lunch," and "Jonathan." The indirect objects are "Laura," "you," "my friends," and "them."

Indirect-Object Pronouns

The indirect-object pronouns in Spanish are very similar to the direct objects. In fact, the only point of confusion may be the third-person object pronouns. Take a look at **TABLE 13-6**, which contains pronouns for direct and indirect objects.

TABLE 13-6	PRONOUNS FOR DIRECT AND INDIRECT OBJECTS		
DIRECT OBJECTS		**INDIRECT OBJECTS**	
me	me	*me*	to me
te	you, informal	*te*	to you, informal
lo	him, it	*le*	to him, it

PRONOUNS FOR DIRECT AND INDIRECT OBJECTS *(continued)*			
DIRECT OBJECTS		**INDIRECT OBJECTS**	
la	her; it; you (formal feminine)	*le*	to her; it; you (formal feminine)
le	you (formal masculine)	*le*	to you (formal masculine)
nos	us	*nos*	to us
los	them	*les*	(to them)
las	them; you (feminine plural)	*les*	to them; you (feminine plural)
les	you (masculine plural)	*les*	to you (masculine plural)

Use le and les for all indirect objects in the third person. Le should be used as any indirect-object pronoun in the singular: to him, her, it, or the formal you (usted); les should be used as any indirect-object pronoun in the plural: to them (whether masculine or feminine), or to you, plural (whether masculine or feminine as well). The following examples will help you see how the indirect-object pronouns should be used.

<u>Me</u> *compré una bicicleta.* (I bought a bicycle **for me**.)
<u>Te</u> *compré una bicicleta.* (I bought **you** a bicycle.)
<u>Le</u> *compré una bicicleta.* (I bought **you/him/her** a bicycle.)
<u>Nos</u> *compré una bicicleta.* (I bought **us** a bicycle.)
<u>Les</u> *compré una bicicleta.* (I bought **you all/them** a bicycle.)

Here are some points to keep in mind about indirect-object pronouns:

- An indirect-object pronoun cannot exist without the presence of a direct object.
- Indirect-object pronouns refer only to people.
- Indirect-object pronouns are always placed before the conjugated verb.
- When *no* is necessary, place it before the indirect object. For example: *No me compró una bicicleta.* (He did not buy me a bicycle.)

- When *me, te,* or *nos* are used within a sentence that also employs a direct-object pronoun, they are placed immediately before the direct-object pronoun. For example: *Me la compró.* (He bought it for me.)
- Much like with the direct-object pronouns, you can use a redundant construction to emphasize who is receiving the completed action. For example: <u>*Me*</u> *compró* <u>*a mí*</u> *una bicicleta.* (He bought me a bicycle.)

When *le* or *les* is used within a sentence that also employs a direct-object pronoun, it is replaced by **se,** which is then placed immediately before the direct-object pronoun. For example: <u>*Le compré la bicicleta.*</u> <u>*Se la compré.*</u> (I bought **her** a bicycle. I bought it **for her.**)

In situations where an infinitive follows an active verb, the indirect-object pronoun may be placed either before the active verb or attached to the end of the infinitive, as follows:

Quiero escribir una carta a Susana. (I want to write a letter to Susana.)
<u>*Le*</u> *quiero escribir una carta.* (I want to write her a letter.)
Quiero escribir<u>le</u> una carta. (I want to write her a letter.)
<u>*Le*</u> *quiero escribir <u>a ella</u> una carta.* (I want to write her a letter.)
Quiero escribir<u>le</u> <u>a ella</u> una carta. (I want to write her a letter.)
<u>*Se*</u> *la quiero escribir.* (I want to write it to her.)
<u>*Se*</u> *la quiero escribir <u>a ella.</u>* (I want to write it to her.)

Indirect-Object Pronouns

Translate these phrases, using the appropriate indirect-object pronouns. (For vocabulary, refer to **TABLE 13-7** following the exercise.) Then, convert all the direct and indirect objects to pronouns.

1. I purchased him a beverage.

2. I will send Samantha to you.

3. I brought you all the book.

4. I recommend them Jonathan.

5. I show Berta the painting.

6. I want to phone my sister.

7. I told her all the news.

TABLE 13-7

VOCABULARY			
bebida	drink, beverage	*comprar*	to buy, purchase
decir	to tell	*hermana*	sister
libro	book	*mandar*	to send
mostrar	to show	*noticia*	news
pintura	painting	*querer*	to want to
recomendar	to recommend	*telefonear*	to phone
todo	all	*traer*	to bring

CHAPTER 14

Family and Friends

In this chapter, you will learn grammatical concepts that will broaden your scope to help you discuss topics related to your family and friends—possessive adjectives and pronouns, the impersonal *ser* construction to help you express possession, and the Spanish diminutives.

Reviewing Possessive Constructions

Recall that part of your identity is dependent on the relationships that you have, the relationships to which you belong. And as you belong to a relationship, the relationship "belongs" to you.

Spanish, as you may remember, does not facilitate the use of contractions to show possession. When you speak of "belonging" *en español*, you often mean that something is part "of" or "from" something else. For example: *Soy hijo de César y Patricia.* (I am the son of Cesar and Patricia.) The preposition *de* links son to parents, where the son is "of" the parents. Another way of expressing this relationship is: *César y Patricia son los padres de Alex.* (Cesar and Patricia are the parents of Alex.)

Possessive Adjectives

You will have to rely on the *de* construction quite often, particularly when speaking of parts of a whole, in general. However, when it becomes redundant, you can always rely on possessive adjectives to do the job—it's quicker and easier. Refer to **TABLE 14-1** for a list of possessive adjectives.

TABLE 14-1

POSSESSIVE ADJECTIVES		
POSSESSION OF ONE OBJECT	POSSESSION OF MULTIPLE OBJECTS	ENGLISH
mi	*mis*	my
tu	*tus*	your (familiar)
su	*sus*	his, her, your (polite)
nuestro	*nuestros*	our (masculine)
nuestra	*nuestras*	our (feminine)
su	*sus*	their, your (plural)

In English, the adjectives used to show possession depend more on the person doing the possessing than on the items being possessed. Thus, you can use "my" to express ownership of a single item as well as many. In Spanish, however, a possessive pronoun will change depending on the number of the noun that it modifies. For example: *mi camisa/mis camisas* (my shirt/my shirts). To see how possessive adjectives work in Spanish, take a look at the following sentences:

> *Tengo <u>mi</u> propio computadora.* (I have **my** own computer.)
> *Compré <u>mis</u> libros en la librería.* (I purchased **my** books at the bookstore.)
> *Soy <u>tu</u> mejor amigo.* (I am **your** best friend.)
> *¿Visitaste a <u>tus</u> padres?* (Did you visit **your** parents?)
> *Conducirá <u>su</u> coche.* (He will drive **his** car.)
> *No conozco a <u>sus</u> hermanos.* (I don't know **her** brothers.)
> *¿Dondé está <u>su</u> libro, Sra. Lopez?* (Where is **your** book, Mrs. Lopez?)
> *Necesito <u>sus</u> consejos, Sr. Garcia.* (I need **your** advice, Mr. Garcia.)
> *Estoy entusiasmado con <u>nuestro</u> viaje.* (I am excited with **our** trip.)
> *Escribiré <u>nuestras</u> nombres, Alicia y Carolina, en el registro.* (I will write **our** names, Alicia and Carolina, on the register.)
> *Contaré <u>su</u> historia, la historia de Manuel y Jacinta.* (I'll tell **their** story, the story of Manuel and Jacinta.)
> *¿Ustedes buscan a <u>sus</u> coches?* (Are you looking for **your** cars?)

Remember to use a possessive adjective in front of every possessed noun listed. For example: *Hablé con <u>tu</u> hermana y <u>tu</u> primo.* (I spoke with **your** sister and cousin.)

Don't worry about the potential for confusion when employing possessive adjectives su and sus—they are generally clear in context. After all, you switch to a possessive adjective only after you've established the subjects or "possessors" in question. You'd never say "her shoes" before you've made it clear to the speaker that you are referring to "Jane's shoes."

Possessive Adjectives

Translate the following phrases, using the appropriate possessive adjectives. If you can't remember a particular word, use the vocabulary listed in **TABLE 14-2**.

1. my radio
2. our (masculine) parents
3. your (informal) food
4. their job
5. her dog
6. my culture
7. your (plural) party
8. his aunt
9. her notebook
10. your (formal) opinions

TABLE 14-2

VOCABULARY			
comida	food	*cuaderno*	notebook
cultura	culture	*fiesta*	party
opinión	opinion	*padres*	parents
perro	dog	*(la) radio*	radio
tía	aunt	*trabajo*	job

Possessive Pronouns

In addition to adjectives, *español* employs pronouns to show possession. Like possessive adjectives, possessive pronouns reflect the number of items possessed. However, they must also agree in gender.

Note that it is the gender and number of the items possessed (*not* the gender and number of the subject or "owner") that determines the gender of the possessive pronoun. Refer to **TABLE 14-3** for a comprehensive list of possessive pronouns.

TABLE 14-3

POSSESSIVE PRONOUNS		
POSSESSION OF ONE OBJECT	**POSSESSION OF MULTIPLE OBJECTS**	**ENGLISH**
mío	*míos*	mine
mía	*mías*	mine
tuyo	*tuyos*	yours (familiar)
tuya	*tuyas*	yours (familiar)
suyo	*suyos*	his
suya	*suyas*	his
suyo	*suyos*	hers
suya	*suyas*	hers
suyo	*suyos*	yours (polite)
suya	*suyas*	yours (polite)
nuestro	*nuestros*	ours
nuestra	*nuestras*	ours
suyo	*suyos*	theirs (masc./fem.)
suya	*suyas*	theirs (masc./fem.)
suyo	*suyos*	yours (plural)
suya	*suyas*	yours (plural)

For example:

Ésta es mi casa. Es la mía.
(This is my house. It's mine.)
Éstos son sus regalos. Son los suyos.
(These are your presents. They are yours.)

Ser and Possession

You've already learned that *ser*, a rather versatile Spanish verb, may express "to be" in six particular ways—personal identity, relationships, profession, origin, personality, and character appearance. To these six, you can also add possession. To review the conjugations of the verb *ser*, refer to **TABLE 14-4**.

TABLE 14-4

CONJUGATING *SER*					
SUBJECT	PRESENT	PRETERITE	IMPERFECT	PRESENT PERFECT	FUTURE
(yo)	soy	fui	era	he sido	seré
(tú)	eres	fuiste	eras	has sido	serás
(él, ella, usted)	es	fue	era	ha sido	será
(nosotros, nosotras)	somos	fuimos	éramos	hemos sido	seremos
(ellos, ellas, ustedes)	son	fueron	eran	han sido	serán

The third person of the verb *ser* allows for a possessive construction, like the following two examples:

El coche es mío. (The car is mine.)
Es mi coche. (It is my car.)
La casa es mía. (The house is mine.)
Es mi casa. (It is my house.)

In the last example, *es* is translated as "it is," with "it" acting as the impersonal subject of the verb *ser*, but in reality the Spanish sentence lacks a subject. This construction works in all of the verb tenses:

Es mi coche. (It is my car.)
Fue mi coche. (It was my car, but no longer.)
Era mi coche. (It was my car, and may or may not be now.)
Ha sido mi coche desde hace cuatro años. (It has been my car since four years ago.)
Será mi coche. (It will be my car.)

What if you were talking about more than one car? How can this impersonal construction be expressed for plural items? Well, you simply use the third-person plural form of *ser*: *son* (in the present tense), and so on. Take a look at the following examples:

Son mis metas. (They are my goals now.)
Son mis metas cada vez que intento. (They are my goals each time I try.)
Fueron mis metas. (They were my goals, but no longer.)
Eran mis metas. (They were my goals.)
Han sido mis metas desde la universidad. (They have been my goals since college.)
Serán mis metas de hoy en delante. (They will be my goals from now on.)

Ser in Possessive Constructions

1. Translate the following sentences, using the appropriate forms of *ser* and possessive adjectives and pronouns (relevant vocabulary appears in **TABLE 14-5**).

1. It is my sweater.

2. The telephone is his.

3. They're my trousers.

4. They're (feminine) yours (informal).

5. Good grades will be mine.

6. The eyeglasses are his.

7. The sandals are hers.

8. The camera is hers.

9. My room used to be my brother's.

10. Your (formal) position will be mine next year.

11. My books used to be my sister's.

TABLE 14-5

VOCABULARY			
año	year	anteojos	eyeglasses
bueno	good	cámara	camera
(la) habitación	room	hermano, hermana	brother, sister
libro	book	nota	grade
pantalones	pants	próximo	next
puesto	position	saco	sweater
sandalias	sandals	teléfono	telephone

2. Now it's your turn. Use *es* or *son* to introduce things that you have.

The Family Gathering

In this section you will practice expressing familial relationships. Take a look at **TABLE 14-6**, which contains some relevant vocabulary. Then, try to read the description of the Gallegos family. See how much you can understand (the translation appears in the back of the book).

TABLE 14-6

VOCABULARY: FAMILIAL RELATIONSHIPS	
abuelo, abuela	grandparent; grandfather, grandmother
ahijado, ahijada	godchild; godson, goddaughter
cuñado, cuñada	brother-in-law, sister-in-law
esposo, esposa	spouse; husband, wife
hermanastro, hermanastra	stepbrother, stepsister
hermano, hermana	sibling; brother, sister
hijastro, hijastra	stepchild; stepson, stepdaughter
hijo, hija	child; son, daughter
madrastra	stepmother
madre, mamá (mami)	mother, mom
marido	husband
mujer	wife, woman, female
nieto, nieta	grandchild; grandson, granddaughter
niño, niña	child; boy, girl
nuera	daughter-in-law
padrastro	stepfather
padre, papá (papi)	father, dad
primo, prima	cousin
sobrino, sobrina	nephew, niece
suegro, suegra	father-in-law, mother-in-law
varón	male, man
yerno	son-in-law

La familia Gallegos

¿Cuál es la relación entre Luis y Fanny Gallegos? Luis y Fanny son esposos. Luis es el esposo de Fanny, y Fanny es la esposa de Luis. Son marido y mujer.

¿Cómo es la familia Luis y Fanny? Luis y Fanny tienen tres hijos. Dos son varones y una es mujer. La mujer se llama Susy, y los varones se llaman Hugo y César.

¿Cuál es la relación entre Cesar, Susy, y Hugo? Son los hermanos.

¿Quién es Marlene? Ella es la esposa de Hugo. Tienen dos hijos, Jonathan y Jennifer. Jonathan es el hijastro de Hugo.

¿Cuáles son las relaciones entre Marlene y la familia de Luis y Fanny? Marlene es la nuera de Luis y Fanny. Luis es su suegro y Fanny es su suegra. Marlene es la cuñada de Susy. Cesar es su cuñado. Jonathan es el sobrino de Susy y Cesar. Jennifer es la sobrina de ellos. Es decir, Susy es la tía de Jonathan y Jennifer, y Cesar es el tío de ellos.

¿Quiénes son los primos de Jonathan y Jennifer? Los primos de Jonathan y Jennifer son Celsito y Estefi, los hijos de Susy.

¿Cuál es la relación entre Luis y Jonathan? ¿Y entre Fanny y Jennifer? Luis es el abuelo de Jonathan. Jonathan es su nieto. Fanny es la abuela de Jennifer. Jennifer es su nieta.

So? How did it feel to be reading in Spanish? Did you understand what was going on? Go back and reread the passage—you might be surprised to discover that each time you read it again, it will become much easier to understand.

In general, there are a few things to remember when speaking of family relationships:

- When talking in general terms, or grouping family members by relationship rather than gender, you will often use the plural of the masculine form of the word. For example: *¿Cuántos hijos tienen Luis y Fanny?* (How many children do Luis and Fanny have?) *¿Quiénes son los padres de Hugo?* (Who are the *parents* of Hugo?)
- When grouping family members by relationship and gender, you will need to use the plural form of the word in the chosen gender. For example: *¿Cuántas sobrinas tiene César?* (How many nieces does Cesar have?)
- Since the masculine form is often used as the default gender of most categories, sometimes it may be necessary to further specify the male

gender. For example: *¿Quiénes son los hijos (varones) de Luis y Fanny?* (Who are the sons of Luis and Fanny?)

FACTS

In some regions, unaccented *mama* and *papa* precede the first names of grandparents (as opposed to *mamá* and *papá*, which refer to parents). For example: Jonathan calls his grandparents *Mama Fanny* and *Papa Luis*; he calls his mother, Marlene, *mamá*, and he calls his father, Hugo, *papá*.

EXERCISE

Members of the Family

1. Translate the following sentences, using the vocabulary you have just learned, and the appropriate forms of *ser*. For additional vocabulary words that do not appear in this section, refer to **TABLE 14-7**.

1. The Garcías were my neighbors last year.

2. I (fem.) am your friend.

3. He is my husband.

4. They are my children.

5. I (masc.) am yours.

6. They are your (informal) friends.

7. Pepe and Alicia have been my friends for years.

8. Alicia was my girlfriend for three months.

9. Pepe has been my barber for years.

TABLE 14-7

	VOCABULARY			
amigo	friend		*año*	year
mes	month		*novio, novia*	boyfriend, girlfriend
pasado	last		*peluquero*	barber
vecino	neighbor			

2. Now it's your turn. Describe your family, and don't forget to include your *mascota* (pet)!

Diminutives

When you hear a family member addressed in Spanish, you may not hear the standard relation terms you just saw above. In fact, you are more likely to hear variations on those terms. This is true because Spanish allows diminutive suffixes to be added to the ends of nouns. These suffixes are there to signal how the speaker feels about the person (or object) being described.

**SSENTIALS**

Although you are probably not aware of it, diminutives also occur in English. For example, compare the following phrases: kitten/kitty, duck/ducky, dog/doggy. The difference is in terms of ease and frequency of usage: In Spanish, any noun can be easily changed to a diminutive by adding the appropriate suffix, and diminutives are used a lot more frequently.

You will often encounter the *-ito* and *-ita* suffixes attached to masculine and feminine nouns and some adjectives. In general, they add a quality of "smallness" or "dearness" to the description of a noun.

When you wish to add a diminutive suffix, you need to keep a few things in mind. In general, nouns that end in vowels have the vowel replaced by the suffix appropriate in gender and number (see **TABLE 14-8** for a few examples).

TABLE 14-8

DIMINUTIVES			
casa	house	*casita*	little house
cuchara	spoon	*cucharita*	teaspoon
gato	(male) cat	*gatito*	(male) kitten
hermana	sister	*hermanita*	little/younger sister
lámpara	lamp	*lamparita*	little lamp
perros	(male) dogs	*perritos*	(male) puppies

As with irregular verbs that require spelling accommodations, some diminutives also require certain modifications to maintain the pronunciation of the transformed nouns. Fortunately, the changes are similar to those you have already encountered.

Recall that if you wish a word to maintain a hard "c" sound, it must be replaced with a *qu* combination when adding a suffix that begins with *e* or *i*: *taco* (taco); *taquito* (little taco). Similarly, *g* is replaced by *gu*: *jugo* (juice); *juguito* (a little juice). Z sometimes needs to be replaced by *c*: *pedazo* (piece); *pedacito* (little piece).

If the noun ends in an *n* or *r*, add a *c* before the suffix:

joven (youth); *jovencito* (young boy)
mujer (woman); *mujercita* (young girl, woman)

If a noun with more than one syllable ends in *e*, you would also need to add a *c* before the suffix: *mueble* (furniture); *mueblecito* (little bridge).

If the first syllable of a two-syllable noun has an *ie* or a *ue*, and the last syllable ends in an *o* or an *a*, add the combination *ec* before the suffix:

cuento (story); *cuentecito* (short story)
pierna (leg); *piernecita* (small leg)

With respect to proper nouns and relationships, diminutives denote a particular closeness or affection for an individual. Most often, diminutives are used as forms of address. Given the affection that the diminutive implies, not using it may characterize a formality within a relationship. For instance, a grandson may call his grandmother *abuelita* (dear grandmother) if he is close to her, and she in turn will add a diminutive ending to his name—for instance, if his name is Paco, she would call him *Paquito*.

Keep in mind that diminutives are largely regional and the uses of *-ito* and *-ita* may differ from one country to the next. Other diminutives employed in addition to or instead of these suffixes include:

1. *-ico/-ica*
   mama (mother); *mamica* (dear mother)
2. *-illo/-illa*
   pan (bread); *panecillo* (bread roll)

Diminutives may also be employed with a limited number of adjectives. However, whereas diminutive nouns show a small size or affection, adding a diminutive suffix to an adjective will generally make its meaning more emphatic. For example:

suave (soft); *suavecito* (very soft)
viejo (old); *viejito* (very old)

CHAPTER 15

Irregular Verbs: Moving Through Time

As you have seen in Chapters 11 and 12, irregular verbs in the present tense undergo various kinds of changes based on spelling modifications, group irregularities, and other irregularities specific to a particular verb. This chapter will introduce you to how irregular verbs behave in the preterite, imperfect, present perfect, and the future.

The Preterite Tense

To review, the preterite tense deals with the actions that occur in the past and have been completed. For regular-verb conjugations in the preterite, refer to **TABLE 15-1**.

TABLE 15-1

VERB CONJUGATIONS IN THE PRETERITE TENSE		
	−AR VERBS	*−ER* AND *−IR* VERBS
yo	-é (canté)	-í (aprendí, viví)
tú	-aste (cantaste)	-iste (aprendiste, viviste)
él, ella, usted	-ó (cantó)	-ió (aprendió, vivió)
nosotros	-amos (cantamos)	-imos (aprendimos, vivimos)
ellos, ellas, ustedes	-aron (cantaron)	-ieron (aprendieron, vivieron)

Spelling Accommodations

Whenever a particular conjugation ending threatens to change its pronunciation, the spelling of the verb must be altered to accommodate the correct pronunciation. The first type of spelling accommodation that you might consider is in the verbs that end in *-car*. Because the *yo* ending is *é*, you need to find some way to accommodate the conjugation so that it keeps the "k" sound in *-car*. (You have already come across similar spelling-accommodation changes when learning about the irregular verbs in the present.) For example, take a look at the verb *buscar* (**TABLE 15-2**).

TABLE 15-2

CONJUGATING *BUSCAR* IN THE PRETERITE		
	-AR	*BUSCAR* (TO SEARCH, LOOK FOR)
yo	-é	busqué
tú	-aste	buscaste
él, ella, usted	-ó	buscó
nosotros	-amos	buscamos
ellos, ellas, ustedes	-aron	buscaron

As you can see, in order to get a conjugation that is pronounced "boos-KEH," the *c* is changed to *qu*, which spells out *busqué*. For other verbs in this category, refer to **TABLE 15-3**.

TABLE 15-3

OTHER –CAR VERBS			
VERB	YO FORM	*ÉL/ELLA/USTED* FORM	ENGLISH
abarcar	abarqué	abarcó	to take on
clarificar	clarifiqué	clarificó	to clarify
explicar	expliqué	explicó	to explain
practicar	practiqué	practicó	to practice
sacar	saqué	sacó	to get, take out
tocar	toqué	tocó	to touch, play (an instrument)

Another spelling accommodation that occurs in the *yo* form of the preterite conjugation applies to verbs that end in *-gar*. In order to avoid the ending *-gé* (which makes the *g* soft), the spelling is modified to *-gué*.

Reviewing pronunciation: *ge* is pronounced as "hheh" and *gu* is pronounced as "gw." However, within the *gué* combination, the *u* becomes silent and produces the sound you are looking for, "gheh."

Because only the *yo*-form ending of these verbs begins with an *e* (the only other vowel that would similarly influence *g* is *i*), only one out of the five conjugations is irregular. **TABLE 15-4** lists the *-gar* verbs, as well as their conjugations in the yo form and the *él/ella/usted* form (used as example of the "default" conjugation).

TABLE 15-4

–GAR VERB CONJUGATIONS			
VERB	YO FORM	*ÉL/ELLA/USTED* FORM	ENGLISH
apagar	apagué	apagó	to turn off, put out
entregar	entregué	entregó	to bring, hand over
jugar	jugué	jugó	to play

llegar	*llegué*	*llegó*	to arrive
madrugar	*madrugué*	*madrugó*	to get up early
pagar	*pagué*	*pagó*	to pay
tragar	*tragué*	*tragó*	to swallow

The last exception for the first-person singular conjugations in the preterite that apply to *-ar* verbs are the verbs that end in *-zar*. When *-é* is added to the base, **z** must be replaced by **c**. This change may seem a bit confusing, since both letters would sound equivalent under this circumstance. Unfortunately, this is but another remnant of Spanish's heritage. Again, this spelling accommodation occurs only in the *yo* form of the preterite. For a list of *-zar* verbs, refer to **TABLE 15-5**.

TABLE 15-5

–ZAR VERB CONJUGATIONS			
VERB	**YO FORM**	**ÉL/ELLA/USTED FORM**	**ENGLISH**
abrazar	*abracé*	*abrazó*	to embrace, hug
almorzar	*almorcé*	*almorzó*	to have lunch
empezar	*empecé*	*empezó*	to begin
rezar	*recé*	*rezó*	to pray

Another spelling-accommodation change occurs in *-er* and *-ir* verbs that have a base that ends in a vowel. In this category, the *i* in third-person endings *-ió* and *-ieron* changes to a **y**. This switch does not indicate a fundamental change so much as it provides a clarification of emphasis. Remember that the *i* is a weak vowel that is often overpowered by stronger vowels (*a, e,* and *o*) to produce a "y" sound. Recall also that the accented *i* maintains its "ee" sound. An accented *i* would actually change the pronunciation of the word, and yet the "vowel + *i* + strong vowel" combination does not seem to produce a strong enough "y" to tame that mess of open sound. The answer therefore is to adopt the **y** formally. Refer to the conjugations of *construir* (to construct) and *sustituir* (to substitute) in **TABLE 15-6**.

TABLE 15-6

	−UIR	CONSTRUIR (TO CONSTRUCT)	SUSTITUIR (TO SUBSTITUTE)
CONJUGATING *CONSTRUIR* AND *SUSTITUIR* IN THE PRETERITE			
yo	-í	construí	sustituí
tú	-iste	construiste	sustituiste
él, ella, usted	-ió	construyó	sustituyó
nosotros	-imos	construimos	sustituimos
ellos, ellas, ustedes	-ieron	construyeron	sustituyeron

In the other verbs that belong to the same category, the *tú* and *nosotros* forms also have an accent mark over the *i*—the accent mark turns the weak *i* ("y") into a strong *i* ("ee"). (For a sample conjugation of *proveer*, go to **TABLE 15-7**. For other verbs in this category, refer to **TABLE 15-8**.)

TABLE 15-7

	−ER	PROVEER (TO PROVIDE)
CONJUGATING *PROVEER* IN THE PRETERITE		
yo	-í	proveí
tú	-iste	proveíste
él, ella, usted	-ió	proveyó
nosotros	-imos	proveímos
ellos, ellas, ustedes	-ieron	proveyeron

TABLE 15-8

VERB	TÚ FORM	ÉL/ELLA/USTED FORM	NOSOTROS FORM	ELLOS/ELLAS/ USTEDES FORM	ENGLISH
OTHER VERBS IN THE *I* TO *Y* CATEGORY					
caer	caíste	cayó	caímos	cayeron	to fall
creer	creíste	creyó	creímos	creyeron	to believe
leer	leíste	leyó	leímos	leyeron	to read
poseer	poseíste	poseyó	poseímos	poseyeron	to possess

Now it's time to take a break and review what you've learned so far. Then, check out the following exercise to help you practice these irregular-verb conjugations.

Practice Your Conjugations #1

Translate the following sentences using the appropriate verb forms. If you don't know a word, check the vocabulary in **TABLE 15-9**.

1. I took on too much.

2. I searched for my book.

3. I clarified the situation.

4. He read the newspaper.

5. I explained the idea.

6. They believed the worst.

7. I practiced all day.

8. You (formal) possessed courage.

9. I touched the iron.

10. I turned off the radio.

11. The foxes fell in traps.

12. I handed over the change.

13. I played chess with my friends.

14. They substituted limes for lemons.

15. I arrived late.

16. I rose early today.

17. I paid with cash.

18. I swallowed the pill.

19. Mr. Wright constructed interesting homes.

20. I embraced my father.

21. I ate lunch with Susana.

22. I prayed at Mass.

23. I began the day well.

TABLE 15-9

VOCABULARY			
ajedrez	chess	*amigo*	friend
bien	well	*cambio*	change
casa	home	*con*	with

demasiado	too much	(el) día	day
en efectivo	in cash	hoy	today
interesante	interesting	libro	book
lima	lime	limón	lemon
lo peor	the worst	misa	Mass
pastilla	pill	periódico	newspaper
plancha	iron	situación	situation
tarde	late	temprano	early
todo	all	trampa	trap
valor	courage	zorro	fox

Group Irregularities

There are several group irregularities in the preterite tense. One category that may be singled out is the group of verbs that end with -ducir. In the case of these verbs, the irregular changes occur in *all* of the conjugations of the preterite tense. For example, take a look at how to conjugate conducir (to drive) in Table 15-10.

TABLE 15-10

CONJUGATING *CONDUCIR* IN THE PRETERITE TENSE	
	CONDUCIR (TO DRIVE)
yo	conduje
tú	condujiste
él, ella, usted	condujo
nosotros	condujimos
ellos, ellas, ustedes	condujeron

As you can see, three major changes have taken place: The *c* at the end of each base has been changed to *j,* the accent marks that generally appear in some of the preterite forms have all been dropped, and the ending in the third-person plural is *-eron* (and not *-ieron,* as in regular *-er* and *-ir* verbs).

Other verbs that belong to this category appear in **TABLE 15-11**.

TABLE 15-11

		−*DUCIR* VERB CONJUGATIONS IN THE PRETERITE		
VERB	YO FORM	*ÉL/ELLA/USTED* FORM	*ELLOS/ELLAS/USTEDES* FORM	ENGLISH
deducir	deduje	dedujo	dedujeron	to deduce
introducir	introduje	introdujo	introdujeron	to introduce
producir	produje	produjo	produjeron	to produce
traducir	traduje	tradujo	tradujeron	to translate

Another verb that is similar to this group (though, technically, it doesn't belong here) is *decir* (to say). In the preterite, its base changes to *dij-*, and its endings are the same as that of the verbs in this category: *-e, -iste, -o, -imos,* and *-eron* (notice that there are no accent marks over these endings).

−*Ir* Verbs with Base Change from *E* to *I*

A few group-based irregularities have to do with vowel modifications. Some of these may be familiar to you from the present-tense irregular verb conjugations. For example, the following group of *-ir* verbs undergoes a base-vowel change from *e* to *i* in the third-person singular and plural forms of the preterite verb. (Compare the base of the *yo* and *nosotros* forms to the *él/ella/usted* and *ellos/ellas/ustedes* forms in **TABLE 15-12**.)

TABLE 15-12

	LIST OF VERBS WITH BASE CHANGE FROM *E* TO *I*				
VERB	YO	*ÉL/ELLA/USTED*	*NOSOTROS*	*ELLOS/ELLAS/USTEDES*	ENGLISH
advertir	advertí	advirtió	advertimos	advirtieron	to warn
medir	medí	midió	medimos	midieron	to measure
mentir	mentí	mintió	mentimos	mintieron	to lie
pedir	pedí	pidió	pedimos	pidieron	to ask
preferir	preferí	prefirió	preferimos	prefirieron	to prefer
repetir	repetí	repitió	repitimos	repitieron	to repeat
seguir	seguí	siguió	seguimos	siguieron	to follow
sentir	sentí	sintió	sentimos	sintieron	to feel
servir	serví	sirvió	servimos	sirvieron	to serve

Verbs with Base Change from *O* to *U*

Although the group of verbs that falls into this category in the present tense is quite large, there are only two verbs (*dormir* and *morir*) that undergo this change in the preterite. Much like with the *e* to *i* change, only the bases of the third-person singular and plural conjugations undergo the change. For the conjugations, see **TABLE 15-13**.

TABLE 15-13

CONJUGATING *DORMIR* AND *MORIR* IN THE PRETERITE			
	—IR	*DORMIR* (TO SLEEP)	*MORIR* (TO DIE)
yo	-í	dormí	morí
tú	-iste	dormiste	moriste
él, ella, usted	-ió	durmió	murió
nosotros	-imos	dormimos	morimos
ellos, ellas, ustedes	-ieron	durmieron	murieron

Practice Your Conjugations #2

Translate the following sentences using the appropriate verb forms. If you don't know a word, check the vocabulary in **TABLE 15-14**.

1. We drove to the party.

----

2. The salesman repeated the offer.

----

3. Did you (informal) translate the speech?

----

4. She introduced her friends.

----

5. They slept all day.

----

6. You (plural) deduced the solution.

----

7. They followed the directions to the museum.

8. Who produced your (formal) movie?

9. The tailor measured his waist.

10. President Kennedy died in 1963.

11. We told the truth.

TABLE 15-14

VOCABULARY			
amigo	friend	*cintura*	waist
(el) dia	day	*discurso*	speech
fiesta	party	*museo*	museum
oferta	offer	*película*	movie
presidente	president	*quién*	who
sastre	tailor	*señas*	directions
(la) solución	solution	*todo*	all
vendedor	salesperson	*(la) verdad*	truth

Innate Irregularities

Some verbs are subject to innate irregularities in their pretérito tense conjugations. Recall that these irregularities are particular to the specific verbs themselves. They do not consistently share irregulaties with any particular conjugation, and are not concerned with consistency of pronunciation. The verbs in this category may be further divided by the irregularity they present. These irregularities may be vowel based, consonant based, mixed, or word based.

Vowel-based Irregularities

Vowel-based irregularities require changes to the vowel or vowels within the base of the verb. Fortunately, most of these innately irregular verbs are few in number and, though not consistent with the regular conjugations, are consistent within each of their own tenses. If a vowel change occurs in the first person, it will more than likely run across all the persons within that tense.

The following verbs (**TABLE 15-15**) undergo a base change with the substitution of a *u* (note that, in some cases, the consonant following the base vowel will change as well, and the endings are also irregular). The *u* base change applies to all preterite conjugations of each of these verbs.

TABLE 15-15

VERBS WITH BASE VOWEL CHANGE TO *U*				
	CABER (TO FIT)	*PODER* (TO BE ABLE TO)	*PONER* (TO PUT)	*SABER* (TO KNOW, LEARN)
yo	cupe	pude	puse	supe
tú	cupiste	pudiste	pusiste	supiste
él, ella, usted	cupo	pudo	puso	supo
nosotros	cupimos	pudimos	pusimos	supimos
ellos, ellas, ustedes	cupieron	pudieron	pusieron	supieron

Another irregularity is the substitution of a base vocalized by an *i*. Again, the best approach for these verbs is to memorize the irregular base and how the endings vary from the regular rule. For the conjugations of *i*-based verbs, refer to **TABLE 15-16**.

TABLE 15-16

VERBS WITH BASE VOWEL CHANGE TO *U*				
	DAR (TO GIVE)	*HACER* (TO DO)	*QUERER* (TO WANT)	*VENIR* (TO COME)
yo	di	hice	quise	vine
tú	diste	hiciste	quisiste	viniste
él, ella, usted	dio	hizo	quiso	vino
nosotros	dimos	hicimos	quisimos	vinimos
ellos, ellas, ustedes	dieron	hicieron	quisieron	vinieron

Practice Your Conjugations #3

Translate the following sentences using the appropriate verb forms.
If you don't know a word, check the vocabulary in **TABLE 15-17**.

1. We gave Susy a gift.

2. I placed the key on the table.

3. I wanted a steak.

4. Julio came to Vita's birthday party.

5. You (formal) knew it.

6. We were able to arrive on time.

7. They learned how newspaper ads work.

8. Ramón did the work.

9. Did you (formal) give alms?

10. You (informal) fit the clothes in the drawer.

11. We wanted to read a magazine.

TABLE 15-17

VOCABULARY			
anuncio	newspaper ad	a tiempo	on time
fiesta de cumpleaños	birthday party	funcionar	to work
leer	to read	limosna	alms
llave	key	llegar	arrive
mesa	table	regalo	gift
revista	magazine	ropa	clothes
bistéc	steak	cajón	drawer

Consonant-Based Irregularities

Consonant-based irregularities are similar to vowel-based ones. They require changes or additions to a letter (in this case a consonant) within the base of the verb. Also, accent marks may be dropped from the first-person singular and third-person singular conjugations. The verbs in the following group (see **TABLE 15-18**) gain a *j*.

TABLE 15-18

	VERBS WITH BASE CONSONANT CHANGE TO *J*			
	ABSTRAER (TO MAKE ABSTRACT)	**ATRAER** (TO ATTRACT)	**CONTRAER** (TO CONTRACT)	**DISTRAER** (TO DISTRACT)
yo	abstraje	atraje	contraje	distraje
tú	abstrajiste	atrajiste	contrajiste	distrajiste
él, ella, usted	abstrajo	atrajo	contrajo	distrajo
nosotros	abstrajimos	atrajimos	contrajimos	distrajimos
ellos, ellas, ustedes	abstrajeron	atrajeron	contrajeron	distrajeron

Mixed Irregularities

Mixed irregularities combine vowel-based and consonant-based irregularities in their verbs. Think back to the *ser* and *estar* chapter. Do you remember how to conjugate *estar* in the preterite? The base of this verb changes to *estuv-*. Verbs that behave the same way are *tener (tuv-)* and *andar* (to walk). To compare the preterite conjugations of *andar*, *estar*, and *tener*, refer to **TABLE 15-19**.

TABLE 15-19	**CONJUGATING *ANDAR*, *ESTAR*, AND *TENER* IN THE PRETERITE TENSE**		
	ANDAR (TO WALK)	*ESTAR* (TO BE)	*TENER* (TO HAVE)
yo	anduve	estuve	tuve
tú	anduviste	estuviste	tuviste
él, ella, usted	anduvo	estuvo	tuvo
nosotros	anduvimos	estuvimos	tuvimos
ellos, ellas, ustedes	anduvieron	estuvieron	tuvieron

Oír is another irregular verb that is hard to categorize (as you might remember from looking at its conjugations in the present tense). **TABLE 15-20** lists the conjugations of *oír* in the preterite.

TABLE 15-20	**CONJUGATING *OÍR* IN THE PRETERITE TENSE**
	OÍR (TO HEAR)
yo	oí
tú	oíste
él, ella, usted	oyó
nosotros	oímos
ellos, ellas, ustedes	oyeron

Irregularities in Other Verb Tenses

In the imperfect tense, the endings always remain the same, just as in the regular-verb conjugations (refer to **TABLE 15-21** for a review of regular conjugations in the imperfect tense). The few irregularities that exist in the imperfect are limited to innate base changes.

TABLE 15-21	**VERB ENDINGS IN THE IMPERFECT TENSE**	
	–AR VERBS	*–ER* AND *–IR* VERBS
yo	-aba (cantaba)	-ía (aprendía, vivía)
tú	-abas (cantabas)	-ías (aprendías, vivías)
él, ella, usted	-aba (cantaba)	-ía (aprendía, vivía)

nosotros	-ábamos (cantábamos)	-íamos (aprendíamos, vivíamos)
ellos, ellas, ustedes	-aban (cantaban)	-ían (aprendían, vivían)

One such example is the verb *ver* (to see). In the imperfect, the base changes from *v-* to *ve-*, so that you have *veía* (I saw) instead of *vía* (which is wrong and, incidentally, means "road" or "street" in Spanish). Look at **TABLE 15-22** to see how *ver* is conjugated in the imperfect.

TABLE 15-22

CONJUGATING *VER* IN THE IMPERFECT TENSE	
yo	veía
tú	veías
él, ella, usted	veía
nosotros	veíamos
ellos, ellas, ustedes	veían

Irregular Verbs in the Present Perfect Tense

As you remember, the present perfect is a composite tense—that is, it's made up of two verb parts: the conjugated form of *haber* and a past participle. You already know how to conjugate *haber* (refer to **TABLE 15-23**).

TABLE 15-23

CONJUGATING VERBS IN PRESENT PERFECT		
	—*AR* VERB	—*ER* VERB	—*IR* VERB
yo	he cantado	he aprendido	he vivido
tú	has cantado	has aprendido	has vivido
él, ella, usted	ha cantado	ha aprendido	ha vivido
nosotros	habemos cantado	habemos aprendido	habemos vivido
ellos, ellas, ustedes	han cantado	han aprendido	han vivido

It follows, then, that the irregularities in the present perfect are really the irregularities in the past participles. **TABLE 15-24** contains a list of verbs that have irregular past participles.

TABLE 15-24

IRREGULAR PAST PARTICIPLES		
INFINITIVE	PAST PARTICIPLE	ENGLISH
abrir	abierto	to open
cubrir	cubierto	to cover
decir	dicho	to say
escribir	escrito	to write
hacer	hecho	to do or make
poner	puesto	to put
resolver	resuelto	to resolve
romper	roto	to break
satisfacer	satisfecho	to satisfy
ver	visto	to see
volver	vuelto	to return

Practice Your Conjugations #4

Translate the following sentences using the appropriate verb forms. If you don't know a word, check the vocabulary in **TABLE 15-25**.

1. I have opened an account.

2. She has put one hundred dollars in the account.

3. They have done the work.

4. The two of them have satisfied the requirements.

5. We have returned to university.

6. The elderly man has seen many difficulties.

7. Ramon has broken with the party.

8. Channel 6 has not covered local news well.

9. The boss has resolved to terminate his employee.

10. We have written to our representatives.

TABLE 15-25

VOCABULARY			
bien	well	*canal*	channel
cuenta	account	*despedir*	to terminate, fire
(la) dificultad	difficulty	*dólar*	dollar
empleado	employee	*jefe*	boss
local	local	*mucho*	many, a lot of
noticia	news	*partido*	party
representante	representative	*requisito*	requirement
trabajo	work	*(la) universidad*	university
viejito	elderly man		

Future Tense Irregularities

In the future tense, irregularities are limited to innately irregular verbs. As a result, the endings employed are the same as those used with regular verbs. For a review, refer to **TABLE 15-26**.

TABLE 15-26

CONJUGATING VERBS IN FUTURE TENSE				
		—AR VERBS	*—ER* VERBS	*—IR* VERBS
yo	-é	*cantaré*	*aprenderé*	*viviré*
tú	-ás	*cantarás*	*aprenderás*	*vivirás*
él, ella, usted	-á	*cantará*	*aprenderá*	*vivirá*
nosotros	-emos	*cantaremos*	*aprenderemos*	*viviremos*
ellos, ellas, ustedes	-án	*cantarán*	*aprenderán*	*vivirán*

There is a group of verbs that gain a *d* in the base that is used to put together the future-tense conjugations. These verbs are *poner, salir, tener,* and *venir.* Since they have regular endings, **TABLE 15-27** includes only some of the future-tense conjugations of these verbs.

TABLE 15-27

VERBS THAT GAIN A *D* IN THE BASE OF THE FUTURE-TENSE CONJUGATIONS

VERB	YO FORM	*ÉL/ELLA/USTED* FORM	*NOSOTROS* FORM	ENGLISH
poner	pondré	pondrá	pondremos	to put
salir	saldré	saldrá	saldremos	to leave
tener	tendré	tendrá	tendremos	to have
venir	vendré	vendrá	vendremos	to come

Another group of verbs modifies its base by dropping an *e.* (A likely explanation might be that dropping this vowel shortened the pronunciation of these verbs by a syllable.) For a list of these verbs, refer to **TABLE 15-28**.

TABLE 15-28

VERBS THAT LOSE AN *E* IN THE BASE OF THE FUTURE-TENSE CONJUGATIONS

VERB	YO FORM	*ÉL/ELLA/USTED* FORM	*NOSOTROS* FORM	ENGLISH
caber	cabré	cabrá	cabremos	to fit
poder	podré	podrá	podremos	to be able to
saber	sabré	sabrá	sabremos	to fit

Finally, there are some verbs that are just hard to classify. You've seen them come up again and again in the chapters on irregular verbs: *decir* (to say), *hacer* (to do), and *querer* (to want). Their conjugations are listed in **TABLE 15-29**.

TABLE 15-29

OTHER VERBS WITH IRREGULAR FUTURE-TENSE CONJUGATIONS

VERB	YO FORM	*ÉL/ELLA/USTED* FORM	*NOSOTROS* FORM	ENGLISH
decir	diré	dirá	diremos	to say
hacer	haré	hará	haremos	to do, make
querer	querré	querrá	querremos	to want

Practice Your Conjugations #5

Translate the following sentences using the appropriate verb forms.
If you don't know a word, check the vocabulary in **TABLE 15-30**.

1. Will you (informal) make the bed?

2. My parents will come on Tuesday.

3. We will not be able to walk more.

4. You will leave soon.

5. They will want to wash their clothes.

6. I will have a raise next year.

7. He will put the radio in the kitchen.

8. I will fit the shoes in the suitcase.

9. She will not say the truth.

10. Next week they will know who won.

TABLE 15-30

VOCABULARY			
cama	bed	*aumento de sueldo*	raise
lavar	to wash	*ganar*	to win
maleta	suitcase	*zapatos*	shoes
pronto	soon	*ropa*	clothes

CHAPTER 16

Impersonal Assertions and the Subjunctive

Y ou probably remember your old English teacher warning everybody about overusing passive-voice sentences like "it was given to me by Eileen" (instead of "Eileen gave it to me"). But sometimes you do need to use these constructions, and the same is true in Spanish. What we don't really pay attention to in English is the subjunctive mood, which you will learn about in this chapter as well.

Impersonal Assertions

Most passive-voice constructions in English come with the verb form of "to be." In Spanish, you will often use *ser* as the equivalent. One type of passive-voice construction that uses *ser* is the impersonal assertion. Impersonal assertions are those statements that are said as general truths. They are not bound to time—they may have been true before, may be true now, and might be true in the future. The general rule is that they are expressed in the third person of the present tense with the verb *ser*.

Recall that the interaction of the verb *ser* (to be) and the object of possession permitted you to say *es mi abrigo* (it's my coat). Following are some examples of impersonal-assertion sentences:

> *Es malo fumar.* (It's bad to smoke.)
> *Es bueno hacer ejercicios.* (It's good to exercise.)
> *Es una persona muy inteligente.* (He/she is a very intelligent person.)

ESSENTIALS

The easiest way to distinguish impersonal constructions is to remember that they do not have a specific subject. Technically, of course, the subject is the pronoun of *ser* (*él* or *ella* for *es*, and *ellos* or *ellas* for *son*, translated into English as "it"), but it does not refer to anything and is never actually present in the meaning of the sentence.

Discussing the Weather

The impersonal construction is often used to discuss *el tiempo* (the weather). However, since the weather is never in a permanent state, the verb *estar* is used instead of *ser*. (If you need to review the differences between *ser* and *estar*, reread Chapters 6 and 7.)

Estar allows you to describe physical conditions; when employed to describe the environment, *estar* may be translated as the impersonal assertion "it is." Take a look at the list of the following questions:

> *¿Cómo está el clima?* (How is the climate?)
> *¿Cómo está el tiempo?* (How is the weather?)

¿Cómo está afuera? (How is it outside?)

In reply, all you need to do is say *Está*... and a word that would describe the weather. For a list of weather-related vocabulary, check out **TABLE 16-1**.

TABLE 16-1	THE VOCABULARY OF WEATHER		
agradable	pleasant	*buen tiempo*	nice weather
caloruso	hot	*claro*	clear
cubierto	covered (with clouds)	*despejado*	without clouds
frío	cold	*helado*	freezing
húmedo	humid	*lluvioso*	rainy
nevado	snowy	*nublado*	cloudy
con mucho viento	windy		

What's the Weather Doing?

You can also use *hacer* to describe what the weather "does" (as opposed to how it "is"). For instance, *hace sol* may be translated as "it's sunny," but this phrase literally stands for "(the weather) makes the sun."

So another way of asking about the weather is *¿Qué tiempo hace?* ("How is the weather?" or "Which weather is going on?") In reply, you would say, *Hace*...

- *buen tiempo* (nice weather)
- *calor* (hot)
- *frío* (cold)
- *llovizna* (drizzling)
- *lluvia* (raining)
- *nieve* (snowing)
- *relámpagos* (lightning)
- *sol* (sunny)
- *viento* (windy)

How would you say "It's very hot (weather)"?
In Spanish, you need to literally say "the weather is making a lot of heat," so you would use *mucho* (many, much): *Hace mucho calor*. However, if you need to say "it's bad weather," you'd use *muy* (very): *Hace muy mal tiempo*.

Using *Hacer*

Translate the following sentences into Spanish, using the verb *hacer*. For additional vocabulary, refer to **TABLE 16-2**.

1. It is cool outside.

2. It is very good weather outside.

3. It is very sunny (weather).

4. It is shady under the tree.

5. It's thundering.

TABLE 16-2

VOCABULARY			
afuera	outside	*arbol*	tree
debajo de	under, underneath	*fresco*	cool, fresh

Other Impersonal Verbs

In addition to *estar* and *hacer*, you can use other verbs that describe the weather in an impersonal construction. Take a look at **TABLE 16-3** for some examples. Notice that most of these verbs look like the adverbs you've learned already to describe the weather.

TABLE 16-3

IMPERSONAL-CONSTRUCTION VERBS		
VERB	ENGLISH	EXAMPLE
amanecer	to grow light (at dawn)	*Amaneció nublado.* (It was cloudy at dawn.)
anochecer	to grow dark (at night)	*Anocheció despejado.* (It was clear at nightfall.)
granizar	to hail	*Graniza.* (It hails.)

helar	to freeze	*Hoy ha helado.* (It has been freezing today.)
llover	to rain	*Llueve a cántaros.* (It rains like cats and dogs.)
lloviznar	to drizzle	*Llovizna.* (It drizzles.)
relampaguear	to flash with lightning	*Relampaguea.* (It is lightning.)
tronar	to thunder	*Truena.* (It is thundering.)

It's Your Turn

Now it's your turn. Describe how the weather has been lately, how it is today, and what you expect in the future. Use the various weather expressions and include references to days, dates, and times of day.

Imperative Constructions

Another type of construction that lacks a voiced subject is the imperative construction. The imperative is often called the command mood, though it is often used in making requests. When you request, ask, or demand something, you are using the imperative.

Imperative commands are always written with exclamation points. In Spanish, you have two exclamation points that act as parentheses, so that you know what part of the sentence is the exclamation or command. For example, "Look!" in Spanish would be written as *¡Mira!*

The imperative mood's concern with the present should make it a fairly easy mood to master. Simply plug in the appropriate endings and place the command within exclamation marks (¡ . . . !).

Tú and the Imperative

The best way to approach the imperative is by learning the *tú* form (see **TABLE 16-4**). That's because it's the most obvious type of command— you are much more likely to use the imperative with somebody you know well, or somebody who is younger than you.

TABLE 16-4

IMPERATIVE *TÚ*			
	−AR	**−ER**	**−IR**
positive command ("Do!")	*¡Camina!* (Walk!)	*¡Bebe!* (Drink!)	*¡Parte!* (Leave!)
negative command ("Don't do!")	*¡No camines!* (Don't walk!)	*¡No bebas!* (Don't drink!)	*¡No partas!* (Don't get!)

It is understandable if you find these a little confusing. The positive command endings are the same for the imperative *tú* form as they are for the indicative present-tense *usted* form. (Look at **TABLE 16-5**.)

TABLE 16-5

POSITIVE *TÚ* COMMANDS AND INDICATIVE *USTED* STATEMENTS			
POSITIVE *TÚ* COMMAND	**ENGLISH**	**INDICATIVE *USTED* STATEMENT**	**ENGLISH**
¡Camina!	Walk!	*Usted camina.*	You (formal) walk.
¡Bebe!	Drink!	*Usted bebe.*	You (formal) drink.
¡Parte!	Leave!	*Usted parte.*	You (formal) leave.

Whereas the positive imperatives for *tú* take the same form as the indicative present-tense conjugations of the more formal *usted*, negative imperatives of *tú* seem to invert the conjugation endings. *Caminar* takes on the *-es* ending, and *beber* and *recibir* take on the *-as* ending. For a comparison, take a look at the verbs in **TABLE 16-6**.

TABLE 16-6

NEGATIVE *TÚ* COMMANDS AND INDICATIVE *TÚ* STATEMENTS			
NEGATIVE *TÚ* COMMAND	ENGLISH	INDICATIVE *TÚ* STATEMENT	ENGLISH
¡No camines!	Don't walk!	*No caminas.*	You (informal) don't walk.
¡No bebas!	Don't drink!	*No bebes.*	You (informal) don't drink.
¡No partas!	Don't leave!	*No partes.*	You (informal) don't leave.

There are only a few verbs that have irregular positive-*tú* command conjugations. These verbs are listed in **TABLE 16-7**.

TABLE 16-7

IRREGULAR VERBS			
VERB	ENGLISH	POSITIVE *TÚ* COMMMAND	NEGATIVE *TÚ* COMMAND
decir	to say	*¡Di!*	*¡No digas!*
hacer	to do	*¡Haz!*	*¡No hagas!*
ir	to go	*¡Ve!*	*¡No vayas!*
poner	to put	*¡Pon!*	*¡No pongas!*
salir	to leave	*¡Sal!*	*¡No salgas!*
ser	to be	*¡Sé!*	*¡No seas!*
tener	to have	*¡Ten!*	*¡No tengas!*
venir	to come	*¡Ven!*	*¡No vengas!*

Usted(es) and *Nosotros(as)* in the Imperative

The commands or requests addressed to *usted, ustedes, nosotros,* and *nosotras* approach the imperative in the same way as the negative *tú* command. That is, you add *-e,-en,* and *-emos* endings to the *-ar* verbs, and *-a, -an,* and *-amos* endings to the *-er* and *-ir* verbs (see **TABLE 16-8**). This rule applies to both positive and negative commands.

TABLE 16-8

	IMPERATIVE *USTED* AND *USTEDES*		
	−AR	*−ER*	*−IR*
usted	¡Camine!	¡Beba!	¡Reciba!
ustedes	¡Caminen!	¡Beban!	¡Reciban!
nosotros, nosotras	¡Caminemos!	¡Bebamos!	¡Recibamos!

In the *nosotros/nosotras* form, the commands may be translated in the form of "let's . . ." In **TABLE 16-8**, *¡Caminemos!, ¡Bebamos!,* and *¡Recibamos!* may be translated as "Let's walk!" "Let's drink!" and "Let's get!"

Genderless Lo

Up to this point, you've only encountered nouns and pronouns that possess gender. In fact you were told that all nouns are either masculine or feminine. While this is true for nouns, it is not true of all object pronouns—*lo* is a case in point. You've seen it before as the direct-object pronoun "him." For example:

Ayer, buscaba a David. (Yesterday, I was looking for David.)
Lo vi en la calle. (I saw him on the street.)

In fact, you will often see *lo* used as "it," when the gender of what is being referenced is not clear. In the following example, *lo* in the second phrase refers to *fui a la tienda ayer*:

Fui a la tienda ayer. (I went to the store yesterday.)
Lo hice a las nueve de la mañana. (I did it at nine in the morning.)

The act of having gone to the store cannot be interpreted in terms of gender, and as a result requires the use of a genderless object. You will often use *lo* when "it" is the appropriate object in English. The genderless object plays a major role in shaping imperative sentences. For example:

¡Estúdialo ahora mismo! (Study it right now!)
¡Bébanlo después de comer! (Drink it after eating!)

¡Ábramoslo mañana! (Let's open it tomorrow!)

Notice how the object is attached to the end of the verb. Keep in mind that this is true for all object pronouns found in *positive* imperative sentences, and it lends itself to some interesting combinations, such as these:

¡Escúchame! (Listen to me!)
¡Dame la blusa! (Give me the blouse!)
¡Dámela! (Give it to me!)

Keep in mind that when you add additional syllables to a word, you also need to add an accent mark—unless you intend to pronounce it differently. For example, take a look at *¡Dame!* and *¡Dámela!* According to accent rules, a word that ends in a vowel should be accented on the next-to-last syllable. When you add *la,* you also need to add an accent mark over the *a* in order to keep the pronunciation "DAH-meh-lah" (and not "dah-MEH-lah").

Also note that in the last example the indirect object *me* (to me) precedes the direct object *la* (it). In the negative, however, the object pronouns precede the imperative verb (though, once again, the indirect object comes first, followed by the direct object). Take a look at the following examples:

¡No me escuches! (Don't listen to me!)
¡No me des la blusa! (Don't give me the blouse!)
¡No me la des! (Don't give it to me.)

Irregular *Nosotros* Conjugations

Please also note that some verbs undergo a spelling accommodation in the *nosotros* form of the imperative. Verbs that end in *-car, -gar,* and *-zar* follow a base consonant change from *c* to *qu, g* to *gu,* and *z* to *ce,* respectively (see **TABLES 16-9**, **16-10**, and **16-11**).

TABLE 16-9

CONSONANT CHANGE IN -CAR VERBS		
VERB	ENGLISH	IMPERATIVE NOSOTROS FORM
abarcar	to take on	abarquemos
buscar	to look for	busquemos
practicar	to practice	practiquemos
sacar	to take out	saquemos

TABLE 16-10

CONSONANT CHANGE IN –GAR VERBS		
VERB	ENGLISH	IMPERATIVE NOSOTROS FORM
apagar	to turn off	apaguemos
entregar	to hand over	entreguemos
jugar	to play	juguemos
llegar	to arrive	lleguemos

TABLE 16-11

CONSONANT CHANGE IN –ZAR VERBS		
VERB	ENGLISH	IMPERATIVE NOSOTROS FORM
abrazar	to embrace	abracemos
almorzar	to eat lunch	almorcemos
empezar	to begin	empecemos
rezar	to pray	recemos

Another group of irregular verbs belong to the -ir category, and the spelling-accommodation changes involved concern the verb's base vowel. The changes usually occur as follows: from e to i, and from o to u (see **TABLES 16-12** and **16-13**).

TABLE 16-12

VOWEL CHANGE FROM E TO I		
VERB	ENGLISH	IMPERATIVE NOSOTROS FORM
advertir	to warn	advirtamos
medir	to measure	midamos
mentir	to lie, deceive	mintamos
pedir	to ask, request	pidamos

TABLE 16-13

VOWEL CHANGE FROM *O* TO *U*		
VERB	ENGLISH	IMPERATIVE *NOSOTROS* FORM
dormir	to sleep	*durmamos*
morir	to die	*muramos*

Please note that all the imperative forms (except for the positive *tú* form) look identical to the conjugations of the present subjunctive tense. For more on subjunctive, go on to the next section.

Reviewing the Imperative

Translate the following sentences, using the information you have just learned. For additional vocabulary, refer to **TABLE 16-14**.

1. Listen (you, informal) to the news!

2. Let's decide on a movie!

3. Wait (you, formal) for me at the door!

4. Come (you, informal) here!

5. Don't cry (you, informal)!

6. Look for (you, formal) the key!

7. Don't put (you, informal) it (masculine) here!

8. Let's travel to Mexico together!

9. Don't buy (you, formal) it for her!

---

10. Bring (you, plural) it to me!

---

11. Tell (you, informal) it to me!

---

12. Don't play (you, informal) soccer in the house!

---

13. Don't open (you, informal) the door!

---

14. Learn (you, plural) the rules!

---

15. Receive (you, formal) the shipment!

---

16. Cover (you, plural) the floor!

---

17. Let's discuss the book!

---

18. Understand (you, plural) the instructions!

---

19. Discuss (you, plural) the problem!

---

20. Write (you, informal) it!

TABLE 16-14

VOCABULARY			
abrir	to open	aquí	here
comprar	to buy	comprender	to understand
cubrir	to cover	envío	shipment

discutir	to discuss	*escribir*	to write
esperar	to wait, hope	*juntos*	together
(la) llave	the key	*llorar*	to cry
noticias	news	*película*	movie
piso	floor	*(el) problema*	problem
puerta	door	*viajar*	to travel

Introducing the Subjunctive

As you saw earlier, an impersonal assertion tries to lend a certain amount of authority or objectivity to a statement. An easy way to create this impression is to use the phrases that lend themselves to its construction. Some of these phrases include:

> *Es evidente que* . . . (It is evident that . . .)
> *Es cierto que* . . . (It is certain that . . .)
> *Es verdad que* . . . (It is true that . . .)
> *Es seguro que* . . . (It is sure that . . .)
> *Es indudable que* . . . (It is indubitable that . . .)
> *Es que* . . . (It is that . . .)

To see how these constructions behave in complete sentences, look at the following examples:

> *Será feliz quien tiene a quien amar.* (One who has someone to love will be happy.)
> *Es indudable que los hijos necesitan a su madre.* (There is no doubt that children need their mother.)
> *Es seguro que la policía lo coje.* (It's sure that the police catches him.)

All of these constructions express opinions of certainty in the indicative mood. As you've seen before, this mood can also express some uncertainty, particularly in the compound tenses using a form of *haber*. Recall, however, that usually the uncertainty that can be created is somewhat limited—a probability by definition implies that there is a chance that the contrary may occur, but the deck is stacked in favor of the outcome. In addition to the compound tenses, the indicative offers the following sentence qualifiers:

- *A lo mejor* ... (probably, maybe)
    A lo mejor voy de vacaciones a Perú. (I may go on vacation
    to Peru.)
- *Quizás* ... (maybe)
    Quizás llega a tiempo el regalo de Navidad.
    (Hopefully the Christmas present arrives on time.)
- *Tal vez* ... (maybe)
    Tal vez no le gusta camarones. (Perhaps she doesn't like shrimp.)
- *Posiblemente* ... (possibly)
    Posiblemente el remedio es demasiado fuerte.
    (Possibly the remedy is too strong.)

Though the ability to express uncertainty can be found in the indicative mood, the degree of doubt or opinion is very constrained. To more forcefully express the gray areas of life, you need to consider the subjunctive mood—a mood that you may find somewhat novel, given its scarce employment in everyday English.

Recall that the mood associated with verbs is the manner by which you decide to communicate or report the world around you. In the indicative, you were concerned with telling how things appeared—a somewhat "objective" accounting.

In contrast, the subjunctive takes on a somewhat "subjective" approach. It allows you to express opinions, personal as well as impersonal. Take a look at **TABLE 16-15** below and examine the endings associated with the present subjunctive.

TABLE 16-15

	CONJUGATING VERBS IN PRESENT SUBJUNCTIVE TENSE				
	–AR	*CANTAR*	*–ER* AND *–IR*	*APRENDER*	*VIVIR*
yo	-e	cante	-a	aprenda	viva
tú	-es	cantes	-as	aprendas	vivas
él, ella, usted	-e	cante	-a	aprenda	viva
nosotros	-emos	cantemos	-amos	aprendamos	vivamos
ellos, ellas, ustedes	-en	canten	-an	aprendan	vivan

When you were first asked to look at the table, you may have dreaded having to learn a whole new set of endings. But did you notice any peculiarities within the tense? Take another look.

The first thing that you may have noticed is that, with the exception of the first person singular, the endings look very familiar. In fact, the -ar present subjunctive endings look remarkably similar to the -er endings of the present indicative. Likewise, the present subjunctive -er and -ir endings are the same as those of the -ar present indicative. These are the same rules you have already learned for the imperatives of usted and ustedes (see pp. 211–212). Keeping this in mind will help you considerably in mastering the subjunctive.

ESSENTIALS

A subjunctive phrase rarely stands alone. At the heart of most sentences that use the present subjunctive, there is an indicative phrase that sets the subjunctive in motion by introducing a need or desire to be met, a doubt to be expressed, or an opinion to be made. The short sentence is largely absent in the subjunctive.

Expressing Uncertainty

As you saw earlier, keywords may be employed to express doubt. Such keywords in the subjunctive include:

- *Quizás* . . . (maybe)
    Quizás llegue a tiempo el regalo de Navidad.
    (Hopefully the Christmas present arrives on time—but there is a good chance that it won't.)
- *Tal vez* . . . (maybe)
    Tal vez no le guste camarones.
    (Perhaps she doesn't like shrimp—but she may.)
- *Posiblemente* . . . (possibly)
    Posiblemente el remedio sea demasiado fuerte.
    (Possibly the remedy is too strong—but it may be otherwise.)

Although the sentences are very similar to the ones you've seen previously, the fact that you are using the subjunctive lends them a sense of uncertainty—hence the additional sentences included in the translations. Other tags of uncertainty specifically useful in the subjunctive include:

- *Es dudoso que* . . . (it's doubtful that)
  Es dudoso que Mario saque buena nota en la prueba.
  (It is doubtful that Mario gets a good grade on the test.)
- *Es posible que* . . . (it's possible that)
  Es posible que lo llame por teléfono mañana.
  (It's possible that I might call him by phone.)
- *Puede ser que* . . . or *Puede que* . . . (it might be that)
  Puede ser que compre un coche usado.
  (It might be that I'll purchase a used car.)
  Puede que el dueño cambie de idea.
  (It could be that the owner changes his mind.)

Notice in the sample sentences above how *que* introduces the subjunctive phrase, a common way of signaling the subjunctive. Often, the subjunctive is found as a dependent clause that relies on a main independent and indicative clause to exist. Take a look at how this works with the following independent indicative phrases:

- *No creer que* . . . (not to believe that)
  No creo que Rafael esté interesado en ir al cine.
  (I don't believe that Raphael is interested in going to the movies.)

Other independent indicative phrases that are followed by a subjunctive clause include:

Dudar que . . . (to doubt that)
No estar seguro . . . (not to be sure that)
No imaginarse . . . (not being able to imagine that)
No parecer que . . . (not to seem like)
No pensar que . . . (not to think that)
Temer que . . . (to fear that)

CHAPTER 17

What You Like to Do

What do you like to do in your "free" time? Of course, you probably have many *deberes* (obligations), but you also entertain yourself with things that you enjoy. This chapter will help you explore your hobbies and pastimes in Spanish.

Likes and Dislikes

Why might someone say, "I like hamburgers"? To begin with, the person is expressing a preference. But what is behind a preference? The hamburger provides some level of satisfaction to the person. It pleases the person.

That is what is communicated in Spanish! And the verb that does that is gustar. So, "I like hamburgers" translates to me gustan las hamburguesas—literally, "hamburgers please me."

Notice that in the Spanish sentence, the subject is "the hamburgers" and "I" is the indirect object, *me*. To say "I (you, he, she, we, you all, or they) like" thus becomes a simple matter. All you need to do is change the indirect object and conjugate the verb according to the thing or things that you like. Take a look at the following examples.

Me gusta el café. (I like coffee.)
Me gustan las flores. (I like flowers.)
Te gusta el café. (You like coffee.)
Te gustan las flores. (You like flowers.)
Le gusta el café. (He/she likes coffee. You like coffee.)
Le gustan las flores. (He/she likes flowers. You like flowers.)
Nos gusta el café. (We like coffee.)
Nos gustan las flores. (We like flowers.)
Les gusta el café. (They like coffee. You all like coffee.)
Les gustan las flores. (They like flowers. You all like flowers.)

What if what you like is an action? For example, how would you say "I like to travel"? Think of it as "I like traveling." Since "traveling" may be thought of in the singular, you would say *Me gusta viajar.*

In Combination with *Gustar*

Keep in mind that as simple as this construction is to use, there are certain combinations of words that may change what you mean to say. For instance, be careful to put the modifier in the right place—generally in back of what you want modified. Compare the following:

Me gusta mucho viajar. (I really like to travel.)
Me gusta viajar mucho. (I like to travel a lot/often.)

Untranslatable redundant constructions may also be used to emphasize or clarify the indirect object. For example:

A mí me gusta el boxeo. El boxeo me gusta a mí. (**I** like boxing.)
A ti te gusta la ópera. La ópera te gusta a ti. (**You** like the opera.)
A él le gusta María. María le gusta a él. (**He** likes Maria.)
A ella le gustan los perros. Los perros le gustan a ella. (**She** likes dogs.)
A usted le gusta la pesca. La pesca le gusta a usted. (**You** like fishing.)
A nosotros nos gusta el vino. El vino nos gusta a nosotros. (**We** like wine.)
A nosotras nos gusta el ajo. El ajo nos gusta a nosotras. (**We** like garlic.)
A ellos les gusta el té. El té les gusta a ellos. (**They** like tea.)
A ellas les gusta el café. El café les gusta a ellas. (**They** like coffee.)
A ustedes les gusta el actor. El actor les gusta a ustedes. (**You all** like the actor.)

FACTS

Notice that there is a small difference between *a mí me gusta el boxeo* and *el boxeo me gusta a mí.* They both mean "I like boxing"; the difference is in emphasis. The first phrase may be translated as "as for me, I like boxing." The second phrase puts more emphasis on boxing: "Boxing is what I like."

To state these statements in the negative, place *no* before the indirect object. "I don't like boxing" may be translated into Spanish in three ways:

No me gusta el boxeo.
A mí no me gusta el boxeo.
El boxeo no me gusta a mí.

The verb *gustar* may also appear in other tenses. For instance, take a look at the following sentences. Can you recognize the tense of each one?

Te gusté callado. (You liked me silent.)
Me gustaba el ajedrez. (I used to like chess.)

Nos ha gustado viajar a Lima desde pequeños. (We have liked to travel to Lima since we were little.)
Te gustará mi amiga. (You will like my girl friend.)

¿Qué te gusta? (What do you like?)

Translate the following sentences, using the appropriate form of *gustar* and vocabulary learned in the previous section. For additional vocabulary, refer to **TABLE 17-1**.

1. I like talking with my friends.

2. They like to work.

3. We like rice and chicken.

4. You (informal) used to like the Johnsons.

5. You all liked Spain.

6. I believe that I will like New York.

7. She has liked Thai food since college.

TABLE 17-1

VOCABULARY			
arroz	rice	*comida*	food
con	with	*desde*	since
hablar	to talk	*pollo*	chicken
que	that	*tailandesa*	Thai
trabajar	to work	*universidad*	college

Just Saying "No"

As you've seen, the act of negating a positive statement is simply a matter of placing a "no" before the verb. The easiest example is the sentence *No hablo.* (I don't speak.) As you know, however, any language has a multitude of ways to express a single point. This is also the case with saying "no."

To understand the negative better, first look at the vocabulary of positive quantities and their negative counterparts in **TABLE 17-2**.

TABLE 17-2

VOCABULARY: POSITIVE AND NEGATIVE QUANTITIES	
POSITIVE	**NEGATIVE**
algo (something)	*nada* (nothing)
alguien (someone)	*nadie* (no one)
alguna vez, otra vez (sometimes, another time)	*ninguna vez* (never)
alguno (some)	*ninguno* (none)
a veces (sometimes)	*jamás* (never)
o (or)	*ni, ni siquiera* (nor, not even)
sí (yes)	*no* (no)
siempre (always)	*nunca* (never)
también (too)	*tampoco* (neither)
todo (all)	*nada* (nothing)
todavía (still)	*ya no* (no longer)
ya (already)	*aún no* (not yet)

Whereas a double negative in English is said to be logically equivalent to a positive statement, it simply confirms the negative in Spanish. For example:

Yo no voy allí nunca. (I don't go there never—I never go there.)
Yo no voy a ningun sitio. (I don't go to no place—I don't go anyplace.)

Yes or No?

Translate the following sentences, using the vocabulary learned in the previous section. For additional vocabulary, see **TABLE 17-3**.

1. I always eat vegetables.

2. I never eat vegetables.

3. Someone waits for you.

4. No one is here.

5. At times, Fred and Ginger go out dancing.

6. Fred and Ethel never go out dancing.

7. They already know the route.

8. They don't know the route yet.

9. I liked the movie also.

10. I did not like the movie (n)either.

TABLE 17-3

VOCABULARY			
aquí	here	*bailar*	to dance
comer	to eat	*conocer*	to know
esperar	to wait	*película*	movie
ruta	route	*salir*	to leave, go out
vegetal	vegetable		

Verbs That Act Like *Gustar*

There is a whole group of verbs in Spanish that behave similarly to *gustar*. The simplest example is the verb *disgustar* (to dislike):

> *Me disgusta viajar.* (I dislike to travel.)
> *Te disgusta el café.* (You dislike coffee.)
> *Nos disgustan las flores.* (We dislike flowers.)

Other verbs that you should know are listed in **TABLE 17-4**:

TABLE 17-4

VERBS THAT ACT LIKE *GUSTAR*		
SPANISH	**ENGLISH**	**EXAMPLE**
agradar	to please	*Nos agradan los perros, pero no los gatos.* (We like dogs but not cats.)
doler	to hurt, be in pain	*Te duele el brazo.* (Your arm hurts.)
encantar	to delight, charm	*Me encantan las flores.* (I'm delighted by flowers.)
faltar	to be lacking	*No le falta ni dinero ni poder.* (He lacks neither money nor power.)
hacer falta	to need	*Me hacen falta mis padres.* (I miss/need my parents.)
interesar	to interest	*Nos interesa el fútbol americano.* (We are interested in football.)
parecer	to seem, appear	*La camisa me parece muy pequeña.* (It seems to me that the shirt is too small.)
sobrar	to be left	*Te sobró la comida.* (You had food left over.)

Practice What You Learned

Translate the following sentences, using the appropriate form of the verbs that behave like *gustar*. For additional vocabulary, refer to **TABLE 17-5**.

1. I was lacking courage.

2. My head hurts.

3. Do you miss your automobile?

4. We are interested in learning Spanish.

5. Are you pleased by romantic films?

6. It looked good to us.

7. I am delighted by Monet's paintings.

TABLE 17-5

VOCABULARY			
ánimo	courage	*aprender*	to learn
automóvil	automobile	*bueno*	good
cabeza	head	*película*	film
pintura	painting	*romántico*	romantic

What Do You Like to Do?

What do you like to do in your free time? What are some hobbies and activities you are interested in? The following section will help you discuss these hobbies and activities.

Going Places

As you remember, the verb "to go" in Spanish is *ir*. Use the expression *ir a . . .* ("to go to . . .") with the words and phrases in **TABLE 17-6**.

TABLE 17-6

IR A . . .	
los almacenes	the department stores
un concierto	concert
las carreras de caballo	the horse races
las carreras de coche	the car races
un casino	a casino
una competencia	a competition
las corridas de toro	the running of bulls
discotecas	discotheques, clubs
un parque de diversiones	an amusement park
un partido de . . .	a game of . . .
la playa	the beach
visitar a amigos	visit friends
visitar a parientes	visit relatives

As you might remember, whenever *a* precedes the definite article *el*, they form the construction *al*. Therefore, *ir a el ballet* should be *ir al ballet* (to go to the ballet). Other examples include *ir al centro* (to go to center/downtown) and *ir al cine* (to go to the movie theater).

A similar construction is *ir de . . .* ("to go . . ."). This construction generally appears with one of the words listed in **TABLE 17-7**.

TABLE 17-7

IR DE . . .			
compras	shopping	*excursión*	on excursions
pesca	fishing	*vacaciones*	on vacation
viaje	on a trip	*visita*	visit

Activities do require you to think of not only who does something and when, but also how that activity is described. Some activities are considered ones that you "play" (*jugar*) and others that you "do" (*hacer*).

Sports-related activities are generally expressed with the verb *hacer* (to do). For instance, *hacer natación* is literally "to do swimming." **TABLE 17-8** contains a list of activities that you "do."

TABLE 17-8

HACER . . .			
aeróbic	aerobics	el alpinismo	mountain climbing
artes marciales	martial arts	aventura	extreme sports
el buceo	scuba diving	el canotaje	rowing
el ciclismo	cycling	ejercicios	exercise
la equitación	horseback riding	el surf	surfing
el esquí	skiing	el levantamiento de pesas	weightlifting
la navegación	sailing	el patinaje (sobre hielo)	(ice)skating

With *jugar,* things are easier. The idea of "playing" sports is the same in Spanish as in English. For instance, *jugar al ajedrez* means "to play chess." (Remember that when you put *a* and *el* together, they merge into *al,* as in this case, when you use the construction *jugar a* . . . and *el ajedrez.*) For other sports terms used in this construction, see **TABLE 17-9**.

TABLE 17-9

JUGAR A . . .			
el baloncesto/ básquetbol	basketball	el balonvolea/ voleibol	volleyball
el béisbol	baseball	el billar	billiards, pool
los bolos	bowling	las cartas	cards
los dardos	darts	el fútbol	soccer
el fútbol americano	American football	el golf	golf
la lotería	the lottery	el póquer	poker
la ruleta	roulette	el solitario	solitaire
el tenis	tennis	el veintiúno	21 (blackjack)

But some of us like more sedentary activities, such as reading. And there is so much to read—just take a look at **TABLE 17-10**.

TABLE 17-10

LEER . . .			
biografías	biographies	*cuentos*	stories, short stories
cuentos de hadas	fairy tales	*libros*	books
novelas policíacas	detective novels	*novelas romanticas*	romance novels
periódicos	newspapers	*la poesia*	poems
resetas	recipes	*revistas*	magazines

For additional vocabulary, refer to **TABLE 17-11**.

TABLE 17-11

OTHER PASTIMES: RELATED VOCABULARY			
asistir a . . .	to attend . . .	*caminar*	to walk
(la) canción	song	*la cocina gastronómica*	gourmet cooking
correr	to run	*dar paseo en bicicleta*	to tour on bicycle
escuchar la radio	listen to the radio	*escuchar música*	to listen to music
mirar la televisión	to watch television	*nadar*	to swim
pasatiempos	pastime	*pasear*	to stroll, go for a walk
la pintura al oleo	oil painting	*tomar clases*	to take classes
trotear	jog	*ver peliculas*	to watch movies

Listening to Music

Let's get more specific here. Many people like to listen to music, but their tastes vary—some people listen to CDs and others to records. Some may prefer hip-hop and others listen to country music. First, take inventory of your equipment. (Use **TABLE 17-12** to help you with vocabulary.)

TABLE 17-12

VOCABULARY: MUSICAL EQUIPMENT			
altavoz	speaker	amplificador	amplifier
los auriculares	headphones	el disco compacto	compact disc, CD
tocacasete	cassette player	tocadiscos CD	CD player
el volumen	volume	el Walkman	Walkman

You can use four related verbs with this equipment: *tocar* (to play), *escuchar* (to listen), *grabar* (to record), and *disfrutar* (to enjoy).

Listening to Music

Here are some questions that may be asked to identify your musical preferences. See if you can answer them in Spanish.

¿Qué tipo de música le gusta?

¿Le gusta el `jazz'?

¿Qué piensa del rock español?

¿Cuáles cantantes son sus favoritos?

¿Le gusta la música movida?

¿Le gustan los boleros?

Sitting Down at the Computer

Using the computer is not always done for fun. Today, many people rely on the computer to work and to study. In Spain, the computer is called *el ordenador* (programmable ordering machine). In Latin America, it is called *el computador* or *la computadora* (the computing machine). For consistency, this book has used *la computadora* throughout.

FACTS

With the technological advances of the past decades, this is a time of great flux in the world of technical Spanish. Words are being created on the spot and discarded just as quickly. Within the computer industry, though, some basic terminology is starting to stick.

Here is some basic terminology related to *la computadora* (see **TABLES 17-13** and **17-14**).

TABLE 17-13

COMPUTER-RELATED TERMS	
@ *(arroba)*	"at" in e-mail addresses
disco duro	hard drive
escáner	scanner
hoja de cálculo	spreadsheet
lector de DVDs	DVD player
impresora láser	laser printer
módem	modem
monitor	monitor
motores de busqueda	search engines
nombre de usario	user name
página Web	Web page
pantalla	screen
PC portátil	notebook computer
proveedor Internet	Internet service provider
ratón	mouse
regrabadora de CDs	CD-RW drive
sitio Web	Web site
sobremesa	desktop
teclado	keyboard
vínculo	link

TABLE 17-14

COMPUTER-RELATED ACTIVITIES	
abandonar un programa	to exit a program
abrir un archivo	to open or start a file
arrancar un progama	to start a program
apretar las teclas	to press and hold the keys
averiguar una dirreción	to search for an address
bajarse programas	to download programs
buscar un fichero	to search for a file
cambiar la configuración actual	to change the present configuration
cargar un programa	to load/start a program
cerrar la ventana de un programa	to close a program's window
chatear con	to chat with
conectar a la Web	to connect to the Web
correr un programa	to run a program
ejecutar un programa	to start a program
elegir el menú	to select from the menu
empezar un programa	to start a program
encender la computadora	to turn on the PC
enviar mensajes	to send messages
hacer clique/clic en una carpeta	to select and click on a file folder
lanzar un programa	to launch a program
leer los mensajes recibidos	to read the messages received
minimizar una ventana	to minimize a window
navegar la Web	to surf the Web
prender la consola	to turn on the PC
presionar la tecla	to press the key
pulsar con el ratón	to tap/click with the mouse
salir de un programa	to leave from a program
seleccionar un icono	to select an icon

CHAPTER 18

Any Questions?

Spanish has various ways for making inquiries, also known as "interrogatives." These include using interrogative pronouns and adverbs, subject-verb switching with interrogative intonation patterns, and interrogative tags. Sound difficult? It's not. This chapter will show you how.

Interrogatives

Most of the questions you have encountered up to this point have begun with an interrogative pronoun or adverb. These interrogatives generally begin the interrogative phrase and identify the object or person about which there is some doubt. It is important to recognize that these pronouns and adverbs are distinguished by their accent. Unaccented, they have similar meanings but often exhibit subtle differences; accented, they also offer an exception to the general intonation patterns described above.

Interrogative pronouns are special in the variety of different factors that guide their use. Whereas number must be considered in the subject and possessive pronouns employed, it is not always available for consideration in some interrogative pronouns. The same is true for considerations of gender. Keep in mind that interrogatives work to fill in the blanks of notions requiring more information to be completely understood.

Interrogatives Without Gender or Number

Some interrogatives function without being gender- or number-specific. For a list of these interrogatives, see **TABLE 18-1**.

TABLE 18-1

INTERROGATIVES WITHOUT GENDER OR NUMBER		
INTERROGATIVE	ENGLISH	EXAMPLE
¿Cómo?	How?	¿Cómo está Mauricio? (How is Mauricio?)
¿Cuándo?	When?	¿Cuándo será Rafico un abogado? (When will Rafico be a lawyer?)
¿Dónde?	Where?	¿Dónde está la iglesia? (Where is the church?)
¿Qué?	What?	¿Qué tenía Gloria en la mano? (What did Gloria have in her hand?)

¿Cómo?

Though generally used to ask "how," *¿cómo?* is one of those small words that have various situational uses. In a question, you may use it to ask about the condition of a noun or manner of an action. If you didn't hear what somebody said, you can say *¿Cómo?* (Excuse me?) This word is also used to express surprise and to inquire as to how that surprise came to occur. (You may also use *¿cómo?* to form a rhetorical question.) For examples, take a look at the following questions:

¿Cómo está el tiempo? (How is the weather?)
¿Cómo es el clima en Vera Cruz? (How is the climate in Vera Cruz?)
¿Cómo le gusta el café? (How does he like his coffee?)
¿Cómo debo cocinar el bistec? (How should I cook the steak?)
¿Cómo? (What? Excuse me?)
¿Cómo así están aquí tus hermanos? (This is unexpected, how is it that your siblings are here?)
¿Cómo no? (Why not? How would it be otherwise?)

¿Cuándo?

The Spanish "when" is much more straightforward. It always refers to a time. (To practice telling time, you can refer back to Chapter 9.)

¿Cuándo estarán en casa los niños? (When will the children be at home?)
¿Cuándo llegaste a casa? (When did you get home?)

¿Dónde?

The Spanish "where," though as simple to use as *¿cuándo?* is interesting in that it often needs help to express a question regarding "place." That is, it is often used with prepositions. For the list of prepositions, as well as some examples, take a look at **TABLE 18-2**.

TABLE 18-2		*¿DÓNDE?* IN COMBINATION WITH PREPOSITIONS	
—	*¿dónde?*	*¿Dónde está Gloria?* (Where is Gloria?)	
a (to)	*¿adónde?*	*¿Adónde fue Marco?* (Where did Marco go to?)	
de (from)	*¿de dónde?*	*¿De dónde es Marisela?* (Where is Maricela from?)	
en (in)	*¿en dónde?*	*¿En dónde se lastimó?* (Where did he hurt himself?)	
por (by)	*¿por dónde?*	*¿Por dónde caminó?* (By which way did she walk?)	

¿Qué?

Qué is another word with many meanings. Within a question, it generally translates to "what." It may:

- Stand on its own as a familiar alternative to ¿cómo?—for example, to ask "What did you/he/she/they say?"
- Precede a noun where the subject is defined within the question.
  ¿Qué hora es? (What time is it?)
  ¿Qué día es hoy? (What day is it?)
  ¿Qué modelo de coche tiene Pedro? (What car model does Peter have?)
  ¿Qué comida hay? (What food is there?)
- Precede a verb where the question refers to something in general terms rather than by a specific instance. It may be assumed that the person making the inquiry possesses no knowledge of the possible responses to his or her question.
  ¿Qué está en la caja? (What is in the box?)
  ¿Qué compraba en el almacén? (What was he purchasing at the store?)

A special combination, *¿por qué?* exhibits several of the meanings that would be assigned to it by literal translation of its components. "By what (reason)," "for what (purpose)," and so on, can all be summed up in the English "why?"

ESSENTIALS

When *por qué* is not used as an interrogative, it changes to *porque* (no accent mark) to mean "because." For instance: *¿Por qué no está Juan en casa?* (Why is Juan not at home?) *Porque está en la escuela.* (Because he is at school.)

Interrogatives with Number but Without Gender

Some interrogatives do possess *número* (number) but not *género* (gender). Interrogatives that comprise this category are listed in **TABLE 18-3**.

TABLE 18-3	INTERROGATIVES WITH NUMBER BUT WITHOUT GENDER		
	INTERROGATIVE	**ENGLISH**	**EXAMPLE**
	¿Cuál?	Which (singular)?	*¿Cuál de los pasteles quiere Marí?* (Which of the pastries does Mari want?)
	¿Cuáles?	Which (plural)?	*¿Cuáles libros prefiere Sebastián?* (Which books does Sebastian prefer?)
	¿Quién?	Who (singular)?	*¿Quién estuvo en la reunion?* (Who was at the gathering/reunion?)
	¿Quiénes?	Who (plural)?	*¿Quiénes aquí tienen treinta años?* (Who here are thirty years old?)

¿Cuál? and *¿Cuáles?*

Cuál is an interrogative pronoun that causes confusion for many beginners. It may be said that it is the Spanish word for "which." However, you will often see it translated as "what." The cause of the confusion, then, is how to choose between *¿cuál?* and *¿qué?* The rules you should follow are:

1. When preceding a verb, *cuál* refers to a specific instance rather than a general idea. It implicitly presupposes prior knowledge of instances and asks that the respondent make a selection.
   ¿Qué está en la caja? (What is in the box?)
   ¿Cuál está en la caja? (Which one is in the box?)
   ¿Qué compraba en el almacén? (What was he purchasing in the store?)
   ¿Cuáles compraba en el almacén? (Which ones was she purchasing at the store?)
2. It may establish the selection more explicitly when used within the combination *¿Cuál(es) + de + (noun/pronoun) . . . ?*
   ¿Cuál de las joyas está en la caja? (Which one of the jewels is in the box?)
   ¿Cuáles de estos videos son buenos? (Which of these videos are good?)
3. When used with a form of **ser** and certain words, *cuál* is always chosen instead of **qué**, despite the vagueness that accompanies these words. Here are some examples:

¿Cuál era la diferencia? (What was the difference?)

¿Cuáles fueron las dificultades? (What were the difficulties?)

¿Cuál ha sido el motivo? (What has been the motive?)

¿Cuáles son los problemas? (What are the problems?)

¿Cuál será la razón? (What will the reason be? I wonder what the reason is?)

¿Cuál es la solución? (What is the solution?)

¿Quién? and *¿Quiénes?*

Quién is much less complicated than most interrogative pronouns. It is translated as "who" or "whom"—all you have to be concerned about is the number of people being represented. Furthermore, keep in mind that *quién* and *quiénes* sometimes appear with a preposition, *a* ("to," or personal preposition), *de* ("of" or "from"), or *en* ("in" or "about"). For some examples, see the following sentences:

¿Quién habló en la recepción? (Who spoke at the reception?)

¿Quiénes participaron? (Who participated?)

¿A quién buscas? (Who are you looking for?)

¿De quién es ese coche? (Whose automobile is it?)

¿En quiénes pensaba Joaquim? (About whom was Joaquim thinking?)

Cuándo, cómo, dónde, and *quién* are never followed immediately by nouns. Noting its exceptions, this is also true of *cuál*. In conversation, however, native speakers appear to break this rule often with *cuál*; in these cases, the construction *¿Cuál(es) + de + (noun/pronoun) . . . ?* is usually implied.

Interrogatives with Number and Gender

This section includes only one interrogative, *cuánto*. This interrogative is a little tricky in that it can have two very similar meanings, "how much" and "how many," depending on the number, singular or plural, employed. Compare the following sentences:

¿Cuánto dinero tiene Javier? (How much money does Javier have?)

¿Cuánta plata tiene Javier? (How much money does Javier have?—colloquial)

¿Cuánto cuesta? (How much does it cost?)

¿En cuánto está lista? (In how much time will she be ready?)

¿Cuántos años tiene Jorge? (How old is Jorge?)

¿Cuántas bufandas tiene Beatriz? (How many scarves does Beatriz have?)

As you can see, the interrogative *cuánto* acts as an adjective by changing in gender and number according to the noun that it modifies, so that, for example, if you want to ask "how many years?" you take *años* (years) and modify *cuánto* accordingly (to *cuántos*).

A with Interrogative Pronouns

A often plays an important role in determining the nature, subject, or object of the information requested. You've seen it translated as "at" and "to." And, as you remember, it may act as a personal particle placed before objects that designate people. Take a look at how *a* behaves with interrogatives in the following sentences:

¿A cómo está la gasolina? (At how much is gasoline?)

¿Adónde viaja Ximena? (To where does Ximena travel?)

¿A qué se refiere la maestra? (To what is the teacher referring?)

¿A cuál fiesta irá Benjamín? (To which party will Benjamin go?)

¿A quién vió Jaime en el concierto? (Whom did Jaime see at the concert?)

¿A cuánto está el agua? (At how much is the water?)

¿A cuántos kilómetors está el museo? (At how many kilometers is the museum?)

Subject-Verb Switch and Interrogative Tags

You are probably unconsciously very familiar with the subject-verb switch that often occurs in English to transform a statement into a question. For example: "Mary is a teacher" can switch to "Is Mary a teacher?" in order to act as an interrogative statement. When accompanied by the intonation of a question, the same transformations are possible in Spanish. Take a look at these examples:

> *La cama está contra la pared.* (The bed is against the wall.)
> *¿Está la cama contra la pared?* (Is the bed against the wall?)
> *Rodrigo no hace ejercicios.* (Rodrigo doesn't do exercises.)
> *¿No hace Rodrigo ejercicios?* (Doesn't Rodrigo do exercises?)

Equally as common in English and in Spanish is the addition of a phrase of doubt to a statement, thereby rendering it, for all intents and purposes, a question. For example:

> *La cama está contra la pared, ¿no?* (The bed is against the wall, isn't it?)
> *Paca no trajaba, ¿o sí?* (Paca does not work, or does she?)
> *Rodrigo no hace ejercicios, ¿verdad?* (Rodrigo doesn't do exercises, right?)

ESSENTIALS Every question is enclosed in two punctuation marks, ¿...? Notice that these marks stake off the territory that is the question. As such, they may mark off an entire sentence or just a portion of one. The same is also true for exclamation marks: ¡...!

Interjections

Exclamatory phrases are set off by ¡...! and often use three of the accented words that you have already encountered in the capacity of interrogatives: *¡Qué!, ¡Cuánto!,* and *¡Cómo!* (Note that the accent marks are also present in these words when they act as exclamatory expressions.) With these simple words, the exclamatory possibilities are endless.

¡Qué!

Qué is used within a variety of structures that express surprise or strong emotion:

1. *¡Qué + (sustantivo)!* What a (noun)!
   ¡Qué espectáculo! (What a show!)
   ¡Qué mujer! (What a woman!)
2. *¡Qué + (adjetivo)!* That's (adjective)! How (adjective)!
   ¡Qué bonito! (That's pretty!)
   ¡Qué maravilloso! (How marvelous!)
3. *¡Qué + (sustantivo) + tan + (adjetivo)!* What a(n) (adjective) (noun)!
   ¡Qué blusa tan cara! (What an expensive blouse!)
   ¡Qué perrito simpático! (What a charming puppy!)
4. *¡Qué + (sustantivo) + más + (adjetivo)!* What a(n) (adjective) (noun)!
   ¡Qué pulsera más fea! (What an ugly bracelet!)
   ¡Qué caballo más veloz! (What a fast horse!)
5. *¡Qué + (adverbio)!* That's (adverb)! How (adverb)!
   ¡Qué bueno! (That's good!)
   ¡Qué lejos! (How far!)
6. *¡Qué + (adjetivo) + (ser)!* How (adjective) + (subject pronoun) am/is/are!
   ¡Qué seria es! (How serious she is!)
   ¡Qué bajo es! (How short he is!)
7. *¡Qué + (adjetivo) + (ser) + (sustantivo)!* How (adjective) + (noun) am/is/are!
   ¡Qué rápido es tu coche! (How fast your car is!)
   ¡Qué linda es mi sobrina! (How pretty my niece is!)
8. *¡Qué + (adjetivo) + (estar)!*
   How (adjective) + (subj. pronoun) am/is/are!
   ¡Qué alegre estoy! (How happy I am!)
   ¡Qué enojado está! (How angry he is!)
9. *¡Qué + (adjetivo) + (estar) + (sustantivo)!* How (adjective) + (noun) am/is/are!
   ¡Qué rudo está Humberto hoy! (How rude is Humberto today!)
   ¡Qué pálido está Alfredo! (How pale is Alfredo!)

10. *¡Qué + (adverbio) + (verbo)!* How (adverb) + (subj. pronoun) + (verb)!
    ¡Qué bien baila! (How well he dances!)
    ¡Qué lento trabajan! (How slowly they work!)

11. *¡Qué + (adverbio) + (verbo) + (sustantivo)!* How (adverb) + (subj. pronoun) + (verb) + (noun)!
    ¡Qué bien baila Lisa! (How well Lisa dances!)
    ¡Qué lento trabajan Juan e Ignacio! (How slowly Juan and Ignacio work!)

¡Qué Fácil! (How Easy!)

Translate the following interjections into Spanish. For additional vocabulary, refer to **TABLE 18-4**.

1. What a tall young man!

2. What a sad story!

3. How far she swims!

4. How lazy she is!

5. What a car!

6. How close!

7. What a delicious steak!

8. How quickly Carmen speaks!

9. How frightening is war!

10. How helpful are tools!

---

11. How small!

---

12. That's soon!

---

13. How well Elena cooks!

---

14. How pale is she!

---

15. What a game!

---

16. What bad luck!

---

17. How charming they are!

---

18. How busy he was!

---

19. How quickly he speaks!

TABLE 18-4

VOCABULARY			
alto	tall	*bien*	well
bistec	steak	*cerca*	close, near
coche	car	*cocinar*	to cook
cuento	story	*delicioso*	delicious
(el/la) joven	young man, young woman	*guerra*	war
hablar	to speak	*herramienta*	tool

malo	bad		*miedoso*	frightening
ocupado	busy		*pálido*	pale
partido	game		*pequeño*	small
perezoso	lazy		*pronto*	soon
rápido	quickly		*simpático*	charming, nice
(la) suerte	luck		*triste*	sad

¡Cómo! and *¡Cuánto!*

The interjections *cómo!* and *cuánto!* use their own structures to express strong emotion. The possible constructions are listed below:

1. *¡Cómo* + (verbo)*!* How + (subject pronoun) + (verb)!
   ¡Cómo canta! (How she sings!)
   ¡Cómo lloró! (How he cried!)
2. *¡Cómo* + (verbo) + (sustantivo)*!* How + (noun) + (verb)!
   ¡Cómo cocina tu mamá! (How your mother cooks!)
   ¡Cómo lloraba el niño! (How the baby was crying!)
3. *¡Cuánto* + (verbo) + (sustantivo)*!* How much + (noun) + (verb)!
   ¡Cuánto habla Juan! (How much Juan talks!)
   ¡Cuánto lloró el niño! (How much the baby cried!)
4. *¡(Cuánto)* + (sustantivo) + (verbo)*!* How much/many + (verb) + (noun)!
   ¡Cuánta gente está aquí! (How many people are here!)
   ¡Cuántos gatos tienes! (How many cats you have!)

¡Cuánto Sabes! (How Much You Know!)

Translate the following interjections into Spanish. For additional vocabulary, refer to **TABLE 18-5**.

1. How much they ran!

2. How I want to be tall!

3. How Marco and Lucía smoked!

----

4. How much I wanted to eat!

----

5. How many chores we have!

----

6. How it was raining!

TABLE 18-5

VOCABULARY			
alto	tall	*comer*	to eat
corer	to run	*fumar*	to smoke
llover	to rain	*querer*	to want
tarea	chore		

What's Better and What's Best?

As you often have to do in English, there will be times when your descriptions of things will require that you make comparisons between two or more items. Comparisons can be made to show equivalency or difference.

Two equal modifiers may be compared by using the construction *tan + adjetivo/adverbio + como* (as + adjective/adverb + as). For example: *Mi coche es tan rápido como el de Raúl.* (My car is as fast as Raul's.)

Comparison of objects tends to center on quantity. As such, the construction above may be slightly altered: *tanto* + noun + *como*. For example: *Mi computadora tiene tanta memoria como la tuya.* (My computer has as much memory as yours.)

The general structure for comparison of unequals uses the adjective qualifier + *que* + noun/adjective/adverb. To show that something is more than another, simply use *más* (more) as the qualifier. For example: *Roberto es más bajo que su hermano.* (Robert is shorter than his brother.)

Likewise, to show that something is less than something else, simply use *menos* (less, minus) as the qualifier. For example: *Hay menos asientos que personas.* (There are less seats than people.)

As you would expect, not all comparisons can be made so simply. Some adjectives and adverbs don't get along with *más* and *menos*. Instead, they are modified into the comparative form. For some examples, see **TABLE 18-6**.

TABLE 18-6

IRREGULAR COMPARISONS			
MODIFIER	ENGLISH	COMPARATIVE	ENGLISH
alto	high	*superior*	higher
bajo	low	*inferior*	lower
bien	well	*mejor*	better
bueno	good	*mejor*	better
grande	big, large	*mayor*	larger, older
joven	young	*menor*	younger
mal	badly	*peor*	worse
malo	bad	*peor*	worse
mucho	much	*más*	more
pequeño	small	*menor*	smaller
poco	little	*menos*	less
viejo	old	*mayor*	older

Here are a few examples of how these irregulars are treated in a sentence:

El trabajo de Sandra es bueno, pero el de Susana es mejor. (Sandra's work is good, but Susana's is better.)

Jaime es viejo, pero César es mayor. (Jaime is old, but Cesar is older.)

Ser pobre es peor que ser feo. (Being poor is worse than being ugly.)

FACTS

There are many other expressions that allow comparison, including:

de la misma manera (in the same way)   *superior a* (superior to)

igual que (the same as)   *parecido a* (similar to)

inferior a (inferior to)

Superlatives

Often you will need to describe things of an exceptional nature or quality. In English, you would add the ending "-est" to a modifier (adjective or adverb) to describe something that is the best—"biggest," "strongest," "smartest," and so on. This form is called the superlative.

In Spanish, the superlative form also relies on the words *más* and *menos,* which appear with a definite article to signify "most" and "least." The superlative construction works as follows: *artículo definido + más/menos + adjetivo/adverbio + de* (definite article "the" + more/less + adjective/adverb + of). For example:

Superman es el más poderoso de los superhéroes. (Superman is the most powerful of the superheroes.)

Javier es el menos responsable de los hermanos. (Javier is the least responsible of the brothers.)

Pepito es el estudiante más vago. (Pepito is the laziest student.)

EXERCISE

¡Cómo Comparas! (How You Compare!)

Translate the following comparisons into Spanish. For additional vocabulary, refer to **TABLE 18-7.**

1. You sing as well as my sister.

----

2. I have as many coins as you.

----

3. There is less work than people.

---

4. Julio has more experience than Pedro.

---

5. Jonathan is older than Jenny.

---

6. Maira is the prettiest of the girls.

---

7. Baseball is the most popular sport in the United States.

TABLE 18-7	VOCABULARY			
	béisbol	baseball	*bonito*	pretty
	cantar	to sing	*los Estados Unidos*	the United States
	experiencia	experience	*(la) gente*	people
	hermana	sister	*moneda*	coin
	muchacha	girl	*popular*	popular
	trabajo	job		

CHAPTER 19
A Day in the Life

The only way to really learn another language is to see it, hear it, and think it—just plain live it on a day-to-day basis. This chapter will help you achieve this by concentrating on what most people do in their daily lives, and will introduce you to the concept of the reflexive verbs.

One Day in the Life of Celso

The following is written by Celso about his day. See how much you can understand of what he is saying.

Hola. Yo soy Celso, el hermano de Estefi. La mañana típica para mi comienza a las seis, la hora que me despierto. Soy un poco lento para levantarme, especialmente cuando hace frío afuera. A veces me quedo acostado y miro hacia el techo de mi dormitorio. Me gusta pensar en el día que me espera mientras escucho la radio.

Por regular, me levanto a las seis y cuarto, cuando sé que no hay nadie en el baño. Después de salir de la cama, me cepillo los dientes y me lavo el sueño de la cara. Ya despierto, saludo a mi mami, mi papi, y a mi hermanita. Como todos nos apresuramos a partir, no hay mucho tiempo para hablar.

Me ducho, me afeito (¡de veras!), y me visto en treinta minutos. A veces desayuno en casa. Pero cuando no tengo tiempo, espero para hacerlo en la escuela. Salgo para la escuela a las siete de la mañana. Tomo el tren y llego allí con tiempo suficiente para hablar con mis amigos antes de mi primera clase.

So, how did you do? How much were you able to understand? If you need help, take a look at the translation in Appendix D.

Did You Notice?

In Celso's story, did you notice the following phrases?

> *la hora que me despierto* (the hour when I wake up)
> *me quedo acostado* (I stay in bed)
> *me levanto a las seis y cuarto* (I get up at 6:15 A.M.)
> *me cepillo los dientes* (I brush my teeth)
> *me ducho, me afeito, y me visto* (I take a shower, shave, and get dressed)

You might wonder what the pronoun *me* is doing in these sentences. After all, it can't be a direct-object pronoun, right? Well, not exactly. In this case, *me* acts as a reflexive pronoun. That is, it reflects back to the subject. If the subject is *yo* (as it is in this case), the reflexive pronoun will be *me*. Other reflexive pronouns are outlined in **TABLE 19-1**.

TABLE 19-1

REFLEXIVE PRONOUNS		
SUBJECT PRONOUN	REFLEXIVE PRONOUN	ENGLISH
yo	*me*	myself
tú	*te*	yourself (familiar)
él, ella	*se*	himself, herself
usted	*se*	yourself (polite)
nosotros, nosotras	*nos*	ourselves
ellos, ellas	*se*	themselves
ustedes	*se*	yourselves

Introducing Reflexive Verbs

There is a class of verbs (appropriately called reflexive verbs) that relies on reflexive pronouns to convey their meanings correctly. Reflexive verbs may be categorized in various ways. Celso showed you how you might use them to describe your daily routine. Here is a list of items you probably do without even thinking about them (see **TABLE 19-2**). Try to apply them in sentences that describe what you do daily.

TABLE 19-2

VERBS AND THEIR REFLEXIVE COUNTERPARTS			
VERB	ENGLISH	REFLEXIVE VERB	ENGLISH
acostar	to lay something down	*acostarse*	to lay down, to go to bed
afeitar	to shave someone or something	*afeitarse*	to shave oneself
apresurar	to pressure to hurry up	*apresurarse*	to hurry oneself up
apurar	to hurry to conclusion	*apurarse*	to hurry oneself
arreglar	to put in order, fix	*arreglarse*	to fix one's clothing, makeup, etc.
bañar	to bathe	*bañarse*	to bathe oneself
cepillar	to brush	*cepillarse*	to brush oneself

comportar	to involve	*comportarse*	to behave
despedir	to dismiss, see someone off	*despedirse*	to say goodbye
despertar	to awaken	*despertarse*	to awaken oneself
desvestir	to unclothe	*desvestirse*	to undress oneself
divertir	to amuse	*divertirse*	to enjoy oneself
dormir	to sleep	*dormirse*	to fall asleep
duchar	to shower	*ducharse*	to take a shower
echar	to throw	*echarse*	to throw oneself into
encontrar	to find or encounter	*encontrarse*	to find oneself
engañar	to deceive	*engañarse*	to deceive oneself
enjuagar	to rinse	*enjuagarse*	to rinse oneself (mouth)
fregar	to scrub, wash	*fregarse*	to scrub or wash oneself
frotar	to rub	*frotarse*	to rub oneself
lavar	to wash	*lavarse*	to wash oneself
levantar	to lift	*levantarse*	to get up
limpiar	to clean	*limpiarse*	to clean oneself
llamar	to call	*llamarse*	to be called, to call oneself
llevar	to take, carry	*llevarse*	to carry oneself
maquillar	to apply makeup to someone	*maquillarse*	to apply makeup to oneself
olvidar	to forget	*olvidarse*	to forget oneself
parar	to stand, stop	*pararse*	to stop oneself
peinar	to comb	*peinarse*	to comb oneself
pintar	to paint	*pintarse*	to paint oneself
poner	to put, place	*ponerse*	to put on
preocupar	to worry	*preocuparse*	to worry oneself, get worried
quemar	to burn	*quemarse*	to burn oneself
quitar	to remove, take away (something)	*quitarse*	to get rid of, remove

secar	to dry	*secarse*	to dry oneself off
sentar	to sit	*sentarse*	to sit oneself down
ver	to see	*verse*	to see oneself, imagine oneself
vestir	to wear, dress in	*vestirse*	to dress oneself

One peculiarity in the way parts of the body are treated in Spanish, particularly with the reflexive verbs, involves not expressing possession. So when you wash your hands, the literal translation of what you say in Spanish is not "I wash my hands," but rather "I wash the hands." Since many of the things you do on a daily basis do involve different parts of your body, first look at the table of reflexive verbs and think about how you might describe your routine. Before actually writing down your routine, however, list the various verbs that describe acts that you can perform on the specific body parts listed.

You have always thought that when you grab a toothbrush and toothpaste, you were going to brush your teeth. According to Spanish, however, you are not "brushing" your teeth—you are actually "washing" your teeth ("to brush one's teeth" is translated as *lavarse los dientes*).

Because most reflexive verbs work with parts of the body, it might be useful for you to learn this vocabulary (see **TABLE 19-3**). Don't forget to learn the definite article of each word—it will help you remember the word's gender.

TABLE 19-3

THE HUMAN BODY			
el antebrazo	forearm	*la axila*	armpit
la barbilla	chin	*la boca*	mouth
el brazo	arm	*la cabeza*	head
la cara	face	*la ceja*	eyebrow
el codo	elbow	*el cuello*	neck
el dedo	finger	*el diente*	tooth
la encía	gum	*la frente*	forehead
el labio	lip	*la lengua*	tongue
la mano	hand	*la mejilla*	cheek

la muela	molar		*la muñeca*	wrist
el músculo	muscle		*el muslo*	thigh
la nariz	nose		*la oreja*	outer ear
el pelo	hair		*la pestaña*	eyelash
el pie	foot		*la pierna*	leg
la planta del pie	sole of foot		*la quijada*	jaw
la sien	temple		*el talón*	heel
el tobillo	ankle			

The structure of these reflexive constructions is generally simple: subject + reflexive pronoun + verb. As an example of how reflexive verbs work, refer to the following example:

Lavo los platos.
(I wash the plates.)
Me lavo las manos.
(I wash my hands.)

In the first sentence, the action is done by the subject toward *los platos* (the direct object). In the second sentence, the direct object is *las manos*, which is part of *yo*, so the sentence is reflexive—the action is done to one's self.

FACTS

The reflexive pronoun's position isn't as restricted when used with *voy + a + infinitivo reflexivo*. The pronoun may appear before the active *voy*, or stay as part of the infinitive. For example: *me voy a lavar las manos* is as correct as *voy a lavarme las manos* (I'm going to wash my hands).

The Daily Routine

Translate the following sentences using the appropriate reflexive verbs and pronouns. For additional vocabulary, refer to **TABLE 19-4**.

1. I get up at ten in the morning.

2. We wash our hair every morning.

3. Juan shaved his chin last night.

4. Did you (informal) shave your head?

5. Marco cleaned his nose.

6. You (plural) must wash your hair.

7. Martín likes to rub his feet.

8. I rinse my mouth after brushing my teeth.

9. After dinner, they brush their teeth.

10. Leticia applies makeup on her eyes.

TABLE 19-4	VOCABULARY			
cada	every, each		*cena*	dinner
después de	after		*ojo*	eye
pasado	last		*tener*	to have/have to

Additional Categories of Reflexive Verbs

Not all reflexive verbs are concerned with personal hygiene and the daily routine. Some reflexive verbs are categorized by the standardized manner they are translated into English. One category includes the verbs that may be translated with the words "to get . . ." (see **TABLE 19-5**).

TABLE 19-5

REFLEXIVE VERBS THAT MEAN "TO GET . . ."			
VERB	ENGLISH	REFLEXIVE	ENGLISH
acercar	to bring near	*acercarse*	to get closer
alegrar	to make happy, enliven	*alegrarse*	to get happy
alistar	to ready, prepare	*alistarse*	to get ready
asustar	to frighten	*asustarse*	to get frightened
cansar	to make tired	*cansarse*	to get tired
callar	to quiet a person or situation	*callarse*	to get quiet
emborachar	to make drunk	*emboracharse*	to get drunk
enfermar	to sicken	*enfermarse*	to get sick
enfriar	to make cold	*enfriarse*	to get cold
engordar	to make fatter	*engordarse*	to get fatter
entusiasmar	to excite	*entusiasmarse*	to get enthusiastic, excited
inquietar	to incite	*inquietarse*	to get restless
marear	to make dizzy	*marearse*	to get dizzy
mejorar	to make better	*mejorarse*	to get better

Some reflexive verbs reflect on "each other" rather than on the "self." For example, *casarse* (to get married) is based on the concept of "marrying each other." Other examples include *quererse*, as in *se quieren* (they love each other), and *ayudarse*, as in *mis amigos se ayudan* (my friends help each other).

Another category contains verbs that change meaning radically with the addition of the reflexive pronoun. You really need to learn these pairs separately, since knowing one won't necessarily help you figure out the meaning of the other. (Refer to **TABLE 19-6**.)

TABLE 19-6 OTHER REFLEXIVE VERBS

VERB	MEANING	REFLEXIVE	MEANING
acabar	to finish, end	*acabarse*	to run out of, ruin one's condition
acordar	to agree	*acordarse*	to remember
burlar	to trick	*burlarse*	to make fun of, ridicule
comportar	to involve	*comportarse*	to behave
dar	to give	*darse a*	to devote oneself to
dar	to give	*darse con/contra*	to hit oneself with/against
		darse por	to consider oneself
enojar	to make angry	*enojarse*	to become angry
fiar	to vouch for, to sell on credit	*fiarse*	to confide in
fijar	to fix, fasten	*fijarse*	to settle in, to notice, to put attention to
ir	to go someplace	*irse*	to go away, leave
liar	to tie up	*liarse con (alguien)*	to have an affair with (someone)
llevar	to take, carry	*llevarse*	to get, win
		llevarse bien/mal	to get along well/ poorly
negar	to deny	*negarse*	to refuse
parecer	to seem	*parecerse*	to be alike, look alike
portar	to carry	*portarse bien/mal*	to behave oneself/ be naughty
probar	to prove, test, try, taste	*probarse*	to try on
quedar	to remain, stay, fit, be left over	*quedarse con*	to keep
quemar	to burn	*quemarse*	to burn oneself out
quitar	to remove, take away	*quitarse*	to go away, get rid of something
referir	to tell, relate	*referirse*	to refer to

saltar	to jump	saltarse	to skip, come off
sentir	to feel	sentirse *(mal)*	to feel (ill)
sonreír	to smile (at)	sonreírse	to smile
reír	to laugh (at)	reírse	to laugh

Yet another category of verbs can exist only in the reflexive form. Without the reflexive pronouns, these verbs don't have any meaning. Refer to **TABLE 19-7** for a list of verbs that are always reflexive.

TABLE 19-7

VERBS THAT EXIST ONLY IN THE REFLEXIVE FORM	
REFLEXIVE VERB	ENGLISH
arrepentirse	to regret
atenerse	to abide by, conform, comply
atreverse	to dare
atreverse con (alguien)	to be disrespectful with (someone)
quejarse	to complain
rebelarse	to rebel
resentirse con/contra	to feel resentment toward/against

Constructions with *Ponerse*

One word in particular, *ponerse* (which normally means "to put on," as in clothing), adopts a new meaning ("to start to") when placed in a combination with *a* + infinitive. (For examples, see **TABLE 19-8**.)

TABLE 19-8

PONERSE + *A* + INFINITIVE			
INFINITIVE	ENGLISH	*PONERSE* + *A* + INFINITIVE	ENGLISH
vestir	to dress	*ponerse a vestir*	to start to dress
caminar	to walk	*ponerse a caminar*	to start to walk
llorar	to cry	*ponerse a llorar*	to start to cry
comer	to eat	*ponerse a comer*	to start to eat

Reflecting on the Verb

Translate the following sentences, employing the reflexive pronouns. For additional vocabulary, refer to **TABLE 19-9**.

1. He complained about the noise.

   ....

2. When are you (plural) leaving to Florida?

   ....

3. She dares to steal.

   ....

4. You sit down.

   ....

5. She is called Nancy.

   ....

6. You (informal) started to cry when they left.

   ....

7. She burned her hand.

   ....

8. They regret their words.

   ....

TABLE 19-9	VOCABULARY			
cuando	when		*la mano*	the hand
palabra	word		*robar*	to steal
ruido	noise			

Your Home

A big part of your life is the place where you spend at least some of your free time, and where your Spanish zone is—your home! *¿Dónde vive?* (Where do you live?) You might live in an apartment (*un apartamento*), a

house (*una casa*), or a dormitory (*un dormitorio* or *una residencia*).
TABLES 19-10, **19-11**, and **19-12** will provide you with some vocabulary related to your home, which you can use to answer questions in the next exercise.

TABLE 19-10

VOCABULARY: IN YOUR HOME			
ático	attic	*balcón*	balcony
cocina	kitchen	*comedor*	dining room
cuarto de baño	bathroom	*dormitorio*	bedroom
(el) garaje	garage	*jardín*	garden
lavandería	laundry room	*(la) patio*	patio
piso	level, floor	*sala*	living room
sala de estar	family room	*sótano*	basement
suelo	floor	*techo*	ceiling, roof

TABLE 19-11

VOCABULARY: FURNITURE			
armario	closet	*alfombra*	carpet
almohada	pillow	*anaquel de ropa*	linen shelf
cajón	drawer	*cama*	bed
colchón	mattress	*cuadro*	picture
despertador eléctrico	electric alarm	*espejo*	mirror
estante para libros	bookcase	*lámpara*	lamp

TABLE 19-12

VOCABULARY: IN THE KITCHEN			
batidora	hand mixer	*cafetera eléctrica*	electric coffeemaker
cajón de cubiertos	cutlery drawer	*cocina de gas*	gas stove
congelador	freezer	*escurridor de platos*	dish drainer
estante de las especias	spice rack	*fregadero*	(kitchen) sink
grifo de agua	water tap	*horno*	oven
(el) lavavajillas	dishwasher	*(el) microondas*	microwave
nevera	refrigerator		

Colors

Chances are probably high that most of the things that are in your home are there because they are either functional or pleasing to your eyes. Regardless of function or aesthetics, you probably coordinate much of what you have by color. The colors of the things you choose make you the artist within your home, dabbing a white toaster here and a blue wastebasket there. Take a look at **TABLE 19-13** for some vocabulary and start adding color into your descriptions.

TABLE 19-13

VOCABULARY: COLORS			
amarillo	yellow	anaranjado	orange
azul	blue	azul celeste	sky blue
azul marino	navy blue	azul turqui	indigo
beige	beige	blanco	white
café	brown	claro	light
gris	gray	marrón	brown
morado	purple	negro	black
oscuro	dark	pardo	brown
rojo	red	rosado	pink
verde	green	violeta	violet

As adjectives, colors must agree with the gender and number (singular or plural) of the nouns they describe. Colors ending in -e or a consonant cannot be modified by gender. They can only agree with the items they modify in number. For example: *Elisa tiene camisas azules claros.* (Elisa has light blue shirts.)

What Color Is It?

Describe the items in your home by color, using the vocabulary you have just learned. For additional vocabulary, refer to **TABLE 19-14**.

1. ¿Qué color es tu baño?

   ----

2. ¿Qué color son tus chanclas?

   ----

3. ¿Qué color son tus sábanas?

   ----

4. ¿Qué color son tus cortinas?

   ----

5. ¿Qué color es tu coche?

TABLE 19-14

VOCABULARY			
baño	bathroom	chancla	slipper, flip-flop
coche	car	cortina	curtain
sábana	sheet		

Dining Out

Dining out for the first time at a Spanish restaurant does not have to be a stressful situation where you have to express everything perfectly and in complete sentences. With a smile you should be able to get by on a minimal vocabulary. Often verbs aren't even needed. Simply read out loud the items you want from the *menú* (menu) and add a *por favor* (please) at the end of your request. When the food comes, you say *gracias* (thank you). At the end of the meal, you say *cheque, por favor* (check, please). You pay your bill, you say *muchas gracias,* and you are out the door. Here are a few other phrases that might help you along:

> *Necesito un poco de mostaza para mi perro caliente.* (I need a little bit of mustard for my hot dog.)
>
> *Yo quiero el bistec poco asado.* (I want the steak rare.)

Rocío quería un vino tinto con su cena. (Rocio wanted red wine with
  her dinner.)
Marcos no quiso conducir después de tomar bebidas alcoholicas.
  (Marcos did not want to drive after drinking alcoholic beverages.)
¿Se puede fumar aquí? (Can one smoke here?)

Since you already know how to communicate some common
requests and inquiries, what you need is a quick tour of what to expect.
Here are some phrases that your waiter may say to you:

¿Tiene usted una reservación? (Do you have a reservation?)
¿Cuántos son? (How many of you?—that is, how large is your party?)
¿Prefiere(n) una mesa aquí adentro o afuera? (Do you prefer a table
  here inside or outside?)
¿Desea(n) algo de beber? (Would you like something to drink?)
¿Cómo lo gusta preparado? (How would you like it prepared?)
¿Desean algo más? (Would you care for something more?)
¡Buen provecho! (Bon appetit!)
¿Cómo está todo? (How is everything?)
Si, acceptamos tarjetas de crédito. (Yes, we accept credit cards.)

When looking at a menu, you will see so many dining options that it
is impossible to present a complete list. But here are some foods that
may interest you (**TABLES 19-15**, **19-16**, and **19-17**).

TABLE 19-15	VOCABULARY: MEATS AND SEAFOOD			
almeja	clam	*atún*	tuna
ave	poultry	*bistec*	steak
camarones	shrimp	*(la) carne de res*	beef
cerdo	pork	*chuleta*	chop
cordero	lamb	*hígado*	liver
jamón	ham	*langosta*	lobster
pez	fish	*pollo*	chicken

salchicha	sausage	salmón	salmon
ternera	veal	tiburón	shark
tocino	bacon		

TABLE 19-16

	VOCABULARY: FRUITS AND VEGETABLES		
berenjena	eggplant	brécol	broccoli
cebolla	onion	cereza	cherry
champiñon	mushroom	ciruela	plum
durazno	peach	espinaca	spinach
fresa	strawberry	frijoles	beans
guayaba	guava	lechuga	lettuce
lima	lime	limón	lemon
mango	mango	manzana	apple
melón	melon	naranja	orange
papa	potato	pepino	cucumber
pera	pear	piña	pineapple
uva	grape	zanahoria	carrot

TABLE 19-17

	VOCABULARY: OTHER FOODS		
arroz	rice	arroz con leche	rice pudding
avena	oats	flan	caramel custard
huevos	eggs	galleta	cookie
(la) leche	milk	maíz	corn
manteca	butter	miel	honey
pan	bread	pasas	raisins
pastel	cake, pie	queso	cheese
trigo	wheat		

CHAPTER 20

Means of Communication

You are coming to the end of the book. You have learned a great deal— congratulations! Now, it's time to put all you know into practice. In this chapter, you will see how you might use your newly developed skills to communicate with others, *en persona* (in person), *por carta* (by letter), and *por teléfono* (by telephone).

In Person

The most basic form of communication is conversation. Whether you are chatting with an old friend or making small talk with the person sitting next to you on the bus, you are communicating. Now that it's time to practice what you learned by speaking Spanish, here are some basics you will find useful. First, let's begin by learning the basics of conversation with people whom you already know.

Familiar Greetings

With familiarity comes a multitude of greetings that are often colloquial and may be used interchangeably. Here is a common exchange among two Spanish speakers who know each other well enough to use the *tú* (informal) address:

A. *Hola, ¡qué gusto verte!* (Hi, what a pleasure to see you!)
B. *Hola, ¿cómo estás?* (Hi, how are you?)
A. *Bien, gracias. Y, ¿cómo te va?* (I'm well, thanks. And how is it going?)
B. *Más o menos.* (So-so.)
A. *¿Qué te pasa? ¿Qué hay?* (What's going on? What's new?)
B. *Nada en particular.* (Nothing in particular.)
A. *Adiós.* (Goodbye.)
B. *Chao.* (Bye.)

At a Social Gathering

What makes learning a new language so much fun is that it affords you opportunities to meet people you would not have met before. Again, keep in mind that formality and familiarity act as catalysts to forming relationships. When it comes to *las introducciones* (the introductions), you have many options to choose from. Take a look below at what you have available:

Le presento (a usted) señor Suarez. (I present to you Mr. Suarez.)
Te presento (a ti) a mi amigo Emilio. (I present you to my friend Emilio.)

Les presento (a ustedes) a la señora Perez. (I present you all to Mrs. Perez.)

Les presento (a ustedes) a mi amiga Elena. (I present you all to my friend Elena.)

Other ways of saying this are:

Me gustaría presentarle a señor Zambrano. (I would like to present to you Mr. Zambrano.)

Quisiera presentarte a mi hermano Roberto. (I wanted to present to you my brother Roberto.)

Tengo el gusto de presentarles a María Lorenzo. (I have the pleasure of introducing to you all Maria Lorenzo.)

For a more casual approach, you can simply say, "This is [name]."

Éste es mi hijo, Paco. (This is my son, Paco.)

Ésta es mi esposa, Rosa. (This is my wife, Rose.)

The response to an introduction is generally the same for formal and familiar situations. When somebody has just been introduced to you, you might respond as follows:

Mucho gusto en conocerle, señor Cardoza. (It is a pleasure to meet you, Mr. Cardoza.)

Mucho gusto, Rita. (It's a pleasure, Rita.)

Es un placer. (It's a pleasure.)

Encantado. (I am, masculine, charmed.)

Encantada. (I am, feminine, charmed.)

In response, you will get something like:

Igualmente. (Likewise.)

El gusto es mío. (The pleasure is mine.)

Introductions

Your name is Juana Mendoza García. You are visiting a cousin (*una prima*) in Mexico. She is unable to pick you up at the airport and sends her assistant, Claudio, whom you have never met. A gentleman approaches you. Please imagine what he might say in Spanish and how you might respond in Spanish.

Señor: _____ (He wishes you a good afternoon.)

Tú: _____ (Respond appropriately.)

Señor: _____ (He asks if you are Daniela
        Espinosa Cárdenas.)

Tú: _____ (Respond appropriately.)

Señor: Disculpe. ("Please pardon me.")

Tú: No se preocupe. ("Not to worry.")

Another person approaches you. Complete the following conversation:

Señor: _____ (He excuses himself and asks for
        your name.)

Tú: _____ (Respond appropriately and state
        where you are from.)

Señor: _____ (He says that he is pleased to meet
        you and that his name is Claudio Jimenez Juarez and he is from
        Guadalajara.)

Tú: _____ (Respond appropriately.)

Señor: _____ (He smiles and welcomes you.)

Tú: _____ (Respond appropriately.)

Señor: _____ (Are those your suitcases?)

Tú: _____ (Say yes. Then apologize for bringing
        four suitcases on your two-week vacation!)

Making Conversation in Spanish

Once introduced, the host would most certainly "welcome" you with a *bienvenido* (if you are male) or a *bienvenida* (if you are female), as well as a smile. It's just that simple. Of course, once the introductions are done, it's time for real conversations to begin.

Once you have met or have been introduced to someone, courtesy extends past the initial meeting and into your entire dealing with the person. Since you are just starting out with Spanish, there will be times when you will need to ask for some clarification. To better understand what the person is trying to communicate to you, you might have to resort to the following strategies:

1. "Get the floor" with a polite interruption.
   Perdón. (Pardon.)
   Perdóneme. (Pardon me—polite.)
   Perdóname. (Pardon me—informal.)
   Disculpe, por favor. (Please excuse me—polite.)

2. Indicate that you are experiencing some confusion because of various circumstances.
   No entiendo. (I don't understand.)
   No comprendo. (I don't comprehend.)
   No le oí. (I didn't hear you—formal.)
   No te escuché. (I wasn't listening to you—informal.)
   No sé. (I don't know.)
   Me olvidé. (I forgot.)

3. Try to remedy the situation by expressing your confusion in the form of a question.
   ¿Cómo? (What did you just say?)
   ¿Qué dijo (usted)? ¿Qué dijiste (tú)? (What did you say?)
   ¿Qué significa . . . ? (What does . . . mean?)
   ¿Cuándo se dice . . . ? (When does one say . . . ?)
   ¿Por qué dice (usted) que . . . ? ¿Por qué dices (tú) que . . . ? (Why do you say that . . . ?)

4. Politely request that the speaker repeat what was said.
   Por favor, repítalo (usted). Por favor, repítelo (tú). (Please repeat it.)

¿Puede (usted) repetirlo? ¿Puedes (tú) repetirlo?
    (Can you repeat it?)
Por favor, dígalo (usted) otra vez. Por favor, dilo (tú) otra vez.
    (Please say it again.)
¿Me lo puede (usted) repetir? ¿Me lo puedes (tú) repetir? (Can you
    repeat it for me?)
Hágame (usted) el favor de hablar más despacio. Hazme el favor de
    hablar más despacio. (Do me the favor of speaking more slowly.)

When you are learning a language, it might seem that everyone is speaking too fast, and you want them to slow down. To ask a person you are speaking with to speak slower, you can say:

Estás hablando muy rápido. (You are speaking too quickly.)
Por favor, ¿me lo repites más despacio? (Will you repeat more
    slowly, please?)

Here are some other phrases that you might find useful:

- When you are passing through a crowd, you can say *con permiso* (excuse me).
- If you need to apologize, you can say *¡Lo siento mucho!* (I am so sorry!)
- When you leave the dining table, and would like to excuse yourself, you can say *con su permiso* (could you excuse me).

Conversation Starters

Suppose you are ready to start communicating, but you don't know how to begin. Here are some conversation starters for you to consider:

- *El tiempo* (the weather)
- *La situación económica* (the current economic situation)
- *La situación internacional* (the current international situation)
- *Las películas que están estrenando en el cine* (the films they are showing at the movies)

The easiest way to get a discussion going is to ask questions. Here are a few—can you think of any others?

¡Qué buen tiempo hace! ¿No lo cree? (What good weather it is. Don't you agree?)

¡Qué mal tiempo hace afuera! ¿No lo cree? (What bad weather it is outside. Don't you agree?)

¿Qué le gusta hacer? (What do you like to do?)

¿Cuál es su comida favorita? (What is your favorite food?)

¿Qué piensa? (What do you think?)

Farewells

All conversations eventually come to an end. Ways of saying goodbye *(despedidas)* may be placed into three general categories:

1. Short-term separations that last between several minutes to a day or two. In such a case, you can say:
   Hasta luego. (I'll see you later.)
   Hasta pronto. (See you soon.)
   Te veo. (I'll see you.)
2. Separations with a determined length (when you know when you'll see each other again). In such a situation, you would say:
   Hasta la proxima. (Bye until the next time.)
   Hasta otro día. (Bye until another day.)
   Hasta mañana. (See you tomorrow.)
3. Separations of indeterminate length. When you don't know when you'll see each other again, you might say:
   Adiós. (Goodbye.)
   Hasta la vista. (Bye, until I see you again.)

Cultural Differences in Conversations

One last point to make about conversations and speaking Spanish is rooted in the fact that the United States is a country where you are exposed to a multitude of ideas, cultures, and opinions. If you are in

Miami, you will probably encounter at least one person of Cuban ancestry within a month's time. In New York, chances are good that you have met at least one *boricua* (a person of Puerto Rican descent). In San Antonio, your friends may be of Mexican extraction. They all may speak conversational Spanish, and speak it "correctly."

However, remember that each has a different cultural experience that is probably reflected in his or her speech, which is peppered with particular colloquial expressions. Many colloquial expressions are universal, but several do mean different things to different people in different regions. As you learn them, try to identify these expressions with the persons who introduced them to you and the cultures they represent.

Communication by Mail

In general, written Spanish is considered highly stylized, more formal, and less forgiving. The reason for this is because of the permanence of the "record." Any *faltas* (mistakes) will appear on the page or in the file for as long as the recipient holds onto it.

You already know all about the formality associated with *tú* and *usted* and the Spanish verbs. Given the facilities the language does provide, not to use them correctly will reflect badly on you. While this may convince you to avoid writing in Spanish as much as possible, it is actually the reason why you must write more—to practice.

Every time you write in Spanish, you make it and the subject matter you write about more concrete within your mind. This is why, regardless of whether you actually send them or not, writing letters is so important. Keeping a daily journal written in Spanish only can also help achieve the same objectives.

The Fundamentals of Good Letter Writing

There are six fundamental parts to every letter, discussed in the following sections.

La Fecha (the Date)

As in English, the date is a standard part of the letter. In Spanish, however, it is not simply a question of the month, date, and year, but also of the place from which the letter originates. Unless this region is incorporated in the letterhead (*membrete*), it generally accompanies and precedes the date near the upper right-hand corner (*la parte superior derecha*) of the paper. Take a look at the date variations you may find in Spanish letters (all referring to June 12, 2002):

12 de junio de 2.002
Chicago, 12 de junio de 2.002
Chicago, 12 junio 2.002
12/6/2.002

When referring to dates, keep in mind that the actual date is always written before the month. If the friendly letter is brief, the date is also found at the end of the letter, near *la parte inferior derecha* (the lower right-hand corner).

El Encabezamiento (the Heading)

As in English, the form that the heading takes depends on the purpose of the letter and the intended recipient. It is located below the date, but on the opposing side. In a business letter, the heading takes the form of a block of information describing the destination. The information in the heading begins with the following:

Nombre de la empresa (name of the firm)
Calle (street address)
Código postal, Ciudad (postal/zip code, city)
País (country)

In more formal business letters, the heading also includes the name and title of the recipient. If the title is not based on position or is unknown, simply use *distinguido(a) señor(a)* (distinguished Mr./Mrs.).

Notice that in a Spanish greeting to the recipient, abbreviations are seldom used. For example:

Distinguido Señor Arellano
Distinguida Señora Méndez

For personal or informal letters, the recipient's address is often skipped, with the salutation being the next printed item. The most common salutations coincide with their English counterparts. Here are a few examples:

Querido Miguel (dear Miguel)
Queridísima Marta (dearest Martha)
Mis queridos Mario y Fernanda (my dear Mario y Fernanda)

FACTS

Many addresses in Latin America and Spain are not of the form that employs a directional reference point in addition to numerals associated with buildings on a street. That is, you will rarely find anything similar to 1029 NE 23rd Place. You will simply find numbers and streets, like *29 calle Ochoa.*

La Introducción (the Introduction)

As in English, it is always good form to provide an introduction to your correspondence. Whereas common courtesy requires it in friendly letters, this is not the case with business letters, where efficiency is at a premium. Here are a few common introductions, running from the most casual to the more formal:

Hola, Fabián, ¿cómo estás? (Hi, Fabian, how are you?)
Le escribo para . . . (I am writing to you to . . .)
Deseo comunicarle que . . . (I wish to communicate to you . . .)
Deseo hacerle saber . . . (I would like to inform you . . .)

El Cuerpo (the Body)

The body of the letter is what will give you the chance to show off your Spanish knowledge! There are no hard-and-fast rules here, but remember to stick to your point and make sure that the tone of your letter is consistent with your message.

La Despedida (the Farewell)

Although the body of the letter doesn't fit into a formula, the farewell does. Friendly letters often exhibit one of the following closing lines:

Besos y abrazos (kisses and hugs)
Con un abrazo para ti (with an embrace for you)
Con todo mi cariño (with all my affection)
Te saludo muy cordialmente (greeting you very cordially)
Un cordial saludo (a cordial greeting)

La Firma (the Signature)

This one's easy: Signatures are the same in Spanish and English.

A Sample Letter

Take a look at the following sample letter. See how much of it you can understand. To see the translation, refer to the answer key.

Querida amiga:

No sabes la alegría que me ha causado recibir tu nueva dirección. Ha pasado demasiado tiempo desde la última vez que hablamos. ¿Cómo están todos?, ¿tu mamá y tu papá? Espero que estén bien. ¿Qué hay de nuevo? Ojalá los vea a ustedes la próxima vez que viajo hacia allá.

Yo también recuerdo todas las veces que charlamos. Espero hacerlo otra vez, pronto.

Con todo mi cariño,
Lisa

Making Phone Calls

Communicating by phone is very similar to communicating in person, but you may need to know some telephone vocabulary. First, you might learn a few words that can be used to talk about telephone sets and phone usage (see **TABLE 20-1**).

TABLE 20-1

VOCABULARY: USING THE PHONE	
el auricular/la bocina	the handset
cabina de teléfono	telephone booth
colgar el teléfono	to hang up the phone
dejar un recado	to leave a message
descolgar el auricular	to pick up the handset
hacer una llamada	to make a phone call
llamar	to call
marcar, oprimir	to dial, press
telefonear	to phone
el teléfono de botones	push-button telephone
el teléfono inalámbrico	cordless telephone
el tono (la señal)	dial tone

Next, identify the components of your phone number and how to place a phone call (see **TABLE 20-2** for related vocabulary).

TABLE 20-2

VOCABULARY: PLACING A PHONE CALL	
asistencia de operador	operator assistance
la clave de área	area code
con tarjeta de crédito	with a credit card
de larga distancia	long distance
de persona a persona	person to person
la guía de teléfono	the phone guide
el número de teléfono	phone number
por cobrar	collect call
el prefijo del país	country code

Speaking on the Phone

As in English, Spanish offers general useful phrases to facilitate the social interaction that may take place during a phone call. When initiating a conversation by phone, be prepared to receive:

- A standard general salutation. For example:
  ¡Buenos días! (Good morning!)
  ¡Buenas tardes! (Good afternoon/evening!)
  ¡Buenas noches! (Good night!)
- A direct acknowledgment of your call. For example:
  ¡Diga! (used primarily in Spain and literally translates to "Say!")
  ¡Dígame! (Tell me!)
  ¡Bueno! (used primarily in Latin American countries, literally translates as "Well!")
  ¡Aló! (Hello!)
  ¡Hola! (Hello!—the least common opening to a phone call)

After the initial greeting, you will want to introduce yourself. Here are a few examples:

Me llamo César Peñaherrera. (My name is Cesar Peñaherrera.)
Soy el Sr. Rios. (It's Mr. Rios.)
Soy la Sra. Velasquez. (It's Mrs. Velasquez.)
Soy la Srta Roldós. (It's Miss Roldos.)
Mi nombre es Jaime Moreno. (My name is Jaime Moreno.)

If the call is to someone whom you don't know and the connection is not clear, you may be asked one of the following questions:

¿Cómo se escribe (su nombre)? (How do you spell it/your name?)
¿Quiere deletreármelo, por favor? (Could you please spell it for me?)

Remember to go slow when spelling out your name. When distinguishing a specific characteristic of a letter, its description follows the letter. (For a review of how to pronounce each letter in the Spanish alphabet, refer back to Chapter 2.) For example: to spell *María*, you may say "*M mayuscula* (capital M), *a, r, i acentuada* (accented i), *a.*"

After the initial greeting, you may want to ask to speak with someone:

¿Puedo hablar con el Sr. Salgado, por favor? (Can I please speak
with Mr. Salgado?)

Quisiera hablar con la Sra. Guzmán, por favor. (I would like to speak
with Mrs. Guzman.)

¿Podría ponerme con el Departamento de Servicio de Agua? (Could
you connect me to the Water Service Department?)

*¿Podría hacerme la fineza de informarle a la Srta. Acevedo que su
hermana la llama, por favor?* (Could you please do me the kind
act of informing Miss Acevedo that her sister is calling?)

¿Puede pasarme al Sr. Estevez? (Can you transfer me to Mr. Estevez?)

Responses to your request may include:

¿De parte de quién? (Who is calling?)

Si, por supuesto. No cuelgue. (Yes, of course. Don't hang up.)

Un momento, por favor, mientras lo/la busco. (One moment, please,
while I look for him/her.)

Lamento hacerlo/hacerla esperar. (I'm sorry for making you wait.)

Se lo/la paso. (I'll transfer you.)

Lo siento, pero no se encuentra. (I'm sorry, but he/she is not in.)

Lo siento, pero está hablando por la otra linea. (I'm sorry, but he/she
is on the other line.)

Lo siento, pero está con un cliente. (I'm sorry, but he/she is with a
client.)

¿Desea dejar un recado? (Would you like to leave a message?)

¿Puede llamar más tarde? (Can you call later?)

¿Quiere esperar? (Do you want to wait?)

¿Quiere hablar con alguna otra persona? (Would you like to speak
with someone else?)

At this point you may either leave your information for a callback or
proceed with a conversation with your intended party. *¡Buena suerte!*
(Good luck!)

Appendix A
Spanish-to-English Glossary

a to, personal pronoun
abajo downstairs
abarcar to take on
abdominal abdominal
abierto open, opened
abogado attorney, lawyer
abrazar to embrace
abril April
abrir to open
abstinencia abstinency
abstraer to make abstract
absurdidad absurdity
abuela grandmother
abuelita little grandmother
abuelito little grandfather
abuelo grandfather
abundancia abundancy
aburrido boring
aburrir to bore
abusivo abusive
acá over here
acabar to finish
acariciar to caress, pet
accesible accessible
accidentar to produce an unexpected event
accidente accident
acciones actions
acecinar to dry-cure
aceituna olive
aceptable acceptable
acomodable adaptable
acompañar to accompany
acondicionar to condition
acostado, a reclined
actividad activity
actor/actriz actor/actress
actuar to act
acudir to frequent a place
adentro inside
adjetivo adjective
adorar to adore
aduana customs
advertir to warn
aéreo aerial
aeróbic aerobics
aeropuerto airport

afectuoso affectionate
afeitar to shave
afluencia affluence
afortunadamente fortunately
África Africa
afuera outside
agilidad agility
agosto August
agotados exhausted
agradable pleasant weather
agradecer to thank (for)
agricultura agriculture
agua, el water
aguas, las waters
águila, el eagle
ahijada goddaughter
ahijado godson
ahijar to adopt
ahora now
ahuyentar to drive away
aire air
aislar to isolate
ajedrez chess
ajo garlic
al fondo de at/in the back of
al lado de to the side of, next to
alargador extension cord
alarmante alarming
albanés Albanian
Albania Albania
alcohol alcohol
alcoholismo alcoholism
alegórico allegorical
alemán German
Alemania Germany
alfabeto alphabet
álgebra algebra
algunas veces sometimes
alma, el soul
almacén store, warehouse
almas, las souls
almorzar to lunch
alpinismo mountain climbing

altar altar
altavoz speaker
altavoz de sonidos agudos tweeter
altavoz de sonidos graves woofer
altavoz de sonidos medios mid-range speaker
alto tall
altura height
aludir to allude (to)
amable kind, amiable
amanecer to grow light (at dawn)
amar to love
amarillo yellow
ambicioso ambitious
ambos both
ambulancia ambulance
América America
americano American
amigo friend
amistoso friendly
amo (de casa) homeowner
amor love
ampliaciones expansions
amplificador amplifier
analista de inventario inventory analyst
analysis, el analysis
ancho wide, broad
anciano elderly
andar to walk
animado animated
animal animal
aniñado childish
aniversario anniversary
año year
año pasado last year
año próximo next year
anochecer to grow dark (at night)
ansioso anxious
anteayer day before yesterday
anticipación anticipation

antigüedad antiquity
antiguo old
antipático unpleasant
anual annual
apacible pleasant, gentle
apagar to turn off
aparecer to appear
aparentemente apparently
apellido last name
apetecer to desire, crave
aplaudir to applaud, to approve
aplicar to apply
apostar to bet, to post
apoyo support
apretar to tighten
aquel that (at a distance)
aquí here
árbol tree
ardor ardor
armas arms
arquería archery
arrendar to rent, lease
arriba upstairs
arrogancia arrogance
artista artist
ascender to ascend
asesinar to murder
así así so-so
asir to seize
asistir attend
astral astral
asustado frightened
ataúd coffin
atención attention
atender to attend to
atleta athlete
atletismo track and field
atontado stunned
atractivo attractive
atraer to attract
atragantar to choke
atrás back
atrasado late
atrocidad atrocity
audaz bold
aullar to howl, shriek

aumento increase
aun even
aún yet, still
auspiciar to sponsor
australiano Australian
austriaco Austrian
auto automobile
autobús bus
autoestima self-esteem
automóvil car
automovilismo car racing
autoritario domineering
ave, el bird
avenida avenue
aventura extreme sports
avergonzado embarrassed
avergonzar to shame
averiguar to inquire
ayer yesterday
ayuda help
ayudar(se) to help (oneself)
bagaje cargo
bailar to dance
baile dance
bajo short
baloncesto basketball
balonmano handball
balonvolea volley ball
barón baron
básquetbol basketball
baúl chest
beber to drink
bebida a drink
béisbol baseball
belga Belgian
Bélgica Belgium
bello beautiful
beneficial beneficial
bicicleta bicycle
bienvivir to live well
bilingüe bilingual
billar billiards
billón trillion
bistec (beef) steak
blanco white
blusa blouse

boda wedding
boleto ticket
bolígrafo pen
bombero fireman
bondad goodness
bondadoso good, kind
bonito, a pretty
botón de reset reset button
boxear to box
bravura bravery
brazo arm
brevedad brevity
brillante brilliant
británico British
broma practical joke
brusco blunt, rude
brutalidad brutality
bucear to scuba dive
buceo scuba diving
buen tiempo nice weather
bueno good
bueno para good for
buscar to look (for)
caballo horse
cabello hair
caber to fit (into)
cabeza head
cable cable
cada each, every
caer to fall
caída fall
cajero cashier
cajón drawer
calabaza pumpkin
calambre cramp
calculable calculable
calcular to calculate
calentar to heat (up)
calificacción grade
californiano Californian
calor heat
caloruso hot
calvo bald
camarero waiter
Cambodia Cambodia
camboyano Cambodian
caminar to walk

camisa shirt
Canadá Canada
canadiense Canadian
canción song
canotaje rowing
cansado tired
cantante singer
cantar to sing
caos chaos
capacidad capacity
capaz capable
capital, el the sum of money (business)
capital, la the capital of a city
capitalismo capitalism
capitalista capitalist
caprichoso capricious
caradura disrespectful person
carcel jail
cardiólogo cardiologist
cariñoso loving
carne flesh, meat
carrera race
carta letter
cartas cards
cartelera listing
casa house, home
casado married
castellano Spanish (from Castille)
cata de vino winetasting
catástrofe catastrophe
catedral cathedral
catorce fourteen
ceder to submit, surrender
celebridad celebrity
celoso jealous
cena dinner
censor censor
centeno rye
central central
cerca near
cerca de . . . close to . . .
cernir to sieve
cero zero
cerrar to close

césped lawn
chanclas slippers
chanza joke
chaquete backgammon
checo Czech
cheque check
chicle chewing gum
chino Chinese
chiste joke
choclo overshoe, corn
chocolate chocolate
chuleta (pork) chop
cicatriz scar
ciclismo cycling
ciclista cyclist
ciego blind
cielo sky
científico scientific
cierto certain, true
cigüeña stork
cinco five
cincuenta fifty
cínico cynical
cintura waist
circunstancia circumstance
ciruela plum
cita appointment
ciudad city
ciudadano citizen
claridad clarity
clarificar to clarify
claro clear
clavado diving
clavar to nail
clavo nail
cocer to cook, boil
coche car
cocina cooking, kitchen
coco coconut, head
coger to grasp, grab
cohibir to inhibit
coincidir to coincide
colchón mattress
cólera, el cholera
colera, la anger
colgar to hang
coma, el coma

coma, la comma
comadre friend, godmother to one's child
combatir to combat
comentario commentary
comenzar to begin
comer to eat
cometa, el the comet
cometa, la the kite
cometer un error to make a mistake
cómico funny
compadre friend, godfather to one's child
compañero companion
competidor competitor
competir to compete
comprar to purchase
comprender to understand
comprensible comprehensible
comprobar to verify, check
comunidad community
con with
concuñada brother-in-law's spouse
concuñado sister-in-law's spouse
conducir to drive
conductor conductor, driver
conector de altavoces speaker jack
conector de auriculares headphone jack
conector de micrófono microphone jack
confesor confessor
confundir to confuse
confusión confusion
congelado frozen
conocer to be acquainted
conseguir to obtain
consejero advisor
consola console

consonante consonant
constipado congested, head cold
consultor de mercadeo marketing consultant
consumir to consume, to use up
contador accountant
contento satisfied
contestar to respond (to)
contraer to contract
contrario contrary
cordial cordial
Corea Korea
coreano Korean
correa leather strap
corregir to correct
correr to run
corresponder to reciprocate, to belong to
corte, el the cut
corte, la the court
cortés courteous
cortina curtain
cosa thing
coser to sew/stitch
costumbre custom
crear to create
crecer to grow
creer to believe
criar to breed and rear
criatura young child
crimen crime
criminal criminal
criquet cricket
crisis, la crisis
cristiano Christian
crudo raw
cruel cruel
cruzar to cross
cuadro frame
cual which
cuando when
cuarenta forty
cuarto fourth
cuatro four
cubierto covered, cloudy

cubrir to cover
cuchillo knife
cuello neck
cuenta account, bill
cuento story
cuerpo body
cuidar to care for
culinario culinary
cultura culture
cumplir to carry out
cuñada sister-in-law
cuñado brother-in-law
cura, el the priest
cura, la the cure
curable curable
curiosidad curiosity
cursi pretentious
curso course
danés, danesa Danish
dar to give
de of, from
deber duty, must, to owe, to ought to
débil weak
decidir to decide
décimo tenth
decir to say
decisión decision
decorado decorated
dedo finger
deducir to appear
defender to defend
defensivo defensive
definir to define
del of the
delante de in front of
delgado thin
delicioso delicious
delito crime
demasiado too, overly
democrático democratic
demostrar to demonstrate
dentista dentist
depender to depend
dependiente clerk
depotismo despotism
desagradecer to be ungrateful (for)

desagüe drain
desahogo emotional relief
desahucio eviction
desaparecer to disappear
descargue an unloading
desconocer not to recognize
desde since
desde hace for (a time frame)
deseo desire/wish
desnudo undressed
desobedecer to disobey
despedir to see off, fire
despejado without clouds
desperdiciar to waste
despierto awake
después later
destructor destroyer
destruir to destroy
detector detector
detrás de . . . behind . . .
deuda debt
devolver to return
día, el day
dialecto dialect
diario daily
dibujar to draw
diccionario dictionary
diciembre December
diecinueve nineteen
dieciocho eighteen
dieciséis sixteen
diecisiete seventeen
diez ten
diferencia difference
diferente different
difícil difficult
digestible digestible
dignatario dignitary
dignidad dignity
Dinamarca Denmark
director director
discernir to discern
disco record
disco compacto compact disc

discutir to discuss

diseñador de software software developer

diseñador designer

disfrutar to enjoy

disquetera diskette drive

distraer to distract

doce twelve

docto learned, expert

doctor a person with a doctorate

dogmatismo dogmatism

dólar dollar

dolor pain

dolorido aching

domingo Sunday

dominó dominoes

dormido asleep

dos two

drástico drastic

duelo sorrow

dulce sweet

durable durable

durante during

ebrio drunk

echar to throw out

edad age

editor editor

educacional educational

EE UU U.S.A.

egipcio Egyptian

Egipto Egypt

egoismo egotism

egoísta selfish

ejecutivo executive

ejemplo example

ejercer to practice (a trade)

ejercicio exercise

el the (masc.)

él he

elefante elephant

elegancia elegance

elegante elegant

elegir to choose decisively

ella she

ellas they (fem.)

ellos they (masc.)

embarazada pregnant

embarazar to impregnate, to hinder

embellecer to embellish, adorn

emerger to emerge

emigrado emigrated

emisario emissary

emitir to emit or give off

emocionado moved, touched

emocional emotional

empezar to begin

empleo employment

empobrecer to impoverish

empresa firm, company

enamorado loved one

encantado delighted

encender to light, turn on

enchufe de corriente electrical outlets

encontrar to encounter

enero January

enfadado disgusted, angered at someone

énfasis, el emphasis

enfermedad sickness

enfermizo sickly

enfermo sick

enfrente in front

enojado angry

enriquecer to enrich

entender to understand

enterrar to bury

entregar to hand over

entretenido amusing

envejecer to grow old

enviar to send

envolver to wrap

equipaje baggage

equipo equipment

equitación horseback riding

esbelto proportioned

esbozo first draft, outline

escala scale

escáner scanner

escocés, escocesa Scottish

Escocia Scotland

escoger to choose

escribir to write

escuchar to listen (to)

escuela school

escultura sculpture

esencia essence

esencial essential

esfuerzo effort

esgrima fencing

eslavo Slav

esnob snob

eso that

especial special

especialista specialist

espectáculo performance, show

esperar to hope, to wait (for)

espíritu spirit

esposo spouse

esquí skiing

establecer to establish

estacionar to park

estado state

Estados Unidos United States

estadounidense American (from the United States)

estanque pond

estar to be

estatura height

este año this year

estilo style

estudiante student

estudiar to study

eternidad eternity

etiope Ethiopian

evidencia evidence

evitable avoidable

exactamente exactly

examen exam

excelente excellent

exhalar to exhale

exhibir to exhibit

exigencia demand

exigir to demand, require

existencia existence

explicable explicable

explicar to explain

explosivo explosive

exportar to export

éxtasis, el ecstasy

extender to extend

extinguir to extinguish

extranjero foreigner

extraño strange

extraordinario extraordinary

fachada façade

fácil easy

fácilmente easily

falseable falsifiable

fama fame

famoso famous

fatal fatal

favor favor

favorecer to favor

febrero February

febril feverish

federal federal

feliz happy

fénix phoenix

feo ugly

ferocidad fierceness

ferrocarril railway

fervor fervor

fiar to trust, lend

fiebre fever

fierro iron

fijar to fasten

Filipinas Philippines

filipino Philippino

filtro protector surge protector

fin de semana weekend

finalmente finally

fingir to fake

finlandés, finlandesa Finnish

Finlandia Finland

física physics

físico physical, physicist

fisiculturismo bodybuilding

flaco thin, skinny

florecer to flower, flourish

fonógrafo phonograph

fractura fracture

fragilidad fragility

francés French

Francia France

frecuente frequent

frecuentemente frequently

fregar to rub

freír to fry

frenar to brake

frente, el the front line in battle

frente, la forehead

fresco fresh

frío cold/I fry

fruta, el fruit

fuerte strong

fundamental fundamental

fundir to fuse, to cast

fútbol soccer

fútbol americano football

futuro future

galés, galesa Welsh

garaje garage

gato cat

generalmente generally

generoso generous

genial pleasant

gente people

gentil courteous

gerente manager (masc. and fem.)

gesto facial gesture

gimnasia gymnastics

girasol sunflower

gloria glory

glosario glossary

golf golf

golpe blow, hit

golpeado bruised

gordo fat

gorrión sparrow

gozar to enjoy

grabadora de casete cassette recorder

grabar to record

gracioso amusing

gran grand, great

Gran Bretaña Great Britain

grande big, large

granizar to hail

Grecia Greece

griego Greek

gringo a person from a non-Spanish country

gripe influenza

grúa crane

grueso thick, stout

guapo handsome

guardar to store

guedeja lion's mane

guerra war

guía, el the person who guides

guía, la the book, booklet

guiñar to wink

guisado stew

guitarra guitar

gusano worm, caterpillar

gustar to please

gusto pleasure

haber to have (aux. verb)

hábil skillful

hábito habit

hablar to speak

hacer to do, to be, to make

hacia toward

Haití Haiti

haitiano Haitian

halagüeño attractive, flattering

hallar to find

halterofilia y potencia weightlifting and strength

hambre hunger

hamburguesa hamburger

hay there is, there are

hecho fact, deed

helado freezing

helar to freeze

herir to injure

hermana sister

hermanastra stepsister

hermanastro stepbrother

hermano brother

hermoso beautiful, handsome

hervir to boil

hija daughter

hija política daughter-in-law

hija única only child

hijastra stepdaughter

hijastro stepson, stepchild

hijo child, son

hijo político son-in-law

hipo hiccup

hola hi

holandés, holandesa Dutch

Holanda Holland

honrado honorable

horticultura horticulture

hospedar to receive the needy

hospital hospital

hotel hotel

hoy today

huella a trace

hueso bone

huésped guest

huevo egg

huída escape

huir to flee

húmedo humid

humildad humility

humor humor

ideal ideal

idealismo idealism

idealista idealist

idioma language

igual equal

igualdad equality

ilegal illegal

ileso unharmed

impaciencia impatience

impaciente impatient

impedir to hinder

importante important

importar to import, to cause to matter

impresora láser laser printer

inactivo sedentary

incendiario incendiary

incomparable incomparable

independencia independence

India India

indio Indian

individualismo individualism

infancia infancy

informar to inform

ingeniero químico chemical engineer

Inglaterra England

inglés, inglesa English

inocencia innocence

institucion de beneficencia charity

interruptor power switch

intolerancia intolerance

introducir to desire, crave

inventar to invent

inventor inventor

inversión inversion

invierno winter

invitación invitation

invitado invited

ir to go

iraní Iran (masc. and fem.)

Iraq Iraq

iraquí Iraqi (masc. and fem.)

Irlanda Ireland

irlandés, irlandesa Irish

irritable irritable

israelí Israeli (masc. and fem.)

italiano Italian

jabón soap

Japón Japan

japonés, japonesa Japanese

jerosolimitano Jerusalemite

joven young

jovial jovial, jolly

joya jewel

jueves Thursday

juez judge

jugar to play

juguetón playful

julio July

junio June

justicia justice

juventud youth

kárate karate

kilo, kilogramo kilogram

kilómetro kilometer

kilovatio kilowatt

la the (fem.)

menor smallest, youngest

lago lake

lamentable lamentable

lastimado hurt

laúd lute

lector de DVDs DVD player

leer to read

legítimo legitimate

lejos far

lenguaje language

letra letter (of the alphabet)

levantamiento de pesas weightlifting

ley, la law

libra pound (weight)

libro book

limpio clean

linaje lineage

lingüistica linguistics

lío mess

listo prepared

llamar(se) to call (oneself)

llegar to arrive

lleno full

llevar to carry, to wear

llover to rain

llovizna drizzling

lluvia raining

lluvioso rainy

loco crazy, outgoing

lógico logical

los auriculares headphones

luchador fighter, wrestler

lucir to shine, brighten

luna moon

lunes Monday

luterano Lutheran

luz (luces) light(s)

luz del disco duro hard drive light

madera wood

madrastra stepmother

madre mother

madrina godmother

madrugar to rise early

maduro mature, ripe, wise

maestro teacher

magnetismo magnetism

maíz corn

mal educado ill-mannered

maleta suitcase

malhablado foul-mouthed

mami mommy

mañana tomorrow

mano, la hand

manzana apple, city block

mapa, el map

máquina machine

mareado dizzy

marido husband

marino marine

martes Tuesday

marzo March

más more

masaje massage

mascota pet

mayo May

mayor older

mecer to sway, rock

mediano medium

médico doctor, physician

mediodía noon

medir to measure

mejor better

mejor dicho rather, said more accurately

melancólico melancholic

mentir to lie, deceive

mentor mentor

menú menu

mercader merchant

merced mercy

merecer to deserve

merendar to snack in the afternoon

mesero waiter

meter to put (in)

meticuloso meticulous

metro meter

mexicano Mexican

México Mexico

mi(s) my

mía(s), mío(s) mine

miembro member

mientras while

miércoles Wednesday

millar billion

millón million

millonario millionaire

mínimo minimum

mirar to look (at), watch

modista dressmaker

molesto annoyed

molestoso a bothersome person

moneda coin

montaña mountain

montañismo mountain sports

moreno dark-haired, dark-complexioned

mortal fatal

mosquitos mosquito

mostrar to show, exhibit

motor motor

mozo waiter

muchas veces many times

mucho much, a lot

muebles furniture

muerto dead

mujer woman, wife

multicine movie multiplex

mundo world

música music, woman musician

musical musical

músico musician

musulmán, musulmana Moslem

muy very

nacer to be born

nacional national

nacionalidad nationality

nacionalismo nationalism

nadar to swim

nadie no one

naranja orange

natación to swim

natural natural

naturalmente naturally

navegación sailing

navegar to sail

necesariamente necessarily

necesario necessary

necesitar to need

negar to deny, refuse

negativo negative

negociable negotiable

negocio business

negro black

nervioso nervous

neumático tired

neutral neutral

nevado snowy

nieto, nieta grandson, granddaughter

nieve snowing

niño, niña child, boy, girl

niñez childhood

no no

nombre name

norteamericano North American

Noruega Norway

nosotros, nosotras us, ours

nota grade, note

noticias news

novela de ciencia ficción science fiction novels

novela histórica historical novel

novela policíaca detective novel

novela romantica romance novel

noveno ninth

noventa ninety

noviembre November

nube cloud

nublado cloudy

nuera daughter-in-law

nuestro(s) our

nueve nine

nunca never

obedecer to obey

obra work, product

oscuro dark, obscure

obsequio gift

obstruir to block

obviamente obviously

ochenta eighty

ocho eight

octavo eighth

octubre October

ocupado busy

oficial official

ofrecer to offer

oído internal ear

oigo I hear

oír to hear

ojo eye

oler to smell

olor smell

olvidar to forget

once eleven

opinión opinion

oponer to oppose

oportunidad opportunity

opositor opponent

optar to choose

optimista optimist

orden, el order (as opposed to chaos)

orden, la command, request

oreja exterior ear

orgánico organic

organizable organizable

original original

oro gold

ostensible ostensible

otoño autumn, fall

otro other, another

paciente patient

pacífico pacifist

padecer to suffer

padrastro stepfather

padre father

paella Spanish rice dish

pagar to pay (for)

país country

País de Gales Wales

paisaje landscape

pájaro bird

pálido pale

panadería bakery

pantalla screen

pantalones trousers

papá father

Papá Noel Santa Claus

papel paper

paperas mumps

papi daddy

Paquistán Pakistan

para for, to

parada stop, parade

parapente paragliding

parcial partial

parecer to seem, to appear

pared, la wall

parentesco kinship

parque a park

parra grapevine

pasado mañana day after tomorrow

pasear to stroll through

pastor pastor

paterno paternal

patético pathetic

patinaje skating

patinaje sobre hielo ice skating

patriotismo patriotism

PC portátil notebook computer

peaje toll

pedazo piece

pediatra pediatrician

pelea fight

peligro danger

pelirrojo redhead

peluquero barber

pensar to think

peor worse

pequeño small

perder to lose

pereza laziness

periódico newspaper

periodista journalist

pero but

perro dog

perseguir to pursue

pesca fishing

peso weight

pez, el fish (swimming in water)

pez, la tar

pianista pianist

piano piano

pie foot

piedad pity/mercy

piel skin

piloto pilot

pingüino penguin

pintar to paint

piragüismo sailing by light canoe

piso floor

pista trail, hint

placa license plate

plan plan

plancha iron (for ironing)

plantaje planting

platicar to chat

pletina cassette deck

plomo lead

plumaje plumage

pobre poor

poco little

poder to be able to do; power

poema, el poem

polaco Polish

policía the police officer (masc. and fem.)

Polonia Poland

poner to place, to put

póquer poker

porcentaje percentage

porque because

porra stick

posibilidad possibility

posiblemente possibly

postura posture

potente potent

precisamente precisely

preferible preferable

preferir to prefer

preguntar to ask

preocupación worry

preocupado worried

primo, prima cousin

primario primary

primavera spring

primero first

primogénito firstborn

problema, el problem

proceder to proceed

producir to produce

profesor professor

programador programmer

prometer to promise

pronto soon

propio own

protector protector

proteger to protect

próximo next

púa barb

pueblo town/village

puerta door

pulir to polish

puño fist

que that

qué what

quebrar to break

quedar to remain

queja complaint

quejarse to complain

quemar to burn
querer to want, or love
querido beloved
queso cheese
quien who
quiero I want
quijada jaw
quince fifteen
quinto fifth
quitar to take away
quizás perhaps
rabo tail
radio, el the radius, the physical radio
radio, la the radio programming
radiocasete portátil portable stereo
radiografía X-ray picture
raíz root, origin
ranura de la disquetera diskette slot in drive
ratón mouse
raya line
razón reason
reaccionar to react
reanudar to renew
rebatir to refute
receta recipe
recibir to receive
recoger to gather
recordar to remember
redactar to compose, edit
redondo round
reembolsar to reimburse
régimen regimen
regla rule
regrabadora de CDs CD-RW drive
regular regular
rehusar to refuse, reuse
reino kingdom
reír(se) to laugh
rejilla de ventilación ventilation grill
relampagos lightning
relativamente relatively

rellenar to fill out
reloj watch
remitir to send
rendir to hand over
reñir to quarrel
renunciar to quit
reo criminal
repetidas veces repeatedly
repetir to repeat
repisa shelf
repostero pastry maker
reproductor de discos compactos CD player
republicano republican
requisito requirement
resfriado sick with a cold
residencia residence
resistir to resist, to tolerate
resolver to resolve
respetable respectable
resto de mi vida the rest of my life
restringir to limit
resumir to sum up
retirado retired person
reto challenge
retrato portrait
retroceder to turn back
reunión gathering
revisar to check
revista magazine
rey king
rezar to pray
riesgo risk
rincón corner
robado stolen
robusto robust
roedor rodent
rogar to beg, to plead
romper to break
roña scab
ropa clothes
rosa rose
rosado rosy
rubio blond(e)
rueda wheel

ruido noise
ruleta roulette
rumi rummy
rumiar to ruminate
rumor rumor
sábado Saturday
saber to know
sacar to draw, take out
sacerdote priest
sahumar to perfume with incense
sala living room
salario salary
salir to leave, go out
salpicar to sprinkle
salud, la health
santo saint
sarampión measles
sastre, sastra tailor
satisfacer to satisfy
saudita Saudi Arabian
secundario secondary
sed, la thirst
sediento thirsty
seductor seducer
seguir to follow
segundo second
seis six
sentado seated
sentir to feel
septiembre September
séptimo seventh
ser to be
serie series
serio serious
serpiente serpent
servir to serve
sesenta seventy
setenta sixty
sexto sixth
si if
sí yes
siempre always
siete seven
siguiente following
sílaba syllable
simpático agreeable
síntesis synthesis

sintonizador tuner
sintonizar to tune
sinvergüenza shameless
siquiera at least
sistemas hidráulicos hydraulic systems
sobre over, on top of
sobremesa desktop
sobrevivir to overcome
sobrina niece
sobrino nephew
sobrio sober
socio associate
sol, el sun
soledad solitude
solo alone, only
sólo only
soltar to release
soltero single
soñar to dream
sonreír(se) to smile
sorprender to surprise
sosegado calmed
su(s) your (polite), his, her, their
subir to ascend
sudafricano South African
sudar to sweat
Suecia Sweden
sueco Swedish
suegra mother-in-law
suegro father-in-law
suela sole
sueldo salary
sueño dream, sleep, sleepiness
suerte luck
sufrir to suffer
Suiza Switzerland
suizo Swiss
surf surfing
surgir to surge, appear
sustantivo noun
suya(s), suyo(s) yours (polite), his, hers, theirs
tabernero barkeeper
tailandés, tailandesa Thailandese

Tailandia Thailand
talentoso talented
también also
tampoco neither
tanto so much
tapa cover, lid
tarde afternoon, evening
tarjeta de navidad Christmas card
tasa measure
tasador de bienes inmuebles realty appraiser
taxi taxi
taza cup, bowl
techo roof
teclado keyboard
tejer to knit
tela fabric
telefonear to telephone
teléfono telephone
temer to fear
temeroso fearful
tenedor fork
tener to have (to be)
tenis de mesa table tennis
tenor tenor
tercer third
terciopelo velvet
terreno land, field
texano Texan
tez, la complexion, skin
tío, tía uncle, aunt
tigre tiger
tinta tint, dye
tinto tinged, red (wine)
tiro con arco archery
tiro fusil shooting
toalla towel
tocacasete cassette player
tocadiscos (analógico) turntable
tocadiscos CD CD player
tocar to touch, to play
toda la vida the whole life, all the time

todo all, every
tomar to take
tomate tomato
tornado tornado
torre, la tower, tower console
tos, la a cough
trabajo work
trabalenguas, el tongue twister
tradicional traditional
traducir to translate
traer to bring
tragantones gluttonous person
tragar to swallow
tranquilo calm
transcurrir to pass, to elapse
travieso mischievous
trece thirteen
treinta thirty
tres three
trigo wheat
triste sad
tristeza sadness
tronar to thunder
trotear jog
tú you (familiar)
tu(s) your (familiar)
tubo tube
turco Turk, Turkish
turista tourist
Turquía Turkey
tutear to treat informally
tuya(s), tuyo(s) yours (familiar)
último last
uña fingernail
unir to unite
universal universal
uno one, a
usar to use
usted you (polite)
ustedes you all
usualmente usually
útil useful
vaca cow

vaciar to empty
valer to be valued
valor valor
vandalismo vandalism
vapuleo a beating
varias veces several times
varios various
varón male
vaso glass
vecino neighbor
vegetariano vegetarian
veinte twenty
veintiuno 21 (blackjack)
vela sailing
velocidad velocity
vencer to conquer
vendedor salesperson
vender to sell
venir to come
ver to see
ver televisión watch television
verano summer
verbo verb
verdad, la truth
verduras vegetables
vergüenza shame
vestido dress
vestir to dress
vez, veces time(s)
viajar to travel
vice presidente vice president
vida life
videocámara video camera
viejo old
viento wind
viernes Friday
vigor vigor
visible visible
viuda widow
vocal, la vowel
volante badminton, steering wheel
volar to fly
voleibol volleyball
volumen volume

voluntad will
voluntario voluntary
volver to return
vuelo en ala delta hang-gliding
Wáshington Washington
xilófono xylophone
y and
yanquis an American
yegüita small mare
yerno son-in-law
yo I
Yugoslavia Yugoslavia
yugoslavo Yugoslavian
zambullir to dive
zapato shoe
zarzamora blackberry
zoológico zoo

APPENDIX B

English-to-Spanish Glossary

21 (blackjack) *veintiúno*
abbreviate, to *abreviar*
abdominal *abdominal*
abstinency *abstinencia*
absurdity *absurdidad*
abundancy *abundancia*
abundant *abundante*
abusive *abusivo*
acceptable *aceptable*
accessible *accesible*
accident *accidente*
accompany, to *acompañar*
account, bill *cuenta*
accountant *contador*
aching *dolorido*
act, to *actuar*
action *acción*
activity *actividad*
actor, actress *actor,*
  actriz
adaptable *acomodable*
adjective *adjetivo*
admiration *admiración*
admissible *admisible*
adolescent *adolescente*
adopt, to *ahijar*
adorable *adorable*
adore, to *adorar*
adult *adulto*
adversary *adversario*
aerial *aéreo*
aerobics *aeróbic*
affable *afable*
affectionate *afectuoso*
affectionate form of a name
  hipocorístico
affluence *afluencia*
Afghan *afgano*
Afghanistan *Afganistán*
Africa *África*
African *africano*
afternoon/evening *tarde, la*
age *edad, la*
agent *agente*
agility *agilidad*
agreeable *simpático*
agriculture *agricultura*
August *agosto*

air *aire*
airport *aeropuerto*
Albania *Albania*
Albanian *albanés,*
  albanesa
alcohol *alcohol*
alcoholism *alcoholismo*
algebra *álgebra*
all, every *todo*
allude (to), to *aludir*
alone, only *solo*
alphabet *alfabeto*
alphabetic letter *letra*
also *también*
altar *altar*
always *siempre*
ambitious *ambicioso*
ambulance *ambulancia*
America *América*
American *americano*
American, an *yanquis*
amplifier *amplificador*
amusing *entretenido,*
  gracioso
analysis *análisis, el*
and *y*
anger *colera, la*
angry *enojado*
animal *animal*
animated *animado*
anniversary *aniversario*
annoyed *molesto*
annual *anual*
anticipation *anticipación*
antiquity *antigüedad*
anxious *ansioso*
apparently
  aparentemente
appear, to *aparecer,*
  deducir
applaud (to), to approve
  aplaudir
apple, city block *manzana*
apply, to *aplicar*
appointment *cita*
April *abril*
archery *arquería,*
  tiro con arco

architect *arquitecto*
ardor *ardor*
arm *brazo*
arms *armas*
arrive, to *llegar*
arrogance *arrogancia*
artist *artista*
ascend, to *ascender,*
  subir
ask, to *preguntar*
asleep *dormido*
associate *socio*
association *asociación*
astral *astral*
astronaut *astronauta*
at least *siquiera*
athlete *atleta*
Atlantic *Atlántico*
atrocity *atrocidad*
attend, to *atender,*
  asistir
attention *atención, la*
attorney, lawyer *abogado*
attract, to *atraer*
attractive *atractivo*
attractive, flattering
  halagüeño
auditor *auditor*
aunt *tía*
Australia *Australia*
Australian *australiano*
Austria *Austria*
Austrian *austriaco*
authentic *auténtico*
author *autor*
automobile *auto*
autumn, fall *otoño*
avenue *avenida*
avoidable *evitable*
awake *despierto*
back *atrás, de vuelta*
back of . . . (at/in the) *al*
  fondo de(l) . . .
backgammon *chaquete*
badminton *bádminton*
badminton, steering wheel
  volante
baggage *equipaje*

bakery *panadería*
bald *calvo*
barb *púa*
barber *peluquero*
barkeeper *tabernero*
baron *barón*
baseball *béisbol*
basketball *baloncesto,*
  básquetbol
be able (to), to *poder*
be acquainted, to *conocer*
be born, to *nacer*
be ungrateful (for), to
  desagradecer
be valued, to *valer*
be, to *estar, ser, hacer*
beating, (a) *vapuleo*
beautiful *bello*
beautiful, handsome
  hermoso
because *porque*
beef steak *bistec*
beg, to *rogar*
begin, to *comenzar,*
  empezar
behind . . . *detrás de . . .*
Belgian *belga (masc. y*
  fem.)
Belgium *Bélgica*
believe, to *creer*
beloved *querido*
beneficial *beneficial*
bet, to *apostar*
better *mejor*
beverage *bebida*
beyond . . . *más allá*
  de . . .
bicycle *bicicleta*
big, large *grande*
bilingual *bilingüe*
billiards *billar*
billion *millón*
biodegradable
  biodegradable
biography *biografía*
bird *pájaro; ave, el*
black *negro*
blackberry *zarzamora*

blind *ciego*
block, to *obstruir*
blond(e) *rubio*
blouse *blusa*
blow/hit *golpe*
blunt, rude *brusco*
boating *pasear en barco*
body *cuerpo*
bodybuilding
  fisiculturismo
boil, to *cocer, hervir*
bold *audaz*
bone *hueso*
book *libro*
booklet *guía, la*
bore, to *aburrir*
boring *aburrido*
both *ambos*
bothersome person
  molestoso
bowling *los bolos*
box, to *boxear*
boy, child *niño*
boyfriend *novio,*
  enamorado
brake, to *frenar*
bravery *bravura*
break, to *quebrar,*
  romper
breed and rear, to *criar*
brevity *brevedad*
brilliant *brillante*
bring, to *traer*
British *británico*
brother *hermano*
brother-in-law *cuñado*
brother-in-law's spouse
  concuñada
bruised *golpeado*
brutality *brutalidad*
Burma *Birmania*
Burmese *birmano*
burn, to *quemar*
bury, to *enterrar*
bus *autobús*
business *negocio*
busy *ocupado*
but *pero*

cable *cable*
calculable *calculable*
calculate, to *calcular*
Californian *californiano*
call (oneself), to *llamar(se)*
calm *tranquilo*
calmed *sosegado*
Cambodia *Cambodia*
Cambodian *camboyano*
Canada *Canadá*
Canadian *canadiense*
capable *capaz*
capacity *capacidad*
capital of a city *capital, la*
capitalism *capitalismo*
capitalist *capitalista*
capricious *caprichoso*
car *automóvil, coche,*
  carro
car racing *automovilismo*
cards *cartas*
care for, to *cuidar*
caress, to *acariciar*
cargo *bagaje*
carry out, to *cumplir*
carry, to wear *llevar*
cashier *cajero*
cassette deck *pletina*
cassette player *tocacasete*
cassette recorder
  grabadora de casete
cat *gato*
catastrophe *catástrofe*
cathedral *catedral*
CD player *reproductor*
  de discos compactos,
  tocadiscos CD
CD-RW drive *regrabadora*
  de CDs
celebrity *celebridad*
censor *censor*
central *central*
cereal *cereal*
certain, true *cierto*
challenge *reto*
chaos *caos*
charity *institución de*
  beneficencia

chat, to *platicar*
check *cheque*
check, to *revisar*
checkers *las damas*
cheese *queso*
chemical engineer
  ingeniero químico
chess *ajedrez*
chest *baúl*
chewing gum *chicle*
child, son *hijo*
childhood *niñez*
childish *aniñado*
China *China*
Chinese *chino*
chocolate *chocolate*
choke, to *atragantar*
cholera *cólera, el*
choose, to *escoger,*
  optar
choose decisively, to *elegir*
chop (pork) *chuleta*
Christian *cristiano*
Christmas card *tarjeta de*
  navidad
circumstance
  circunstancia
citizen *ciudadano*
city *ciudad*
clarify, to *clarificar*
clarity *claridad*
class *clase*
clean *limpio*
clear *claro*
clerk *dependiente*
close to . . . *cerca de . . .*
close, to *cerrar*
closed *cerrado*
clothes *ropa*
cloud *nube*
cloudy *nublado*
coconut *coco*
coffin *ataúd*
coin *moneda*
coincide, to *coincidir*
cold *frío*
color *color*
coma *coma, el*

combat, to *combatir*
come, to *venir*
comet *cometa, el*
comma *coma, la*
command, request *orden,*
  la
commentary *comentario*
commercial *comercial*
community *comunidad*
compact disc *disco*
  compacto
companion *compañero*
company *compañía*
compete, to *competir*
competitor *competidor*
complain, to *quejarse*
complaint *queja*
complexion, skin *tez, la*
compose/edit, to *redactar*
comprehensible
  comprensible
concert *concierto*
concur, to *concurrir*
condition, to
  acondicionar
conductor, driver
  conductor
confess, to *confesar*
confessor *confesor*
confuse, to *confundir*
confusion *confusión*
congested, head cold
  constipado
conquer, to *vencer*
conscience *consciencia*
consecutive *consecutivo*
conservatism
  conservadorismo
console *consola*
consonant *consonante*
constant *constante*
construct, to *construir*
consume, to *consumir*
contagious *contagioso*
continue, to *continuar*
contract, to *contraer*
contradictory
  contradictorio

contrary *contrario*
contribute, to *contribuir*
convert, to *convertir*
convertible *convertible*
cordial *cordial*
corn *maíz*
corner *rincón*
correct, to *corregir*
cough *tos, la*
country *país*
course *curso*
court *corte, la*
courteous *cortés, gentil*
cousin *primo, prima*
cover, lid *tapa*
cover, to *cubrir*
covered (with clouds) *cubierto*
cow *vaca*
cramp *calambre*
crane *grúa*
crazy, outgoing *loco*
create, to *crear*
cricket *criquet*
crime *crimen, delito*
criminal *criminal, reo*
crisis *crisis, la*
cross, to *cruzar*
CD-ROM player *unidad de CD-ROM*
cruel *cruel*
culinary *culinario*
cultural *cultural*
culture *cultura*
cup, bowl *taza*
curable *curable*
cure, the *cura, la*
curiosity *curiosidad*
curious *curioso*
curtain *cortina*
custom *costumbre*
customs *aduana*
cut, the *corte, el*
cycling *ciclismo*
cyclist *ciclista*
cynical *cínico*

Czech Republic *República Checa*
Czech *checo*
daddy *papi*
daily *diario*
dance *baile*
dance, to *bailar*
Dane, Danish *danés, danesa*
danger *peligro*
dark, obscure *oscuro*
dark-haired *moreno*
darts *los dardos*
DAT recorder *pletina digital*
daughter *hija*
daughter-in-law *hija política, nuera*
day *día, el*
day after tomorrow *pasado mañana*
day before yesterday *anteayer*
dead *muerto*
debate, to *debatir*
debt *deuda*
December *diciembre*
decide, to *decidir*
decision *decisión, la*
decorated *decorado*
defend, to *defender*
defensive *defensivo*
define, to *definir*
delegated *delegado*
delicious *delicioso*
delighted *encantado*
demand *exigencia*
demand, to *exigir*
democratic *democrático*
demonstrate, to *demostrar*
Denmark *Dinamarca*
dentist *dentista*
deny, refuse, to *negar*
depend, to *depender*
despotism *depotismo*
deserve, to *merecer*

designer *diseñador*
desire, crave, to *apetecer, introducir*
desire/wish *deseo*
desktop *sobremesa*
destroy, to *destruir*
destroyer *destructor*
detective novel *novela policiaca*
detector *detector*
dialect *dialecto*
dice *los dados*
dictionary *diccionario*
difference *diferencia*
different *diferente*
difficult *difícil*
digestible *digestible*
dignitary *dignatario*
dignity *dignidad*
dinner *cena*
director *director*
disappear, to *desaparecer*
discern, to *discernir*
discuss, to *discutir*
disgusted, angered at someone *enfadado*
diskette drive *disquetera*
diskette slot in drive *ranura de la disquetera*
disobey, to *desobedecer*
disrespectful *caradura*
distract, to *distraer*
dive, to *zambullir*
diving *clavado*
dizzy *mareado*
do, to *hacer*
doctor *médico*
dog *perro*
dogmatism *dogmatismo*
dollar *dólar*
domineering *autoritario*
dominoes *dominó*
door *puerta*
downstairs *abajo*
drain *desagüe*
drastic *drástico*
draw or take out, to *sacar*

draw, to *dibujar*
drawer *cajón*
dream, sleep, sleepiness *sueño*
dream, to *soñar*
dress *vestido*
dress, to *vestir*
dressmaker *modista*
drink, to *beber*
drive, to *conducir*
drive away, to *ahuyentar*
drizzle, to *lloviznar*
drizzling *llovizna*
drunk *ebrio*
dry-cure, to *acecinar*
durable *durable*
during *durante*
during the day *de día*
Dutch *holadés, holandesa*
duty *obligación, deber*
DVD player *lector de DVDs*
each, every *cada*
each one *cada uno, cada una*
eagle *águila, el*
easily *fácilmente*
easy *fácil*
eat, to *comer*
ecstasy *éxtasis, el*
editor *editor*
educational *educacional*
effort *esfuerzo*
egg *huevo*
egotism *egoismo*
Egypt *Egipto*
Egyptian *egipcio*
eight *ocho*
eighteen *dieciocho*
eighth *octavo*
eighty *ochenta*
elderly *anciano*
electrical outlets *enchufe de corriente*
elegance *elegancia*
elegant *elegante*
elephant *elefante*

eleven *once*
embarrassed *avergonzado*
embellish, to *embellecer*
embrace, to *abrazar*
emerge, to *emerger*
emigrated *emigrado*
emissary *emisario*
emit or give off, to *emitir*
emotional *emocional*
emotional relief *desahogo*
emphasis *énfasis, el*
employment *empleo*
empty, to *vaciar*
enamored *enamorado*
encounter, to *encontrar*
England *Inglaterra*
English *inglés, inglesa*
enjoy, to *disfrutar, gozar*
enrich, to *enriquecer*
enter, to *entrar*
episode *episodio*
equal *igual*
equality *igualdad*
equipment *equipo*
error *error*
escape, the *huida, la*
essence *esencia*
essential *esencial*
establish, to *establecer*
eternity *eternidad*
Ethiopia *Etiopía*
Ethiopian *etiope*
euphoria *euforia*
Europe *Europa*
European *europeo*
evangelism *evangelismo*
even *aun*
eviction *desahucio*
evidence *evidencia*
exactly *exactamente*
exam *examen*
example *ejemplo*
excellent *excelente*
executive *ejecutivo*
executive assistant *asistente ejecutivo*
exercise *ejercicio*

exhale, to *exhalar*
exhausted *agotado*
exhibit, to *exhibir*
existence *existencia*
expansion *ampliación*
explain, to *explicar*
explainable *explicable*
explosive *explosivo*
export, to *exportar*
extend, to *extender*
extension cord *alargador*
exterior ear *oreja*
extinguish, to *extinguir*
extraordinary *extraordinario*
extreme sports *aventura*
eye *ojo*
fabric *tela*
façade *fachada*
facial gesture *gesto*
fact, deed *hecho*
fairy tales *cuentos de hadas*
fake, to *fingir*
fall *caída*
fall, to *caer*
falsifiable *falseable*
fame *fama*
famous *famoso*
far *lejos*
far from *lejos de . . .*
fasten, to *fijar*
fat *gordo*
fatal *fatal, mortal*
father *padre, papá*
father-in-law *suegro*
favor *favor*
favor, to *favorecer*
fear, to *temer*
fearful *temeroso*
February *febrero*
federal *federal*
feel, to *sentir*
fencing *esgrima*
fervor *fervor*
fever *fiebre*
feverish *febril*
fierceness *ferocidad*

fifteen *quince*
fifth *quinto*
fifty *cincuenta*
fight *pelea*
fighter, wrestler *luchador*
fill out, to *rellenar*
finally *finalmente*
find, to *hallar*
finger *dedo*
fingernail *uña*
finish, to *acabar*
Finland *Finlandia*
Finlander *finlandés, finlandesa*
fireman *bombero*
firm, company *empresa*
first *primer*
firstborn *primogénito, primogénita*
first cousin *primo hermano, prima hermana*
first draft, outline *esbozo*
fish *pez, el*
fishing *pesca, la*
fist *puño*
fit (into), to *caber*
five *cinco*
flash with lightning, to *relampaguear*
flee, to *huir*
flesh, meat *carne, la*
floor *piso*
flower or flourish, to *florecer*
fly, to *volar*
follow, to *seguir*
following *siguiente*
foot *pie*
football *fútbol americano*
for (time frame) *desde hace*
for, to *para*
forehead *frente, la*
foreigner *extranjero*
forget, to *olvidar*
fork *tenedor*

fortunately *afortunadamente*
forty *cuarenta*
four *cuatro*
fourteen *catorce*
fourth *cuarto*
fracture *fractura*
fragility *fragilidad*
frame *cuadro*
France *Francia*
freeze, to *helar*
freezing *helado*
French *francés, francesa*
frequent *frecuente*
frequent a place, to *acudir*
frequently *frecuentemente*
fresh *fresco*
Friday *viernes*
friend *amigo*
friend, godfather to one's child *compadre*
friend, godmother to one's child *comadre*
friendly *amistoso*
frightened *asustado*
front, in *enfrente*
front line in battle *frente, el*
frozen *congelado*
fruit *fruta*
fry, to *freír*
full *lleno*
full of life *lleno de vida*
fundamental *fundamental*
funny *cómico*
furniture *muebles*
fuse, to cast *fundir*
future *futuro*
garage *garaje*
garlic *ajo*
gather, to *recoger*
gathering *reunión*
generally *generalmente*
generous *generoso*
German *alemán, alemana*
Germany *Alemania*

gift *obsequio, regalo*
girl *niña*
girlfriend *novia, enamorada*
give, to *dar*
glass *vaso*
glory *gloria*
glossary *glosario*
gluttonous person *tragantones*
go, to *ir*
goddaughter *ahijada*
godmother *madrina*
godson *ahijado*
gold *oro*
golf *golf*
good *bueno*
good for *bueno para*
good, kind *bondadoso*
goodness *bondad*
gourmet cooking *cocina gastronómica*
grade *calificación, nota*
grand, great *gran, grande*
granddaughter *nieta*
grandfather *abuelo, abuelito*
grandmother *abuela, abuelita*
grandson *nieto*
grapevine *parra*
grasp or grab, to *coger*
Great Britain *Gran Bretaña*
Greece *Grecia*
Greek *griego*
grow, to *crecer*
grow dark (at night), to *anochecer*
grow light (at dawn), to *amanecer*
grow old, to *envejecer*
guest *huésped*
guitar *guitarra*
gymnastics *gimnasia*
habit *hábito*
hail, to *granizar*
hair *cabello*

Haiti *Haití*
Haitian *haitiano*
hamburger *hamburguesa*
hand *mano, la*
hand over, to *entregar, rendir*
handball *balonmano*
hang-gliding *vuelo en ala delta*
handsome *guapo*
hang, to *colgar*
happy *feliz*
hard drive light *luz del disco duro*
have, to *tener, haber (aux.)*
he *él*
head *cabeza*
headphone jack *conector de auriculares*
headphones *los auriculares*
health *salud, la*
hear, to *oír*
heat (up), to *calentar*
heat *calor*
height *altura, estatura*
help *ayuda*
help oneself, to *ayudar(se)*
here *aquí*
hereditary *hereditario*
hi *hola*
hiccup *hipo*
hi-fi system *equipo de alta fidelidad*
hinder, to *impedir*
historical novel *novela histórica*
Holland *Holanda*
homeowner *amo (de casa)*
honorable *honorable, honrado*
hope or wait for, to *esperar*
horse *caballo*

horseback riding *equitación*
horticulture *horticultura*
hospital *hospital*
hot *caloruso*
hotel *hotel*
house, home *casa*
how *como*
howl or shriek, to *aullar*
humid *húmedo*
humility *humildad*
humor *humor*
hunger *hambre*
hurt *lastimado*
husband *esposo, marido*
hydraulic system *sistema hidráulico*
I *yo*
iceskating *patinaje sobre hielo*
idea *idea*
ideal *ideal*
idealism *idealismo*
idealist *idealista*
if *si*
illegal *ilegal*
ill-mannered *mal educado*
impatience *impaciencia*
impatient *impaciente*
import, to, or to cause to matter *importar*
important *importante*
impoverish, to *empobrecer*
impregnate or hinder, to *embarazar*
impressionism *impresionismo*
in agreement *de acuerdo*
in fashion *de moda*
in front of . . . *delante de . . .*
incendiary *incendiario*
incentive *incentivo*
incomparable *incomparable*
increase *aumento*

independence *independencia*
India *India*
Indian *indio*
individualism *individualismo*
inevitable *inevitable*
infancy *infancia*
inferior *inferior*
influenza *gripe*
inform, to *informar*
information *información*
inhibit, to *cohibir*
injure, to *herir*
innocence *inocencia*
inquire, to *averiguar*
inside *adentro*
insistence *insistencia*
inspector *inspector*
instructor *instructor*
internal ear *oído*
internist *internista*
interrupt, to *interrumpir*
intolerance *intolerancia*
invent, to *inventar*
inventor *inventor*
inventory analyst *analista de inventario*
inversion *inversión*
investment advisor *consejero(a) de inversiones*
invitation *invitación*
invited *invitado*
Iran *Irán*
Iranian *iraní (masc. y fem.)*
Iraq *Iraq*
Iraqi *iraquí (masc. y fem.)*
Ireland *Irlanda*
Irish *irlandés, irlandesa*
iron (metal) *fierro*
iron (appliance) *plancha*
irritable *irritable*
isolate, to *aislar*
Israel *Israel*
Israeli *israelí (masc. y fem.)*

Italian *italiano*
Italy *Italia*
jail *carcel*
Jamaica *Jamaica*
Jamaican *jamaicano*
January *enero*
Japan *Japón*
Japanese *japonés,*
japonesa
jaw *quijada*
jealous *celoso*
Jerusalemite
jerosolimitano
jewel *joya*
jog *trotear*
joke *chanza,*
chiste
journalist *periodista*
jovial, jolly *jovial*
judge *juez*
July *julio*
June *junio*
justice *justicia*
karate *kárate*
kerosene *keroseno*
keyboard *teclado*
kilogram *kilo,*
kilogramo
kilometer *kilómetro*
kind, amiable *amable*
kinesiology *kinesiologia*
king *rey*
kingdom *reino*
kinship *parentesco*
kite *cometa, la*
kneeling *de rodillas*
knife *cuchillo*
knit, to *tejer*
know, to *saber*
Korea *Corea*
Korean *coreano*
Kurd, Kurdish *kurdo*
lake *lago*
lamentable *lamentable*
land/field *terreno*
landscape *paisaje*
language *idioma,*
lenguaje

laser printer *impresora*
láser
last *último*
last name *apellido*
last week *semana*
pasada
last year *año pasado*
late *atrasado*
later *después*
laugh, to *reír(se)*
law *ley, la*
lawn *césped*
laziness *pereza*
lead *plomo*
learned/expert *docto*
leather strap *correa*
leave or go out, to *salir*
left of . . . (to the) *a la*
izquierda de . . .
left side, on the *a mano*
izquierda
legitimate *legítimo*
letter *carta*
liberalism *liberalismo*
license plate *placa*
lie, deceive, to *mentir*
life *vida*
light (adj.) *claro*
light(s) *luz, luces*
light or turn on, to
encender
lightning *relampagos*
lightning flash
relampagueo
limit, to *restringir*
line *raya*
lineage *linaje*
linguistics *lingüistica*
lion's mane *guedeja*
listen (to), to *escuchar*
listing *cartelera*
literary *literario*
literature *literatura*
little *poco*
live well, to *bienvivir*
living room *sala*
local *local*
logical *lógico*

look (for), to *buscar*
look at, to watch *mirar*
lose, to *perder*
lottery *lotería*
love *amor*
love, to *amar*
loving *cariñoso*
luck *suerte, la*
lunch *almuerzo*
lunch, to *almorzar*
lute *laúd*
Lutheran *luterano*
lying on the back *de*
espaldas
machine *máquina*
magazine *revista*
magnetism *magnetismo*
make, to *hacer*
make a mistake, to
cometer un error
make abstract, to *abstraer*
male *varón*
manager *gerente (masc.*
y fem.)
many times *muchas veces*
map *mapa, el*
March *marzo*
marketing consultant
consultor de
mercadeo
married *casado*
marry, to *casar(se)*
martial arts *artes*
marciales
massage *masaje*
materialism *materialismo*
mattress *colchon*
mature, ripe, wise *maduro*
May *mayo*
measles *sarampión*
measure *tasa*
measure, to *medir*
mechanic(al) *mecánico*
medium *mediano*
medium height *estatura*
mediana
melancholic *melancólico*
member *miembro*

mentally *mentalmente*
mentor *mentor*
menu *menú*
merchant *mercader*
mercy *merced, la*
mess *lío*
meter *metro*
meticulous *meticuloso*
Mexican *mexicano*
Mexico *México*
microphone jack *conector*
de micrófono
mid-range speaker *altavoz*
de sonidos medios
million *millón*
millionaire *millonario*
mine *mío(s), mía(s)*
minimum *mínimo*
mischievous *travieso*
miserable *miserable*
missionary *misionario*
modem *módem*
mom *mamá*
mommy *mami*
Monday *lunes*
monitor *monitor*
moon *luna*
moralist *moralista*
more *más*
morning *mañana*
mortgage banker *banquero*
hipotecario
mosquito *mosquito*
mother *madre*
mother-in-law *suegra*
motor *motor*
mountain *montaña*
mountain climbing
alpinismo
mountain sports
montañismo
mouse *ratón*
moved, touched
emocionado
movie multiplex *multicine*
much, a lot *mucho*
mumps *paperas*
murder, to *asesinar*

THE EVERYTHING LEARNING SPANISH BOOK

music teacher *profesor de música*
music *música*
musical *musical*
musician *músico*
my *mi(s)*
nail *clavo*
nail, to *clavar*
name *nombre*
national *nacional*
nationalism *nacionalismo*
nationality *nacionalidad*
natural *natural*
naturally *naturalmente*
near *cerca*
necessarily *necesariamente*
necessary *necesario*
neck *cuello*
need, to *necesitar*
negative *negativo*
negotiable *negociable*
neighbor *vecino*
neither *tampoco*
nephew *sobrino*
nervous *nervioso*
neutral *neutral*
never *nunca*
news *noticias*
newspaper *periódico*
next *próximo*
next week *semana próxima*
next year *año próximo*
nice weather *buen tiempo*
niece *sobrina*
night (after sunset) *noche*
nine *nueve*
nineteen *diecinueve*
ninety *noventa*
ninth *noveno*
no *no*
no one *nadie*
noise *ruido*
noon *mediodía*
normally *normalmente*
North American *norteamericano*

Norway *Noruega*
Norwegian *noruego*
noun *sustantivo*
not recognize, to *desconocer*
notebook computer *PC portátil*
novelist *novelista*
November *noviembre*
now *ahora*
oasis *oasis*
obey, to *obedecer*
obtain, to *conseguir*
obviously *obviamente*
October *octubre*
of, from *de*
of the *del*
of the age of maturity *mayor de edad*
offend, to *ofender*
offer, to *ofrecer*
official *oficial*
often *a menudo*
oil painting *pintura al oleo*
old *antiguo, viejo*
older *mayor*
olive *aceituna*
omission *omisión*
on button *botón de encendido*
on duty *de guardia*
on one's way back *de regreso*
on top *sobre*
once in a while *de vez en cuando*
one *uno*
only *solo (adv.), único (adj.)*
open, to *abrir*
opened *abierto*
operate, to *operar*
opinion *opinion, la*
opponent *opositor*
opportunity *oportunidad, la*
oppose, to *oponer*

optimist *optimista*
orange *naranja*
order *orden, el*
ordinary *ordinario*
organic *orgánico*
organizable *organizable*
original *original*
ostensible *ostensible*
other, another *otro*
our *nuestro(s)*
outside *afuera*
over, on top of . . . *sobre . . .*
over here *acá*
overcome, to *sobrevivir*
overshoe, corn *choclo*
own *propio*
pacifist *pacífico*
pain *dolor*
paint, to *pintar*
Pakistan *Paquistán*
Pakistani *paquistaní (masc. y fem.)*
pale *pálido*
paper *papel*
parachuting *paracaidismo*
paragliding *parapente*
park *parque*
park, to *estacionar*
partial *parcial*
participate, to *participar*
pass, to elapse *transcurrir*
passable *pasable*
pastor *pastor*
pastry maker *repostero*
paternal *paterno*
pathetic *patético*
patient *paciente*
patriotism *patriotismo*
pay (for), to *pagar*
pediatrician *pediatra (masc. y fem.)*
pen *bolígrafo*
penguin *pingüino*
people *gente, la*
percentage *porcentaje*

perfectly *perfectamente*
performance, show *espectáculo*
perfume with incense, to *sahumar*
perhaps *quizás*
permit, to *permitir*
person *persona*
person from a non-Spanish country *gringo*
person who guides *guía, el*
person with doctorate, Ph.D. *doctor*
personally *personalmente*
pet *mascota*
Philippines *Filipinas*
Philippino *filipino*
phoenix *fénix*
phonograph *fonógrafo*
physical, physicist *físico*
physician *medico (masc. y fem.)*
physics *física*
pianist *pianista*
piano *piano*
piece *pedazo*
pilot *piloto*
pity/mercy *piedad*
place, to put *poner*
plan *plan*
planting *plantaje*
play a sport or game, to *jugar*
playful *juguetón*
pleasant *genial*
pleasant, gentle *apacible*
pleasant weather *agradable*
please, to *gustar*
pleasure *gusto*
plum *ciruela*
plumage *plumaje*
poem *poema, el*
poetry *poesía*
poker *póquer*
Poland *Polonia*
police force *policía, la*

police officer *policía (masc. y fem.)*

Polish *polaco*

polish, to *pulir*

poncho, cape *poncho*

pond *estanque*

poor *pobre*

popular *popular*

portable stereo *radiocasete portátil*

portrait *retrato*

possession *posesión, la*

possibility *posibilidad, la*

possible *posible*

possibly *posiblemente*

posture *postura*

potent *potente*

potty mouth *malhablado*

pound *libra*

power *poder*

power switch *interruptor*

practical jokes *bromas*

practice (a trade), to *ejercer*

practice, to *practicar*

pray, to *rezar*

precisely *precisamente*

prefer, to *preferir*

preferable *preferible*

preference *preferencia*

pregnant *embarazada*

prepare, to *preparar*

prepared *listo*

Presbyterian *presbiteriano*

presentable *presentable*

president *presidente*

pretentious *cursi*

pretty *bonito*

priest *sacerdote; cura, el*

primary *primario*

principally *principalmente*

probably *probablemente*

problem *problema, el*

proceed, to *proceder*

produce, to *producir*

produce an unexpected event, to *accidentar*

professor *profesor*

programmer *programador*

progressive *progresivo*

promise, to *prometer*

proportioned *esbelto*

protect, to *proteger*

protector *protector*

prudent *prudente*

pumpkin *calabaza*

purchase, to *comprar*

pursue, to *perseguir*

put (in), to *meter*

quarrel, to *reñir*

quit, to *renunciar*

race *carrera*

radicalism *radicalismo*

radio programming *radio, la*

radius, the physical radio *radio, el*

railway *ferrocarril*

rain *lluvia*

rain, to *llover*

rainy *lluvioso*

rather, said more accurately *mejor dicho*

rational *racional*

raw *crudo*

react, to *reaccionar*

read, to *leer*

ready for *listo para*

realty appraiser *tasador de bienes inmuebles*

reason *razón, la*

receive, to *recibir*

receive the needy, to *hospedar*

recipes *recetas*

reciprocate, to belong to *corresponder*

reclined *acostado*

recommend, to *recomendar*

record *disco*

record, to *grabar*

redheaded *pelirrojo*

re-examine, to *reexaminar*

reflector *reflector*

refuse or reuse, to *rehusar*

refute, to *rebatir*

regimen *régimen*

region *región*

regular *regular*

reimburse, to *reembolsar*

relatively *relativamente*

release, to *soltar*

remain, to *quedar*

remember, to *recordar*

renew, to *reanudar*

rent, lease, to *arrendar*

repeat, to *repetir*

repeatedly *repetidas veces*

republican *republicano*

requirements *requisitos*

reset button *botón de reset*

residence *residencia*

resist, to tolerate *resistir*

resolve, to *resolver*

respectable *respetable*

respond (to), to *contestar*

rest of my life *resto de mi vida*

retired person *retirado*

return, to *devolver, volver*

right of . . . (to the) *a la derecha de . . .*

right side, on the *a mano derecha*

rise early, to *madrugar*

risk *riesgo*

robust *robusto*

rodent *roedor*

romance novel *novela romantica*

roof *techo*

root, origin *raíz, la*

rosy *rosado*

roulette *ruleta*

round *redondo*

rowing *canotaje*

rub, to *fregar*

rugby *rugby*

rule *regla*

ruminate, to *rumiar*

rummy *rumi*

rumor *rumor*

run, to *correr*

rye *centeno*

sad *triste*

sadness *tristeza*

sailing *navegación, vela*

sail, to *navegar*

sailing by light canoe *piragüismo*

saint *santo*

salary *salario, sueldo*

salesperson *vendedor*

same time, at the *a la vez*

Santa Claus *Papá Noel*

satisfied *contento*

satisfy, to *satisfacer*

Saturday *sábado*

Saudi Arabia *Arabia Saudita*

Saudi Arabian *saudita*

say, to *decir*

scab *roña*

scale *escala*

scanner *escáner*

scar *cicatriz*

school *escuela*

science fiction novel *novela de ciencia ficción*

scientific *científico*

Scotland *Escocia*

Scottish *escoces, escocesa*

screen *pantalla*

scuba dive, to *bucear*

scuba diving *buceo*

sculpture *escultura*

seated *sentado*

second *segundo*

second cousin *primo segundo*

secondary *secundario*

sedentary *inactivo*

seducer *seductor*
see, to *ver*
see off or fire, to *despedir*
seem, to appear *parecer*
seize, to *asir*
seldom *contadas veces*
self-esteem *autoestima*
selfish *egoísta*
sell, to *vender*
send, to *enviar, remitir*
sensational *sensacional*
September *septiembre*
series *serie*
serious *serio*
serpent *serpiente*
serve, to *servir*
seven *siete*
seventeen *diecisiete*
seventh *séptimo*
seventy *sesenta*
several times *varias veces*
sew or stitch, to *coser*
shame *vergüenza*
shame, to *avergonzar*
shameless person *sinvergüenza*
shave, to *afeitar*
she *ella*
shelf *repisa*
shine, to brighten *lucir*
shirt *camisa*
shoe *zapato*
shooting *tiro fusil*
short *bajo*
show, to exhibit *mostrar*
sick *enfermo*
sick with a cold *resfriado*
sickly *enfermizo*
sickness *enfermedad*
side of (to the), next to *al lado de(l) . . .*
sieve, to *cernir*
simple *simple*
since *desde*
sing, to *cantar*

singer *cantante*
single *soltero*
sister *hermana (hermanita)*
sister-in-law *cuñada*
sister-in-law's spouse *concuñado*
six *seis*
sixteen *dieciséis*
sixth *sexto*
sixty *setenta*
skate (over ice), to *patinar (sobre el hielo)*
skating *patinaje*
skiing *esquí*
skillful *hábil*
skin *piel, la*
sky *cielo*
Slav *eslavo*
slippers *chanclas*
small *pequeño*
small mare *yegüita*
smell *olor*
smell, to *oler*
smile, to *sonreír(se)*
snack in the afternoon, to *merendar*
snob *esnob*
snowing *nieve*
snowy *nevado*
so many times *tantas veces*
so much *tanto*
soap *jabón*
sober *sobrio*
soccer *fútbol*
socialism *socialismo*
software developer *diseñador de software*
sole *suela*
solitaire *solitario*
solitude *soledad*
sometimes *algunas veces*
song *canción*
son-in-law *hijo politico, yerno*
soon *pronto*

sorrow *duelo*
so-so *así así*
soul *alma, el*
South Africa *África del Sur*
South African *sudafricano*
Spanish (from Castille) *castellano*
sparrow *gorrión*
speak, to *hablar*
speaker *altavoz*
speaker jack *conector de altavoces*
special *especial*
specialist *especialista*
spirit *espíritu*
sponsor, to *auspiciar*
spring *primavera*
sprinkle, to *salpicar*
standing *de pie, parado*
state *estado*
stepbrother *hermanastro*
stepdaughter *hijastra*
stepfather *padrastro*
stepmother *madrastra*
stepsister *hermanastra*
stepson, stepchild *hijastro*
stereo system *equipo estereofónico*
stew *guisado*
stick *porra*
stolen *robado*
stop, parade *parada*
store, to *guardar*
store, warehouse *almacén*
stork *cigüeña*
story *cuento*
strange *extraño*
stroll through, to *pasear*
strong *fuerte*
student *estudiante*
study, to *estudiar*
stunned *atontado*
stupendously *estupendamente*
style *estilo*

submit or surrender, to *ceder*
suffer, to *padecer, sufrir*
suitcase *maleta*
sum of money (business) *capital, el*
sum up, to *resumir*
summer *verano*
Sunday *domingo*
sunflower *girasol*
sunny *sol*
superior *superior*
supervisor *supervisor(a)*
support *apoyo*
surfing *surf*
surge protector *filtro protector*
surprise, to *sorprender*
swallow, to *tragar*
sway, to rock *mecer*
sweat, to *sudar*
Sweden *Suecia*
Swedish *sueco*
sweet *dulce*
swim, to *nadar*
swimming *natación*
Swiss *suizo*
Switzerland *Suiza*
syllable *sílaba*
synthesis *síntesis*
Syria *Siria*
Syrian *sirio*
table tennis *tenis de mesa*
tail *rabo*
tailor *sastre*
take, to *tomar*
take a trip on a boat, to *dar paseo en barco*
take away, to *quitar*
take on, to *abarcar*
talented *talentoso*
tall *alto*
tar *pez, la*
taxi *taxi*
teach, to *enseñar*
teacher *maestro*
telephone *teléfono*
telephone, to *telefonear*

temperature *temperatura*

ten *diez*

tennis *tenis*

tenor *tenor*

tenth *décimo*

terrorism *terrorismo*

Texan *texano*

Thailand *Tailandia*

Thailandese *tailandés, tailandesa*

thank (for), to *agradecer*

that *eso, que*

that (at a distance) *aquel*

that is *o sea*

the *el, la*

there is/are *hay*

they *ellos, ellas*

thick, stout *grueso*

thin *delgado*

thin, skinny *flaco*

thing *cosa*

think, to *pensar*

third *tercero*

thirst *sed*

thirsty *sediento*

thirteen *trece*

thirty *treinta*

this time *esta vez*

this week *esta semana*

this year *este año*

three *tres*

throw out, to *echar*

thunder, to *tronar*

Thursday *jueves*

ticket *boleto*

tiger *tigre*

tighten, to *apretar*

time(s) *vez, veces*

time, epoch *época*

time, on *a tiempo*

tinged *tinto*

tired *neumático, cansado*

to *a*

today *hoy*

tolerance *tolerancia*

toll *peaje*

tomato *tomate*

tomorrow *mañana*

tongue twister *trabalenguas*

too, overly *demasiado*

tornado *tornado*

touch or play, to *tocar*

tour on bicycle, to *dar paseo en bicicleta*

tourist *turista*

toward *hacia*

towel *toalla*

tower, tower console *torre*

town, village *pueblo*

trace *huella*

track and field *atletismo*

traditional *tradicional*

trail, hint *pista*

translate, to *traducir*

transmit, to *trasmitir*

travel, to *viajar*

treat informally, to *tutear*

tree *árbol*

trillion *billón*

trip, on a *de viaje*

trousers *pantalones*

trust, or to lend *fiar*

truth *verdad, la*

tube *tubo*

Tuesday *martes*

tune, to *sintonizar*

tuner *sintonizador*

Turk, Turkish *turco*

Turkey *Turquía*

turn back, to *retroceder*

turn off, to *apagar*

turntable *tocadiscos (analógico)*

tweeter *altavoz de sonidos agudos*

twelve *doce*

twenty *veinte*

two *dos*

U.S. citizen *estadounidense*

U.S.A. *EE UU*

ugly *feo*

under(neath) *debajo*

under ... *debajo de ...*

understand, to *comprender, entender*

undressed *desnudo*

unharmed *ileso*

unite, to *unir*

United States *Estados Unidos*

universal *universal*

unload, to *descargar*

unpleasant *antipático*

upstairs *arriba*

use, to *usar*

useful *útil*

usual *usual*

usually *usualmente*

vacation, on *de vacaciones*

valor *valor*

vandalism *vandalismo*

various *varios*

vegetables *verduras*

vegetarian *vegetariano*

velocity *velocidad*

velvet *terciopelo*

ventilation grill *rejilla de ventilación*

verbo *verb*

verify or check, to *comprobar*

very *muy*

vice president *vice presidente*

video camera *videocámara*

vigor *vigor*

visible *visible*

volleyball *balonvolea, voleibol*

volume *volumen*

voluntary *voluntario*

vowel *vocal*

waist *cintura*

waiter *mesero, mozo, camarero*

Wales *País de Gales*

walk, to *caminar, andar*

wall *pared, la*

want, or love, to *querer*

war *guerra*

warn, to *advertir*

Washington *Wáshington*

waste, to *desperdiciar*

watch *reloj*

watch television, to *mirar la televisión*

water *agua, el*

water skiing *esquí acuático*

weak *débil*

wedding *boda*

Wednesday *miércoles*

weekend *fin de semana*

weight *peso*

weightlifting *levantamiento de pesas*

weightlifting and strength *halterofilia y potencia*

well mannered *bien educado*

Welsh *galés, galesa*

what *qué*

wheat *trigo*

wheel *rueda*

when *cuando*

where *dónde*

which *cual*

while *mientras*

white *blanco*

who *quién*

whole life *toda la vida*

wide, broad *ancho*

widow *viuda*

wife *esposa, mujer*

will *voluntad, la*

wind *viento*

windsurfer *windsurfista*

windsurfing *windsurf*

winetasting *cata de vino*

wink, to *guiñar*

winter *invierno*

with *con*

without clouds *despejado*

woman *mujer*
wood *madera*
woofer *altavoz de sonidos graves*
work *trabajo*
work, product *obra*
work, to *trabajar*
world *mundo*
worm, caterpillar *gusano*
worried *preocupado*
worry *preocupación*

worse *peor*
wrap, to *envolver*
write, to *escribir*
X-ray picture *radiografía*
xylophone *xilófono*
year *año*
yellow *amarillo*
yes *sí*
yesterday *ayer*
yet, still *aún*
you (familiar) *tú*

you (polite) *usted*
you all *ustedes*
young *joven*
young child *criatura*
youngest *menor*
your (familiar) *tu(s)*
your (polite) *su(s)*
yours (familiar) *tuya(s), tuyo(s)*
yours (polite) *suya(s), suyo(s)*

youth *juventud, la*
Yugoslavia *Yugoslavia*
Yugoslavian *yugoslavo*
zero *cero*
zoo *zoológico*

Spanish Idioms

J ust like any other language, Spanish
has phrases that, literally translated,
will leave you in a quandary. This
chapter lists some of the idioms found in
everyday Spanish—you might be surprised
to find out that many have a direct coun-
terpart in English. Sample sentences have
been provided for better understanding.

A causa de

MEANING: On account of

EXAMPLE: *La fiesta se canceló a causa de un inesperado viaje.* (The party was canceled on account of an unexpected trip.)

A ciegas

MEANING: Blindly

EXAMPLE: *Caminar en una noche tan oscura es igual a caminar a ciegas.* (Walking on such a dark night is the same as walking blindly.)

A ciencia cierta

MEANING: With certainty

EXAMPLE: *El maestro presenta la materia a ciencia cierta.* (The teacher presents the topic with certainty.)

A crédito

MEANING: On credit

EXAMPLE: *Voy a comprar a crédito mi coche nuevo.* (I'm going to buy my new car on credit.)

A escondidas de

MEANING: Without the knowledge of

EXAMPLE: *Los novios se veían a escondidas de sus padres.* (The couple saw each other without the knowledge of their parents.)

A espaldas

MEANING: Behind one's back

EXAMPLE: *El joven habló muy mal a espaldas de su amigo.* (The young man spoke ill of his best friend behind his back.)

A la carrera

MEANING: In haste, or hastily

EXAMPLE: *Estoy de prisa y voy a tener que comer a la carrera.* (I'm in a hurry and will have to eat hastily.)

A la moda

MEANING: In the latest fashion

EXAMPLE: *Ella siempre está a la moda.* (She is always dressed in the latest fashion.)

Al lado de

MEANING: Beside

EXAMPLE: *Las dos jovenes siempre se sientan una a lado de la otra.* (The two young girls always sit beside each other.)

A menudo

MEANING: Often, frequently

EXAMPLE: *Hay gente que viene a este restaurante muy a menudo.* (There are people who come to this restaurant very frequently.)

A mi entender

MEANING: As I understand

EXAMPLE: *A mi entender, la crisis fue solamente una exageración.* (As I understand, the crisis was just an exaggeration.)

A mi modo de ver

MEANING: In my opinion

EXAMPLE: *A mi modo de ver, la comedia no estaba muy buena.* (In my opinion, the comedy was not very good.)

A ojos cerrados

MEANING: Blindly

EXAMPLE: *Ella se dejó llevar por sus amigas a ojos cerrados.* (She allowed her friends to guide her blindly.)

A ojos vistas

MEANING: Visibly, clearly

EXAMPLE: *En la noche las estrellas se ven a ojos vistas.* (At night you can see the stars clearly.)

A perder

MEANING: To spoil

EXAMPLE: *La cena se va echar a perder si se queda mucho tiempo fuera.* (The meal will spoil if it's left out for too long.)

A pesar de que

MEANING: In spite of the fact that, despite, even though

EXAMPLE: *A pesar de que salí una hora antes de la casa, todavía llegué tarde al trabajo.* (Even though I left the house an hour earlier, I still arrived at work late.)

A punto fijo

MEANING: With certainty

EXAMPLE: *El reportero habló a punto fijo.* (The reporter spoke with certainty.)

A ratos

MEANING: From time to time, at times

EXAMPLE: *A ratos se siente bien, a ratos no.* (At times she feels fine, at other times she does not.)

A toda hora

MEANING: At all times

EXAMPLE: *La farmacia esta abierta a toda hora.* (The pharmacy is open at all times.)

A todo correr

MEANING: At full speed

EXAMPLE: *Salió a todo correr para alcanzar al autobús.* (He left at full speed to catch the bus.)

A vistas

MEANING: On approval, with approval

EXAMPLE: *Fue recibido a vistas buenas.* (He was greeted with approval.)

A vuelta de correo

MEANING: By return mail

EXAMPLE: *Su respuesta vendrá a vuelta de correo.* (His response will arrive by return mail.)

Acabar de

MEANING: To have just done something

EXAMPLE: *Acaba de llegar del exterior.* (She just arrived from abroad.)

Acerca de

MEANING: With regard to, about the

EXAMPLE: *El comprador llamó acerca de la casa.* (The buyer called about the house.)

Agua cruda

MEANING: Hard water

EXAMPLE: *Este agua cruda necesita tabletas de sal.* (This hard water needs salt tablets.)

Agua salada

MEANING: Seawater, salty water

EXAMPLE: *El acuario necesitó agua salada para mantener a los peces tropicales vivos.* (The aquarium required salty water in order to keep the tropical fish alive.)

Ahora mismo

MEANING: Right now

EXAMPLE: *Necesito salir ahora mismo.* (I need to leave right now.)

Al cabo de

MEANING: Finally, at the end of

EXAMPLE: *Viene cansado al cabo de una jornada muy larga.* (He arrives tired at the end of a long day's journey.)

Al contrario

MEANING: To the contrary

EXAMPLE: *Al contrario, yo gané la apuesta.* (To the contrary, I won the bet.)

Al día

MEANING: Per day, up-to-date

EXAMPLE: *Todas sus cuentas están al día.* (All his bills are up-to-date.)

Al escape

MEANING: Rapidly or quickly

EXAMPLE: *Tuve que salir al escape de la casa.* (I had to leave the house quickly.)

Al fin

MEANING: At last

EXAMPLE: *Al fin se compró un carro nuevo.* (At last he bought himself a new car.)

Al menos

MEANING: At least

EXAMPLE: *Al menos pide un nuevo*

uniforme. (At least ask for a new uniform.)

Al pie de la letra

MEANING: Literally, to the letter

EXAMPLE: *El juez aplaca la ley al pie de la letra.* (The judge applies the law literally, to the letter.)

Al sereno

MEANING: In the night air

EXAMPLE: *Me gusta caminar al sereno.* (I like to walk in the night air.)

Algunas veces

MEANING: Sometimes

EXAMPLE: *Algunas veces desayuno en ese restaurante.* (Sometimes I have breakfast in that restaurant.)

Ante todo

MEANING: Above all

EXAMPLE: *Ante todo, sigo creyendo que ella no es culpable.* (Above all, I continue to believe that she is not guilty.)

Antes de que

MEANING: Before

EXAMPLE: *Antes de que vengan los invitados, me voy a cambiar de ropa.* (I'm going to change clothes before the guests arrive.)

Así-así

MEANING: So-so.
Example: Estoy así-así. (I am just so-so.)

Así y todo

MEANING: In spite of, even so, anyhow

EXAMPLE: *Así y todo los problemas seguimos luchando diariamente.* (In spite of all the problems, we continue our daily struggles.)

Atrás de

MEANING: Behind

EXAMPLE: *Siempre se queda atrás de los demas.* (She always falls behind the rest.)

Aun cuando

MEANING: Even though

EXAMPLE: *Aun cuando tenía un paraguas me mojé.* (Even though I had an umbrella, I still got wet.)

Baja el radio

MEANING: Turn the radio down

EXAMPLE: *Baja el radio, que me estás poniendo sordo.* (Turn the radio down, you're making me deaf.)

Beber a pulso

MEANING: To gulp down

EXAMPLE: *Estaba tan sediento que se bebió a pulso la botella entera*

de cerveza. (He was so thirsty that he gulped down the entire bottle of beer.)

Cada perico a su estaca, cada changa a su mecate.

MEANING: To each his own.

EXAMPLE: *No me gusta su compañia, pero cada perico a su estaca, cada changa a su mecate.* (I don't like the company he keeps, but to each his own.)

Cada uno

MEANING: Apiece, each one

EXAMPLE: *La recompensa será de cien dólares a cada uno.* (The reward will be one hundred dollars apiece.)

Caer en cama

MEANING: To fall ill, to get sick

EXAMPLE: *Me resfrié y caí en cama.* (I had chills and ended up ill.)

¡Cállate la boca!

MEANING: Shut up!

EXAMPLE: *¡Cállate la boca si no sabes lo que dices!* (If you don't know what you are saying, shut up!)

Carne de gallina

MEANING: Goose bumps

EXAMPLE: *De pronto sentí tanto frío que la piel se me puso como carne de gallina.* (Suddenly it became so cold that I got goose bumps.)

Casa de locos

MEANING: Insane asylum, madhouse

EXAMPLE: *¿Por qué hay tanto desorden? Parece una casa de locos.* (Why is there such disarray? It looks like a madhouse.)

Cerca de

MEANING: Close to

EXAMPLE: *El tren me deja cerca de casa.* (The train leaves me close to home.)

Como si

MEANING: As if

EXAMPLE: *Salió como si fuera perseguido por alguien.* (He left as if someone was following him.)

Como último recurso

MEANING: As a last resort

EXAMPLE: *Como último recurso, acudió a las autoridades.* (She went to the authorities as a last resort.)

Con anticipación

MEANING: In advance

EXAMPLE: *Pagó su cuenta con anticipación de la fecha que se venía.* (She paid her bill in advance of the due date.)

¡Con razón!

MEANING: No wonder!

EXAMPLE: *¡Con razón que no tengo dinero, tengo un hueco en mi bolsillo!* (No wonder I don't have any money, there is a hole in my pocket!)

Cumplir su palabra

MEANING: To keep one's word

EXAMPLE: *Ella hace lo que sea con tal de cumplir su palabra.* (She does whatever it takes to keep her word.)

De sol a sol

MEANING: Sunrise to sunset

EXAMPLE: *El campesino trabaja de sol a sol para alimentar a su familia.* (The farmer works from sunrise to sunset to feed his family.)

De todos modos

MEANING: At any rate

EXAMPLE: *De todos modos, ella no quiso ir.* (At any rate, she did not want to go.)

De un golpe

MEANING: All at once

EXAMPLE: *Robaron el banco de un golpe.* (They robbed the bank all at once.)

De uso

MEANING: Secondhand

EXAMPLE: *Compró un carro de uso.* (He bought a secondhand car.)

De venta

MEANING: On sale

EXAMPLE: *Tuvieron suerte al encontrar la máquina de lavar en venta.* (They were lucky to find the washing machine on sale.)

Dentro de poco

MEANING: In a little while

EXAMPLE: *Dentro de poco tengo que ir al trabajo.* (I have to go to work in a little while.)

Desayunarse con la noticia

MEANING: To get the scoop

EXAMPLE: *No le importó quedarse todo el día con tal de desayunar con la noticia.* (In order to get the scoop, she didn't mind staying the whole day.)

Desde entonces

MEANING: Ever since

EXAMPLE: *Ganó la lotería hace tres meses, no trabaja desde entonces.* (He won the lottery three months ago; he has not worked since then.)

Día de campo

MEANING: Picnic

EXAMPLE: *Estamos planeando un día de campo con toda la familia.* (We're planning a picnic with the entire family.)

Día de raya

MEANING: Payday
EXAMPLE: *El próximo día de raya me voy de fiesta con todos mis amigos.* (Next payday, I'm going out with all my friends.)

Donde no

MEANING: Otherwise
EXAMPLE: *Ven conmigo, donde no, me iré solo.* (Come with me, otherwise, I'll go alone.)

Echar al olvido

MEANING: To purposefully forget
EXAMPLE: *Echó al olvido su cita y se fue con sus amigos.* (He purposefully forgot his date and went with his friends.)

Echar de menos

MEANING: To long for
EXAMPLE: *Ahora que ya no están juntos, él la echa de menos muchísimo.* (Now that they are no longer together, he longs for her a lot.)

Echar la casa por la ventana

MEANING: To spare no expense
EXAMPLE: *Ganaremos, aunque tengamos que echar la casa por la ventana.* (We will spare no expense in order to win.)

Echar la llave

MEANING: To lock the door

EXAMPLE: *No te olvides de echar llave cuando salgas.* (Don't forget to lock the door when you leave.)

Echar la mano

MEANING: To seize, to give a helping hand
EXAMPLE: *Échale la mano a tus estudios y termina el colegio ya.* (Seize your studies and finish school already.)

Echar un sueño

MEANING: To take a nap
EXAMPLE: *Estoy muy cansado, me voy a echar un sueño.* (I'm too tired; I'm going to take a nap.)

Echar un terno

MEANING: To swear, curse
EXAMPLE: *Cuando se enoja, comienza a echar unos ternos.* (When he is mad, he begins to swear.)

Echar un trago

MEANING: To take a drink
EXAMPLE: *Tanta calor merece echarse un buen trago.* (Such heat deserves a good drink.)

Echar una siesta

MEANING: To take a siesta or nap
EXAMPLE: *Después de ese gran almuerzo, me da ganas de tomar una siesta.* (After that good lunch, I feel like taking a nap.)

El día menos pensado

MEANING: When least expected
EXAMPLE: *El día menos pensado te caigo de visita.* (I'll come to visit you when it's least expected.)

El sol poniente

MEANING: The setting sun
EXAMPLE: *El sol poniente se luce en la playa.* (The setting sun looks great on the beach.)

En cueros

MEANING: Naked, stark naked
EXAMPLE: *Traía el traje de baño tan suelto que se quedó en cueros en la piscina.* (Her swimming suit was so loose that she ended up naked in the pool.)

En cuerpo

MEANING: Without a coat or hat
EXAMPLE: *La temperatura subió suficientemente para estar en cuerpo.* (The temperature increased enough to stay without a coat or hat.)

En estado interesante

MEANING: Pregnant
EXAMPLE: *Fue fácil ver que estaba en estado interesante.* (It was easy to see that she was pregnant.)

En grueso

MEANING: In bulk, wholesale
EXAMPLE: *Me gusta comprar las cosas en grueso.* (I like to buy things wholesale.)

En lo más crudo del invierno

MEANING: In the dead of winter
EXAMPLE: *En lo más crudo del invierno se me perdieron mis guantes.* (In the dead of winter I lost my gloves.)

En marcha

MEANING: In progress
EXAMPLE: *Todo está en marcha para la fiesta de sorpresa.* (Everything is in progress for the surprise party.)

En otros términos

MEANING: In other words
EXAMPLE: *En otros términos, no quiero volver a verte aquí.* (In other words, I don't want to see you here.)

En pleno día

MEANING: In broad daylight
EXAMPLE: *El secuestro ocurrió en pleno día.* (The kidnapping took place in broad daylight.)

En poder de

MEANING: In the hands of
EXAMPLE: *El caso está en poder de los abogados.* (The case is in the hands of the lawyers.)

En realidad

MEANING: As a matter of fact
EXAMPLE: *En realidad, todavía soy menor de edad.* (As a matter of fact, I'm still underaged.)

En un soplo

MEANING: In a jiffy
EXAMPLE: *El carro me lo reparó en un soplo.* (He repaired my car in a jiffy.)

En vez de

MEANING: Instead of
EXAMPLE: *En vez de un trago me tomé un café.* (Instead of a drink I had a cup of coffee.)

En voz alta

MEANING: Aloud
EXAMPLE: *La única forma de hablar en el estadio fue en voz alta.* (The only way to talk in the stadium was aloud.)

Enajenamiento de los sentidos

MEANING: Loss of consciousness
EXAMPLE: *El choque de los dos futbolistas resultó en un enajenamiento de los sentidos.* (The collision between the two soccer players resulted in a loss of consciousness.)

Entre paréntesis

MEANING: By the way
EXAMPLE: *El juego estuvo tremendo. Entre paréntesis, perdiste la apuesta.* (The game was great. By the way, you lost the bet.)

Entre tanto

MEANING: Meanwhile, in the meantime
EXAMPLE: *El carro está en la mecánica, entre tanto voy a caminar.* (The car is in the shop, in the meantime I'm going to walk.)

Escribir a máquina

MEANING: To typewrite
EXAMPLE: *En todas mis clases, las tareas tienen que escribirse a máquina.* (In all my classes, the homework must be typewritten.)

Eso es.

MEANING: That's right.
EXAMPLE: *Eso es, no hay nada más que decir.* (That's it; there is nothing else to say.)

Eso es el colmo.

MEANING: That's the limit.
EXAMPLE: *Eso es el colmo, no vuelvo a hablar con ellos.* (That's the limit; I will not talk to them again.)

Espuma de jabón

MEANING: Suds
EXAMPLE: *No te escondas en la espuma de jabón.* (Don't hide in the suds.)

Estar a la mira de

MEANING: To be on the lookout for
EXAMPLE: *Estamos a la mira del primer caballo en la carrera.* (We're on the lookout for the first horse in the race.)

Estar al cabo de

MEANING: To be well informed
EXAMPLE: *Estamos al cabo de todos los antecedentes.* (We are well informed of the antecedents.)

Estar de goma

MEANING: To have a hangover
EXAMPLE: *Bebió tanto que está de goma.* (He drank so much that he has a hangover.)

Estar de malas

MEANING: To be out of luck
EXAMPLE: *Toda la semana ella ha estado de malas.* (She's been unlucky all week.)

Estar en camino

MEANING: To be in the way
EXAMPLE: *Por favor, retírate, que estás en mi camino.* (Please move, you are in my way.)

Falta de conocimientos

MEANING: Lack of instructions
EXAMPLE: *Se nota tu falta de conocimientos sobre el tema.* (Your lack of knowledge is evident.)

Fuegos artificiales

MEANING: Fireworks
EXAMPLE: *Cada cuatro de julio encendemos fuegos artificiales.* (Every Fourth of July we light fireworks.)

Fuera de propósito

MEANING: Irrelevant
EXAMPLE: *El contrato nuevo está fuera de propósito a lo que estamos hablando.* (The new contract is irrelevant to what we're discussing.)

Ganar para comer

MEANING: To earn a living
EXAMPLE: *¿Cómo piensas ganar para comer?* (How do you plan to earn a living?)

Ganar tiempo

MEANING: To save time
EXAMPLE: *Voy a usar la nueva pista para ganar tiempo.* (I'm planning to use the new road to save time.)

Hace aire.

MEANING: It is windy.
EXAMPLE: *Hace aire fuerte, debe venir una tormenta.* (It is very windy; a storm must be approaching.)

Hace buen tiempo.

MEANING: It is good weather.
EXAMPLE: *Estos últimos días ha hecho buen tiempo.* (We've had good weather during these last few days.)

Hace frío.

MEANING: It is cold.
EXAMPLE: *Hace mucho frío para ser solamente septiembre.* (It is too cold for being only September.)

Hace mal tiempo.

MEANING: The weather is bad.
EXAMPLE: *No sé por qué hace mal tiempo.* (I don't know why the weather is bad.)

Hace mucho tiempo

MEANING: A long time ago
EXAMPLE: *Hace mucho tiempo vivió aquí un gran héroe.* (A long time ago a great hero lived here.)

Hacer cocos

MEANING: To make eyes at
EXAMPLE: *Todas las muchachas en la escena le hacen cocos a ese actor.* (All the girls on the stage make eyes at the actor.)

Hacer cola

MEANING: To form a line

EXAMPLE: *Tuvimos que hacer cola para las entradas de la nueva película.* (We had to form a line to get tickets to the new movie.)

Hacer cuco a

MEANING: To make a fool of

EXAMPLE: *Los amigos se reunieron para hacerle cuco al extraño.* (The friends got together to make a fool of the stranger.)

Hacer falta

MEANING: To lack, to be needed, to miss

EXAMPLE: *Mi hija me hace falta desde que se fue al extranjero.* (I miss my daughter ever since she went abroad.)

Hacer por escrito

MEANING: To put into writing

EXAMPLE: *Hizo por escrito todos sus planes.* (He put all his plans in writing.)

Hacer puente

MEANING: To take a long weekend

EXAMPLE: *Para hacer puente libre, se tomó vacaciones el viernes.* (He took off Friday in order to take a long weekend.)

Hacer una mala jugada

MEANING: To play a bad trick

EXAMPLE: *No se llevan bien desde que el uno le hizo una mala jugada al otro.* (They don't get along ever since one played a bad trick on the other.)

Huellas digitales

MEANING: Fingerprints

EXAMPLE: *Encontraron huellas digitales en el arma que estaba cerca del difunto.* (They found fingerprints on the firearm found next to the dead man.)

Huevos revueltos

MEANING: Scrambled eggs

EXAMPLE: *Me encantan los huevos revueltos de desayuno.* (I love scrambled eggs for breakfast.)

Ida y vuelta

MEANING: Round trip

EXAMPLE: *El viaje de ida y vuelta me costó mil dolares.* (The round trip cost me a thousand dollars.)

Ímpetu de ira

MEANING: Fit of rage

EXAMPLE: *En un ímpetu de ira, le golpeo al policía.* (He struck the police officer in a fit of rage.)

Ir de compras

MEANING: To go shopping

EXAMPLE: *Hoy tengo que ir de compras.* (I need to go shopping today.)

Ir para atrás

MEANING: To back up

EXAMPLE: *Para sacar el carro, tuvo que ir para atrás y para adelante.* (He had to back up and pull forward in order to take the car out.)

Juego de té

MEANING: Tea set

EXAMPLE: *Ese juego de té es muy fino.* (That tea set is very expensive.)

Juego limpio

MEANING: Fair play

EXAMPLE: *Los dos equipos jugaron un juego limpio.* (Both teams played a fair game.)

Juego sucio

MEANING: Foul play

EXAMPLE: *No son amigos porque el uno le jugó sucio al otro.* (They are not friends because one foul-played the other.)

Jugador de manos

MEANING: Juggler

EXAMPLE: *Ese jugador de manos es un artista de calidad.* (That juggler is an artist of quality.)

Junto a

MEANING: Near to

EXAMPLE: *Junto a su cuerpo encontraron mucho dinero.* (They found a lot of money next to his body.)

La mera idea de

MEANING: The very idea of
EXAMPLE: *La mera idea de salir de viaje no me agrada.* (The very idea of traveling does not appeal to me.)

La rutina diaria

MEANING: The daily grind, the daily routine
EXAMPLE: *Ya me cansé de la rutina diaria.* (I'm tired of the daily grind.)

La semana antepasada

MEANING: The week before last
EXAMPLE: *Fui de vacaciones la semana antepasada.* (I went on vacation the week before last.)

La semana que viene

MEANING: Next week
EXAMPLE: *La semana que viene tengo otra semana de vacaciones.* (I have another week of vacation next week.)

La verdad clara y desnuda

MEANING: The whole truth
EXAMPLE: *Dime la verdad clara y desnuda.* (Tell me the whole truth.)

Pena de muerte

MEANING: Capital punishment
EXAMPLE: *Ese crimen se merece la pena de muerte.* (That crime deserves capital punishment.)

Perder el juicio

MEANING: To lose one's mind
EXAMPLE: *El joven perdió el juicio al ver a su chica con otro.* (The young man lost his mind when he saw his girlfriend with another man.)

Por lo tanto

MEANING: Therefore
EXAMPLE: *Ya dijimos todo lo que queríamos. Por lo tanto, no hay nada mas que hablar.* (We said all that we wanted to say. Therefore, there is nothing else to say.)

Por menudo

MEANING: In detail
EXAMPLE: *Cuéntame todo por menudo.* (Tell me everything in detail.)

Por mi parte

MEANING: As far as I'm concerned
EXAMPLE: *Por mi parte todo ha terminado.* (As far as I'm concerned, everything is finished.)

Por su cuenta

MEANING: All by himself

EXAMPLE: *Él pagará el coche por su cuenta.* (He will pay for the car all by himself.)

Primeros auxilios

MEANING: First aid
EXAMPLE: *Los paramédicos llegaron justo a tiempo para darle primeros auxilios.* (The paramedics arrived just in time to provide first aid.)

Prohibida la entrada

MEANING: No trespassing
EXAMPLE: *Está prohibida la entrada al parque al anochecer.* (There is no trespassing inside the park after dark.)

Pues bien

MEANING: Well, then
EXAMPLE: *Pues bien, me voy a mi casa.* (Well, then, I am going home.)

Puesto que

MEANING: Since, inasmuch as
EXAMPLE: *Puesto que ya no me necesitan, entonces me voy.* (Since they no longer need me, I'm leaving.)

Punto de inspección

MEANING: Checkpoint
EXAMPLE: *Ese punto de inspección está bien situado.* (That checkpoint is well placed.)

Quien ríe el ultimo, ríe mejor.

MEANING: He who laughs last, laughs best.

EXAMPLE: *No importa. Quien ríe el ultimo, ríe mejor.* (It doesn't matter. He who laughs last, laughs best.)

Rara vez

MEANING: Seldom

EXAMPLE: *El doctor viene a estos lugares muy rara vez.* (The doctor comes here very seldom.)

Reírse a carcajadas

MEANING: To laugh one's head off

EXAMPLE: *La muchacha se rió a carcajadas.* (The girl roared with laughter.)

Saltarse un semáforo

MEANING: To run a red light

EXAMPLE: *Recibió una multa porque se saltó un semáforo.* (He received a fine because he ran a red light.)

Salto de agua

MEANING: Waterfall

EXAMPLE: *Ese salto de agua es muy bonito.* (That waterfall is very beautiful.)

Si esta víbora te pica, no hay remedio en la botica.

MEANING: You're playing with fire.

EXAMPLE: *Cuidado que no se entere, si esa víbora te pica, no hay remedio en la botica.* (Be careful that she does not find out; you are playing with fire.)

Tener buena cara

MEANING: To look well

EXAMPLE: *Debes sentirte mejor, tienes buena cara.* (You must feel better; you look well.)

Tener calor

MEANING: To be hot

EXAMPLE: *Tengo calor con tanta ropa puesta.* (I'm hot with all these clothes that I'm wearing.)

Tener celos

MEANING: To be jealous

EXAMPLE: *Tiene muchos celos de verme con otras muchachas.* (She is very jealous to see me with other girls.)

Tener el pico de oro

MEANING: To be eloquent

EXAMPLE: *Todos reconocen que tiene el pico de oro.* (Everyone is aware of his eloquence.)

Tener en la mente

MEANING: To have in mind, to have a thought

EXAMPLE: *¿Tú sabes lo que tengo en la mente?* (Do you know what I have in mind?)

Tener en poco a

MEANING: To hold in low esteem

EXAMPLE: *Lo tiene en poco a su aspecto físico.* (He holds in low esteem his physical appearance.)

Tener éxito

MEANING: To be successful

EXAMPLE: *Trabajó muy duro para tener éxito.* (He worked very hard to be successful.)

Tener lástima de

MEANING: To pity

EXAMPLE: *Todo el mundo tiene lástima de ver niños abandonados.* (Everyone has pity on seeing abandoned children.)

Tener lugar

MEANING: To take place

EXAMPLE: *Esa presentación va a tener lugar en un mes.* (That show will take place in a month.)

Tener vergüenza

MEANING: To be ashamed, to be shy

EXAMPLE: *Ella tiene mucha vergüenza de hablar en público.* (She is very shy about speaking in public.)

Tirar la riendas

MEANING: To tighten the reins
EXAMPLE: *Su madre tira las riendas en su casa.* (His mother tightens the reins at home.)

Todas las veces

MEANING: Whenever
EXAMPLE: *Todas las veces que voy a ese restaurante, salgo demasiado lleno.* (Whenever I go inside to that restaurant, I come out too full.)

Todo el mundo

MEANING: Everyone
EXAMPLE: *Todo el mundo sabe un poco de Español.* (Everyone knows a little bit of Spanish.)

Todo el tiempo

MEANING: All the time
EXAMPLE: *Yo salgo de compras todo el tiempo.* (I go shopping all the time.)

Tomar a pecho

MEANING: To take something to heart, to take it personally
EXAMPLE: *Cuidado con lo que le digas, no vaya a tomarlo a pecho.* (Be careful with what you say to him, he might take it to heart.)

Un día sí y otro no

MEANING: Every other day
EXAMPLE: *Tengo un trabajo flex- ible, trabajo un día si y otro no.* (My job is very flexible; I work every other day.)

Un par de

MEANING: A couple of
EXAMPLE: *Son un par de gemelos.* (They are a couple of twins.)

Una negativa rotunda

MEANING: A flat denial
EXAMPLE: *No le dieron el prés- tamo, fue una negativa rotunda.* (They did not give him the loan; it was a flat denial.)

Una y otra vez

MEANING: Over and over again
EXAMPLE: *Hace lo mismo una y otra vez.* (He does the same thing over and over again.)

Uno por uno

MEANING: One by one
EXAMPLE: *Repartió los regales de Navidad uno por uno.* (He distrib- uted his Christmas gifts one by one.)

Unos pocos

MEANING: A few
EXAMPLE: *Tan solo fueron unos pocos los que fueron escogidos.* (Only a few were selected.)

Valer la pena

MEANING: To be worthwhile
EXAMPLE: *Después de conocer lindas chicas, valió la pena ir a la playa.* (After meeting some pretty girls, going to the beach was worthwhile.)

Valer más

MEANING: To be worth more
EXAMPLE: *Algunos objetos antiguos valen más hoy que antes.* (Some antiques are worth more today than before.)

Varias veces

MEANING: Several times
EXAMPLE: *Te llamé por teléfono varias veces.* (I called you on the phone several times.)

Venta pública

MEANING: Auction
EXAMPLE: *Algunas obras de arte están a la venta pública.* (Some works of art are up for auc- tion.)

Visto que

MEANING: Seeing that
EXAMPLE: *Visto que no llegó, me fui sola a la fiesta.* (Seeing that he did not arrive, I went to the party on my own.)

Volver loco

MEANING: To drive crazy
EXAMPLE: *Este desorden me vuelve loco.* (This mess is driving me crazy.

Appendix D

Answer Key

CHAPTER 3

Practice Your Accent Marks

re-vis-ta	*llana*
vo-lun-tad	*aguda*
fá-cil-men-te	*sobresdrújula*
fe-rro-ca-rril	*aguda*
hués-ped	*llana*
es-pí-ri-tu	*esdrújula*
pá-sa-se-la	*sobresdrújula*
trái-ga-me-los	*sobresdrújula*
mí-ni-mo	*esdrújula*

2.

atrás	ah-TRAHS	behind
después	dehs-PWEHS	later
cárcel	CAHR-sehl	jail
tía	TEE-ah	aunt
José	hhoh-SEH	Joseph
legítimo	leh-HHEE-tee-moh	legitimate
pagar	pah-GAHR	to pay
juventud	hhoo-vehn-TOOD	youth
álgebra	AHL-hheh-brah	algebra

CHAPTER 4

Exercise: *Tú* or *Usted?*
1. Grandmother: *Usted*
2. Younger brother: *Tú*
3. Your local bank's president: *Usted*
4. The family pet: *Tú*
5. A deacon: *Usted*
6. Your best friend: *Tú*
7. Your spouse: *Tú*

CHAPTER 5

Practicing Conjugations
(Yo) abro la puerta para entrar. (I open the door to come in.)

Nosotros debemos estudiar mejor. (We should study better.)

Sandra y sus amigas caminan hacia la parada de autobus. (Sandra and her friends are walking to the bus stop.)

¿Ustedes asisten la universidad? (Do you attend the university?)

(Yo) estudio los fines de semana. (I study on weekends.)

Carlos, ¿por qué (tú) acudes los restaurantes italianos? (Carlos, why do you frequent Italian restaurants?)

Juan promete hacer sus tareas. (Juan promises to do his chores.)

Mañana (nosotros) caminamos al trabajo. (Tomorrow we will walk to work.)

Usted siempre cumple con sus promesas. (You always keep your promises.)

(Yo) aprendo la lección. (I am learning the lesson.)

(Tú) bebes demasiado. (You drink too much.)

(Ellas) buscan la calle Main. (They are looking for Main Street.)

¿Ustedes trabajan en la ciudad? (Do you work in the city?)

Él recibe cartas cada día. (He receives letters every day.)

(Yo) vivo feliz si gano la lotería. (I will live happily if I win the lottery.)

Ellos comen manzanas en el parque. (They are eating apples in the park.)

Él compra leche y galletas en el supermercado. (He buys milk and cookies at the supermarket.)

María y Luis hablan por teléfono. (Maria and Luis are talking on the telephone.)

Mi marido y yo discutimos las noticias durante la cena. (My husband and I discuss the news during dinner.)

(Tú) temes la verdad. (You are afraid of the truth.)

¿Usted comprende mis instrucciones? (Do you understand my instructions?)

CHAPTER 7

Exercise: Prepositions and *Estar*

1. I am here with a friend. *Estoy aquí con un amigo.*
2. We are returning with Rita. *Estamos de regreso con Rita.*
3. You (plural) are against government waste. *Ustedes están en contra del desperdicio gubernativo.*
4. Today I am not having luck. *Hoy no estoy de suerte.*
5. She is cold. *Ella está fría.*
6. I am a lawyer, but today I am a professor. *Yo soy abogado, pero hoy estoy de profesor.*
7. They don't have even a penny. *Ellos están sin ni un centavo.*
8. I am in a hurry. *Estoy de prisa.*
9. Today I am without problems. *Hoy estoy sin problemas.*
10. We are standing outside. *Estámos de pie afuera.*

Exercise: *Ser* and *Estar*

1. We are sick. *Nosotros estamos enfermos.*
2. Miguel's friend is French. *El amigo de Miguel es francés.*
3. He is boring. *Él es aburrido.*
4. I am very tired. *Estoy muy cansado (cansada).*
5. He is eating in the Italian restaurant on the left-hand side. *Él esta comiendo en el restaurante italiano al lado izquierdo.*
6. You (formal) are sober. *Usted está sobrio (sobria).*
7. I am (a) sober (person). *Soy sobrio (sobria).*
8. Venezuelans are friendly. *Los venezolanos son amistosos.*
9. They are always happy. *Ellos siempre están felices.*

10. You (informal) are embarrassed. *Tú estás avergonzado (avergonzada).*
11. The building is on Main Street, close to Grove Street. *El edificio está en la calle Main, cerca a la calle Grove.*
12. I am crazy today. *Estoy loco (loca) hoy.*
13. The car is a block from here. *El coche está a una manzana de aquí.*
14. You (plural) are never here. *Ustedes nunca están aquí.*

CHAPTER 9

Exercises: Practice Counting

1. Sample Answers
    1. *¿Cuántos automóviles tiene usted? Tengo dos automóviles.*
    2. *¿Cuántas hijas tiene usted? Tengo una hija.*
    3. *¿Cuántas monedas tiene usted? Tengo doce monedas.*
    4. *¿Cuántos sombreros tiene usted? Tengo quatro sombreros.*

2. Write out the following numbers in Spanish:

eighteen—*dieciocho*
ninety-nine—*noventa y nueve*
three hundred and forty-five—*trescientos cuarenta y cinco*
ten thousand five hundred and eighty-seven—*diez mil quinientos ochenta y siete*
twenty-two thousand seven hundred and thirteen—*veintidós mil setecientos trece*
three million and eighty thousand—*tres millones ochenta mil*

Exercise: Days of the Week

1. Yesterday I was in a hurry (all day, but not today). *Ayer estuve de prisa.*

2. Saturday, I was with Elena. *El sábado estaba con Elena.*

3. Sunday I will be in Florida. *El domingo estaré en la Florida.*

4. I am better since last week. *Estoy mejor desde la semana pasada.*

5. I work Tuesdays. *Trabajo los martes.*

6. The birthday party is on the twenty-fifth. *La fiesta de cumpleaños es el veinticinco.*

7. We traveled more this year. *Viajamos más este año.*

8. I will begin the diet the day after tomorrow. *Comenzaré la dieta el día pasado mañana.*

Exercise: What Time Is It?

1. It's a quarter to three in the afternoon. *Son las tres menos cuarto de la tarde.*

2. It's seven-thirty in the morning. *Son las siete y media de la mañana.*

3. It's a quarter after eleven at night. *Son las once y cuarto de la noche.*

4. It's midnight. *Es la medianoche.*

5. 14:36 *Son las tres menos veinticuatro de la tarde.*

6. 8:23 *Son las ocho y veintitrés de la mañana.*

7. 13:28 *Es la una y veintiocho de la tarde.*

8. 4:42 *Son las cinco menos dieciocho de la madrugada.*

9. 23:08 *Son las once y ocho de la noche.*

10. 12:00 noon *Es el mediodía.*

CHAPTER 10

Exercises: Working with *Tener*

1. Translations

   1. I have to drive the car. *Tengo que conducir el coche.*

   2. You (formal) will have to go at four. *Usted tendrá que ir a las cuatro.*

3. They had to read the book (and did). *Ellos tuvieron que leer el libro.*

4. I have to dance with Fabian. *Tengo que bailar con Fabián.*

5. You (informal) have to attend the wedding. *Tú tienes que assistir la boda.*

---

2. Sample Answer

Tengo que acompañar a mi mamá a la tienda. Tengo que ahorrar para poder comprar una nueva bicicleta. Tengo que aprender a nadar. Tengo que hacer más ejercicio y cuidarme mejor. Tengo que devolver el libro a la biblioteca. Tengo que hacer un pago a la compañía de gas. Tengo que hacer arreglar el coche.

(I have to accompany my mother to the store. I have to save to be able to buy a new bicycle. I have to learn how to swim. I have to exercise more and take better care of myself. I have to return the book to the library. I have to make a payment to the gas company. I have to get the car fixed.)

Exercise: Using *Ir*

1. We intend to wait for them in the store. *Vamos a esperar a ellos en la tienda.*

2. I am going to listen to the music. *Voy a escuchar la música.*

3. She is going to go to the concert today. *Ella va a ir al concierto hoy.*

4. They were going to swim, but it did not happen. *Iban a nadar, pero no ocurrió.*

5. We are going to leave on vacation. *Vamos a salir de vacaciones.*

Exercise: Using *Saber* and *Conocer*

1. I know how old Antonio is. *Sé cuantos años tiene Antonio.*

2. María knows how to drive well. *María sabe conducir bien.*

3. I don't know his brother. *No conozco a su hermano.*

4. We know that respect and communication are

essential in a relationship. *Sabemos que el respeto y la comunicación son esenciales en una relación.*

5. He knows Acapulco well because he travels there a lot. *Él conoce Acapulco bien porque viaja allí mucho.*

CHAPTER 11

Practice What You've Learned #1

1. I rent my dwelling. *Arriendo mi vivienda.*
2. What (are) you (informal) think(ing)? *¿En qué piensas?*
3. Today you (formal) start the new job. *Hoy comienza el nuevo trabajo.*
4. On Fridays we scrub the floors. *Los viernes fregamos los pisos.*
5. They want to go out to eat. *Ellos quieren salir a comer.*
6. We warn of the danger. *Advertimos del peligro.*
7. Tomorrow I snack with my brother. *Mañana meriendo con mi hermano.*
8. I recommend the chicken. *Recomiendo el pollo.*
9. You (plural) turn on your computers. *Ustedes encienden sus computadoras.*
10. She (is) los(ing) her patience. *Ella pierde la paciencia.*
11. We prefer green vegetables. *Preferimos verduras.*

Practice What You've Learned #2

1. I eat lunch at noon. *Almuerzo al mediodía.*
2. Tomorrow they fly to San Diego. *Mañana ellos vuelan a San Diego.*
3. I hang the shirts. *Cuelgo las camisas.*
4. You (informal) show houses. *Muestras casas.*
5. She finds a coin on the floor. *Ella encuentra una moneda en el piso.*

6. I don't dream much. *No sueño mucho.*
7. We beg María for ice cream. *Rogamos a María por helado.*
8. I (am) return(ing) the book. *Devuelvo el libro.*
9. Something smells bad. *Algo huele mal.*
10. You (formal) dig the earth. *Usted remueve la tierra.*
11. He doesn't bite. *Él no muerde.*
12. We can swim. *Podemos nadar.*
13. I will return Monday. *Vuelvo el lunes.*
14. Can you (plural) help? *¿Pueden ustedes ayudar?*
15. Priests absolve sins. *Sacerdotes absuelven los pecados.*

Practice What You've Learned #3

1. I (am) boil(ing) eggs. *Hiervo huevos.*
2. We elect the president. *Elegimos al presidente.*
3. You (formal) always follow all the rules. *Ustedes siempre siguen las reglas.*
4. They follow the soaps. *Ellos siguen las telenovelas.*
5. I (am) dress(ing) a baby. *Visto a un bebé.*
6. How tall are you (informal)? (Literally: How much do you measure?) *¿Cuánto mides?*
7. This restaurant serves Mexican food. *Este restaurante sirve comida Mexicana.*

CHAPTER 12

Practice What You've Learned #1

1. I take the small piece. *Cojo el pedazo pequeño.*
2. I choose the yellow apple. *Escojo la manzana amarilla.*
3. I protect the family. *Protejo a la familia.*
4. I gather the clothes from the floor. *Recojo la ropa del piso.*
5. I demand attention. *Exijo la atención.*

Practice What You've Learned #2

1. I follow the news. *Sigo las noticias.*
2. Tomorrow I obtain a ticket for the concert. *Mañana consigo el boleto para el concierto.*
3. I pursue justice. *Persigo la justicia.*

Practice What You've Learned #3

1. Intolerance destroys society. *La intolerancia destruye la sociedad.*
2. You (plural) construct homes. *Construyen casas.*
3. We flee from the police. *Huimos de la policía.*
4. Michelle contributes to her church. *Michelle contribuye a su iglesia.*
5. You (informal) flee from responsibility. *Huyes de la responsabilidad.*

Practice What You've Learned #4

1. Each morning I conquer laziness. *Cada mañana venzo la pereza.*
2. I practice my profession. *Ejerzo mi profesión.*
3. Elena is convincing Juan that tomorrow is Saturday. *Elena convence a Juan que mañana es sábado.*
4. On Sundays I conquer the lawn. *Los domingos venzo el césped.*

Practice What You've Learned #5

1. I give thanks for the help. *Ofrezco gracias por la ayuda.*
2. I am acquainted (with) María. *Conozco a María.*
3. I do exercises in the morning. *Hago ejercicios por la mañana.*
4. I grow older with each worry. *Envejezco con cada preocupación.*
5. I obey the rules. *Obedezco las reglas.*
6. I cook rice, meat, and vegetables. *Cuezo arroz, carne, y vegetales.*
7. I deserve a good grade. *Merezco buena nota.*

Practice What You've Learned #6

1. I drive a yellow car. *Conduzco un coche amarillo.*
2. I am translating a story. *Traduzco un cuento.*
3. Maribel shines at gatherings. *Maribel luce en reuniones.*
4. The cow produces milk. *La vaca produce leche.*
5. The radio program introduces new singers. *El programa de radio introduce a cantantes nuevos.*

Practice What You've Learned #7

1. I send Christmas cards. *Envío tarjetas de Navidad.*
2. Marcela adopts a kitten. *Marcela ahíja a un gatito.*
3. The story continues for another thirty pages. *El cuento continúa por otras treinta páginas.*
4. Sandra pets the zoo animals. *Sandra acaricia a los animales del zoológico.*
5. Adam and Berta study medicine. *Adán y Berta estudian medicina.*

Practice What You've Learned #8

1. I hear noises at night. *Oigo ruidos por la noche.*
2. Do you (formal) hear her? *¿Usted la oye?*
3. I leave from work at five. *Salgo del trabajo a las cinco.*
4. Ricardo does exercises at night. *Ricardo hace ejercicios por la noche.*
5. I have two pets. *Tengo dos mascotas.*
6. They come to visit. *Ellos vienen de visita.*
7. You (informal) say the truth. *Dices la verdad.*
8. She says the truth; she never lies. *Ella dice la verdad; nunca miente.*
9. He hears the ice-cream truck. *Él oye el camión del heladero.*
10. They come to visit their parents. *Vienen para visitar a sus padres.*

CHAPTER 13

Exercise: Object Pronouns

1. You (formal) have two cars. *Usted tiene dos coches. Los tiene.*
2. I am looking for the street. *Busco la calle. La busco.*
3. He makes the beds. *Él hace las camas. Las hace.*
4. I put the book on the shelf. *Pongo el libro en la repisa. Lo pongo en la repisa.*
5. Mr. Muñoz, I will see you tomorrow. *Sr. Muñoz, lo veo a usted mañana. Lo veo.*
6. She saw Alicia and me at the dentist's office. *Ella vió a Alicia y yo en la oficina de dentista. Ella nos vió.*
7. Yesterday I repaired a computer. *Ayer reparé una computadora. Yo la reparé ayer.*
8. Robert has two motorcycles. *Roberto tiene dos motocicletas. Roberto los tiene.*
9. She drives the car. *Ella conduce el coche. Ella lo conduce.*
10. Mom buys milk every Monday. *Mamá compra leche cada lunes. Mamá la compra cada lunes.*

Exercise: Using the Personal *A*

1. I see Ignacio, Amanda, and Pedro. *Yo veo a Ignacio, Amanda, y Pedro.*
2. Who(m) do you (informal) love? *¿A quién amas?*
3. They have a daughter. *Tienen hija.*
4. I am a citizen of the United States. *Soy estadounidense.*
5. I love my cat. *Amo a mi gato.*

Exercise: Indirect-Object Pronouns

1. I purchased him a beverage. *Le compré una bebida. Se la compré.*
2. I will send Samantha to you. *Te mandaré a Samantha. Te la mandaré.*
3. I brought you all the book. *Les traje el libro. Se lo traje.*
4. I recommend them Jonathan. *Los recomiendo a Jonathan. Se los recomiendo.*
5. I show Berta the painting. *Muestro la pintura a Berta. Se la muestro.*
6. I want to phone my sister. *Quiero telefonear a mi hermana. La quiero telefonear.*
7. I told her all the news. *Le dije toda la noticia. Se la dije toda.*

CHAPTER 14

Exercise: Possessive Adjectives

1. my radio—*mi radio*
2. our (masculine) parents—*nuestros padres*
3. your (informal) food—*tu comida*
4. their job—*su trabajo*
5. her dog—*su perro*
6. my culture—*mi cultura*
7. your (plural) party—*su fiesta*
8. his aunt—*su tía*
9. her notebook—*su cuaderno*
10. your (formal) opinions—*sus opiniones*

Exercises: *Ser* in Possessive Constructions

1.

1. It is my sweater. *Es mi saco.*
2. The telephone is his. *El teléfono es suyo.*
3. They're my trousers. *Son mis pantalones.*
4. They're (feminine) yours (informal). *Son las tuyas.*
5. Good grades will be mine. *Las buenas notas serán mías.*
6. The eyeglasses are his. *Los anteojos son suyas.*
7. The sandals are hers. *Las sandalias son suyas.*
8. The camera is hers. *La cámara es suya.*

9. My room used to be my brother's. *Mi cuarto era de mi hermano.*

10. Your (formal) position will be mine next year. *Su puesto será mío el año próximo.*

11. My books used to be my sister's. *Mis libros eran de mi hermana.*

---

2. Sample Answer

El coche es mío. Es mi transporte. La maleta es mía. Los discos compactos son de mi hermano, pero el tocadiscos es mío. Los libros son míos. Las llaves también son mías.

(The car is mine. It is my transportation. The suitcase is mine. The CDs are my brother's, but the CD player is mine. The books are mine. The keys are also mine.)

The Gallegos Family

Which is the relationship between Luis and Fanny Gallegos? Luis and Fanny are spouses. Luis is the husband of Fanny, and Fanny is the wife of Luis. They are husband and wife.

How is the family of Luis and Fanny? Luis and Fanny have three children. Two are men and one is a woman. The woman is named Susy, and the men are named Hugo and Cesar.

Which is the relationship between Cesar, Susy, and Hugo? They are siblings.

Who is Marlene? She is the wife of Hugo. They have two children, Jonathan and Jennifer. Jonathan is Hugo's stepson.

Which is the relationship between Marlene and the family of Luis and Fanny? Marlene is the daughter-in-law of Luis and Fanny. Luis is her father-in-law, and Fanny is her mother-in-law. Marlene is Susy's sister-in-law. Cesar is her brother-in-law. Jonathan is Susy and Cesar's nephew. Jennifer is Susy and Cesar's niece. That is to say, Susy is the aunt of Jonathan and Jennifer, and Cesar is their uncle.

Who are the cousins of Jonathan and Jennifer? The cousins of Jonathan and Jennifer are Celsito and Estefi, the children of Susy.

Which is the relationship between Luis and Jonathan? And between Fanny and Jennifer? Luis is the grandfather of Jonathan. Jonathan is his grandson. Fanny is the grandmother of Jennifer. Jennifer is her granddaughter.

Exercises: Members of the Family

1. Translations

1. The Garcías were my neighbors last year. *Los García fueron mis vecinos el año pasado.*

2. I (fem.) am your friend. *Yo soy tu amiga.*

3. He is my husband. *Él es mi marido.*

4. They are my children. *Ellos son mis hijos.*

5. I (masc.) am yours. *Yo soy tuyo.*

6. They are your (informal) friends. *Ellos son tus amigos.*

7. Pepe and Alicia have been my friends for years. *Pepe and Alicia han sido mis amigos por años.*

8. Alicia was my girlfriend for three months. *Alicia fue mi novia por tres meses.*

9. Pepe has been my barber for years. *Pepe ha sido mi peluquero por años.*

---

2. Sample Answer

Mi familia es pequeña. Mis padres, Luis y Fanny, son de La Paz, Bolivia. Tengo tres hermanos. El mayor es César. Yo soy el menor. Azucena es mi única hermana. Hugo es mi otro hermano. Tenemos cuatro mascotas, tres perros y una gata. Los perros son Ñata, Chap, y Chikis. Candi es nuestra gata.

(My family is small. My parents, Luis and Fanny, are from La Paz, Bolivia. I have three siblings. The oldest is Cesar. I am the youngest. Azucena is my only sister. Hugo is my other brother. We have four pets, three dogs and one cat. The dogs are Ñata, Chap, and Chikis. Candi is our cat.)

CHAPTER 15

Exercise: Practice Your Conjugations #1
1. I took on too much. *Abarqué demasiado.*
2. I searched for my book. *Busqué mi libro.*
3. I clarified the situation. *Clarifiqué la situación.*
4. He read the newspaper. *Él leyó el periódico.*
5. I explained the idea. *Yo expliqué la idea.*
6. They believed the worst. *Ellos creyeron lo peor.*
7. I practiced all day. *Yo practiqué todo el día.*
8. You (formal) possessed courage. *Usted poseyó valor.*
9. I touched the iron. *Toqué la plancha.*
10. I turned off the radio. *Apagué el radio.*
11. The foxes fell in traps. *Los zorros cayeron en las trampas.*
12. I handed over the change. *Entregué el cambio.*
13. I played chess with my friends. *Jugué ajedrez con mis amigo.*
14. They substituted limes for lemons. *Ellos sustituyeron limas por limones.*
15. I arrived late. *Llegué tarde.*
16. I rose early today. *Madrugué hoy temprano.*
17. I paid with cash. *Pagué en efectivo.*
18. I swallowed the pill. *Tragué la pastilla.*
19. Mr. Wright constructed interesting homes. *El Sr. Wright construyó casas interesantes.*
20. I embraced my father. *Abracé a mi papá.*
21. I ate lunch with Susana. *Almorcé con Susana.*
22. I prayed at Mass. *Recé en la misa.*
23. I began the day well. *Comencé el día bien.*

Exercise: Practice Your Conjugations #2
1. We drove to the party. *Condujimos a la fiesta.*
2. The salesman repeated the offer. *El vendedor repitió la oferta.*
3. Did you (informal) translate the speech? *¿Tradujiste el discurso?*
4. She introduced her friends. *Ella introdujo a sus amigos.*
5. They slept all day. *Ellos durmieron todo el día.*
6. You (plural) deduced the solution. *Ustedes dedujeron la solución.*
7. They followed the directions to the museum. *Ellos siguieron las señas al museo.*
8. Who produced your (formal) movie? *¿Quién produjo su película?*
9. The tailor measured his waist. *El sastre midió su cintura.*
10. President Kennedy died in 1963. *El Presidente Kennedy murió en mil novecientos sesenta y tres.*
11. We told the truth. *Dijimos la verdad.*

Exercise: Practice Your Conjugations #3
1. We gave Susy a gift. *Dimos el regalo a Susy.*
2. I placed the key on the table. *Puse la llave sobre la mesa.*
3. I wanted a steak. *Quise un bistec.*
4. Julio came to Vita's birthday party. *Júlio vino a la fiesta de cumpleaños de Vita.*
5. You (formal) knew it. *Usted lo supo.*
6. We were able to arrive on time. *Pudimos llegar a tiempo.*
7. They learned how newspaper ads work. *Supieron como los anuncios funcionan.*
8. Ramón did the work. *Ramón hizo el trabajo.*
9. Did you (formal) give alms? *¿Dió usted una limosna?*
10. You (informal) fit the clothes in the drawer.

Cupiste la ropa en el cajón.

11. We wanted to read a magazine. *Quisimos leer una revista.*

Exercise: Practice Your Conjugations #4

1. I have opened an account. *He abierto una cuenta.*
2. She has put one hundred dollars in the account. *Ella ha puesto cien dólares en la cuenta.*
3. They have done the work. *Ellos han hecho el trabajo.*
4. The two of them have satisfied the requirements. *Los dos de ellos han satisfecho los requisitos.*
5. We have returned to university. *Hemos vuelto a la universidad.*
6. The elderly man has seen many difficulties. *El viejito ha visto muchas dificultades.*
7. Ramon has broken with the party. *Ramón ha roto con el partido.*
8. Channel 6 has not covered local news well. *El canal seis no ha cubierto bien las noticias locales.*
9. The boss has resolved to terminate his employee. *El jefe ha resuelto a despedir su empleado.*
10. We have written to our representatives. *Nosotros hemos escrito a nuestros representantes.*

Exercise: Practice Your Conjugations #5

1. Will you (informal) make the bed? *¿Harás la cama?*
2. My parents will come on Tuesday. *Mis padres vendrán el martes.*
3. We will not be able to walk more. *No podremos caminar más.*
4. You will leave soon. *Saldrás pronto.*
5. They will want to wash their clothes. *Ellos querrán lavar su ropa.*
6. I will have a raise next year. *Tendré un*

aumento de sueldo el año próximo.

7. He will put the radio in the kitchen. *Él pondrá la radio en la cocina.*
8. I will fit the shoes in the suitcase. *Cabré los zapatos en la maleta.*
9. She will not say the truth. *Ella no dirá la verdad.*
10. Next week they will know who won. *La semana próxima ellos sabrán quien ganó.*

CHAPTER 16

Exercise: Using *Hacer*

1. It is cool outside. *Hace fresco. Está fresco afuera.*
2. It is very good weather outside. *Hace buen tiempo. Está buen tiempo afuera.*
3. It is very sunny (weather). *Hace sol. Está soleado.*
4. It is shady under the tree. *Hace sombra debajo del árbol. Está asombreado debajo del árbol.*
5. It's thundering. *Hace truenos. Está tronando.*

Exercise: Reviewing the Imperative

1. Listen (you, informal) to the news! *¡Escucha las noticias!*
2. Let's decide on a movie! *¡Decidamos en la película!*
3. Wait (you, formal) for me at the door! *¡Espéreme por la puerta!*
4. Come (you, informal) here! *¡Ven aquí!*
5. Don't cry (you, informal)! *¡No llores!*
6. Look for (you, formal) the key! *¡Busque la llave!*
7. Don't put (you, informal) it (masculine) here! *¡No lo pongas aquí!*
8. Let's travel to Mexico together! *¡Viajemos a México juntos!*
9. Don't buy (you, formal) it for her! *¡No se lo compre!*

10. Bring (you, plural) it to me! *¡Tráiganmelo!*
11. Tell (you, informal) it to me! *¡Dímelo!*
12. Don't play (you, informal) soccer in the house! *¡No juegues el fútbol en la casa!*
13. Don't open (you, informal) the door! *¡No abres la puerta!*
14. Learn (you, plural) the rules! *¡Aprendan las reglas!*
15. Receive (you, formal) the shipment! *¡Reciba el envío!*
16. Cover (you, plural) the floor! *¡Cubran el piso!*
17. Let's discuss the book! *¡Discutamos el libro!*
18. Understand (you, plural) the instructions! *¡Comprendan las instrucciones!*
19. Discuss (you, plural) the problem! *¡Discutan el problema!*
20. Write (you, informal) it! *¡Escrebalo!*

CHAPTER 17

Exercises: *¿Qué te gusta?* (What do you like?)

1.
1. I like talking with my friends. *Me gusta hablar con mis amigos.*
2. They like to work. *A ellos les gusta trabajar.*
3. We like rice and chicken. *A nosotros nos gustan arroz y pollo.*
4. You (informal) used to like the Johnsons. *Te gustaban los Johnsons.*
5. You all liked Spain. *A ustedes les gustó España.*
6. I believe that I will like New York. *Creo que me gustará Nueva York.*
7. She has liked Thai food since college. *A ella le ha gustado la comida tailandesa desde la universidad.*

Exercise: Yes or No?
1. I always eat vegetables. *Siempre como vegetales.*
2. I never eat vegetables. *Nunca como vegetales.*
3. Someone waits for you. *Alguien te espera.*
4. No one is here. *Nadie está aquí.*
5. At times, Fred and Ginger go out dancing. *A veces, Fred y Ginger salen a bailar.*
6. Fred and Ethel never go out dancing. *Fred y Ethel nunca salen a bailar.*
7. They already know the route. *Ellos ya conocen la ruta.*
8. They don't know the route yet. *Ellos aún no conocen la ruta.*
9. I liked the movie also. *Me gustó la película también.*
10. I did not like the movie (n)either. *No me gustó la película tampoco.*

Exercise: Practice What You Learned
1. I was lacking courage. *Me faltaba ánimo.*
2. My head hurts. *Me duele la cabeza.*
3. Do you miss your automobile? *¿Te hace falta tu automóvil?*
4. We are interested in learning Spanish. *Nos interesa aprender el español.*
5. Are you pleased by romantic films. *¿Te agradan las películas románticas?*
6. It looked good to us. *Nos pareció bueno.*
7. I am delighted by Monet's paintings. *Me encantan las pinturas de Monet.*

Exercises: Listening to Music

Sample Answers
¿Qué tipo de música le gusta? (What type of music do you like?) *Me gusta la música clásica.* (I like classical music.)
¿Le gusta el `jazz'? (Do you like jazz?) *¡Sí, me gusta mucho!* (Yes, I like it very much!)
¿Qué piensa del rock español? (What do you think of Spanish rock?) *Es muy divertido.* (It's a lot of fun.)
¿Cuáles cantantes son sus favoritos? (Which

singers are your favorites?) *Me gustan a Shakira, Carlos Vives, y Rocío Durcal.* (I like Shakira, Carlos Vives, and Rocio Durcal.)

¿Le gusta la música movida? (Do you like fast-paced/rhythmic music?) *No me gusta la música movida.* (I don't like fast-paced music.)

¿Le gustan los boleros? (Do you like slow/sentimental songs?) *¡Sí! muchísimo. Son románticos.* (Yes, a lot. They're romantic.)

CHAPTER 18

Exercise: *¡Qué Fácil!* (How Easy!)

1. What a tall young man! *¡Qué joven tan alto!*
2. What a sad story! *¡Qué cuento más triste!*
3. How far she swims! *¡Qué lejos nada ella!*
4. How lazy she is! *¡Qué perezosa es ella!*
5. What a car! *¡Qué coche!*
6. How close! *¡Qué cerca!*
7. What a delicious steak! *¡Qué bistec más delicioso!*
8. How quickly Carmen speaks! *¡Qué rápido habla Carmen!*
9. How frightening is war! *¡Qué miedosa es la guerra!*
10. How helpful are tools! *¡Qué útiles son las herramientas!*
11. How small! *¡Qué pequeño!*
12. That's soon! *¡Qué pronto!*
13. How well Elena cooks! *¡Qué bien cocina Elena!*
14. How pale is she! *¡Qué pálida está ella!*
15. What a game! *¡Qué juego!*
16. What bad luck! *¡Qué mala suerte!*
17. How charming they are! *¡Qué simpáticos son ellos!*
18. How busy he was! *¡Qué ocupado estaba él!*
19. How quickly he speaks! *¡Qué rápido habla él!*

Exercise: *¡Cuánto Sabes!* (How Much You Know!)

1. How much they ran! *¡Cuánto corrieron!*
2. How I want to be tall! *¡Cuánto quiero ser alto!*
3. How Marco and Lucía smoked! *¡Cuánto fumaron Marco y Lucía!*
4. How much I wanted to eat! *¡Cuánto quería comer!*
5. How many chores we have! *¡Cuántas tareas tenemos!*
6. How it was raining! *¡Cuánto llovía!*

Exercise: *¡Cómo Comparas!* (How You Compare!)

1. You sing as well as my sister. *Tú cantas tan bien como mi hermana.*
2. I have as many coins as you. *Tengo tantas monedas como tu.*
3. There is less work than people. *Hay menos trabajo que gente.*
4. Julio has more experience than Pedro. *Júlio tiene más experiencia que Pedro.*
5. Jonathan is older than Jenny. *Jonathan es mayor que Jenny.*
6. Maira is the prettiest of the girls. *Maira es la más bonita de las muchachas.*
7. Baseball is the most popular sport in the United States. *Béisbol es el deporte más popular en los Estados Unidos.*

CHAPTER 19

One Day in the Life of Celso

Hi. I'm Celso, Estefi's brother. A typical morning for me begins at six, the hour I wake up. I am a little slow to get myself up, especially when it's cold outside. At times I stay in bed and look toward the ceiling of my bedroom. I like thinking about the day that awaits me while I listen to the radio.

I usually get up at 6:15 A.M., when I know that there is no one in the bathroom. After getting myself up from bed, I brush my teeth and wash the sleep from my face. Now awake, I greet my dear mother, father, and sister. Because we are all rushing ourselves to leave, there isn't much time to speak.

I shower, shave (it's true!), and get dressed within thirty minutes. Sometimes I eat breakfast at home. But when I don't have time, I wait to do it at school. I leave for school at 7 A.M. I take the train and arrive there with enough time to speak with my friends before my first class.

Exercise: The Daily Routine

1. I get up at ten in the morning. *Me levanto a las diez de la mañana.*
2. We wash our hair every morning. *Nos lavamos el pelo cada mañana.*
3. Juan shaved his chin last night. *Juan se afeitó la barbilla anoche.*
4. Did you (informal) shave your head? *¿Te afeitaste la cabeza?*
5. Marco cleaned his nose. *Marco se limpió la nariz.*
6. You (plural) must wash your hair. *Ustedes deben lavarse el cabello.*
7. Martín likes to rub his feet. *A Martín le gusta fregarse los pies.*
8. I rinse my mouth after brushing my teeth. *Me enjuago la boca después de lavarme los dientes.*
9. After dinner, they brush their teeth. *Después de la cena, ellos se lavan los dientes.*
10. Leticia applies makeup on her eyes. *Leticia se maquilla los ojos.*

Exercise: Reflecting on the Verb

1. He complained about the noise. *Se quejó del ruido.*
2. When are you (plural) leaving to Florida? *¿Cuándo se van a la Florida?*
3. She dares to steal. *Ella se atreve a robar.*
4. You sit down. *Usted se sienta.*
5. She is called Nancy. *Ella se llama Nancy.*
6. You (informal) started to cry when they left. *Te pusiste a llorar cuando se fueron.*
7. She burned her hand. *Se quemó la mano.*
8. They regret their words. *Se arrepienten de sus palabras.*

Exercise: What Color Is It?
Sample answers:

1. *¿Qué color es tu baño? Mi baño es blanco.*
2. *¿Qué color son tus chanclas? Mis chanclas son anaranjadas.*
3. *¿Qué color son tus sábanas? Mis sábanas son verdes oscuras.*
4. *¿Qué color son tus cortinas? Las cortinas son beiges.*
5. *¿Qué color es tu coche? Mi coche es azul.*

CHAPTER 20

Exercise: Introducciones
Señor: ¡Buenas tardes, Señora! (He wishes you a good afternoon.)
Tú: ¡Buenas tardes! (Respond appropriately.)
Señor: Perdón, pero ¿es usted Daniela Espinosa Cárdenas? (He asks if you are Daniela Espinosa Cardenas.)
Tú: No, no lo soy. (Respond appropriately.)
Señor: Disculpe. ("Please pardon me.")
Tú: No se preocupe. ("Not to worry.")

Another person approaches you. Complete the following conversation:
Señor: Perdón, ¿Cómo se llama usted? (He excuses himself and asks for your name.)
Tú: Me llamo [state your name], *soy de* [state where you are from]. (Respond appropriately and state where you are from.)
Señor: Mucho gusto. Yo soy Claudio Jiménez Juárez, y soy de Guadalajara. (He says that he is pleased to meet you and that his name is Claudio Jimenez Juarez and he is from Guadalajara.)

Tú: Encantada. (Respond appropriately.)

Señor: ¡Bienvenidos a México! (He smiles and welcomes you.)

Tú: Muchas gracias. (Respond appropriately.)

Señor: ¿Son sus maletas? (Are those your suitcases?)

Tú: Sí. Por favor, discúlpeme por traer las quatro maletas por una vacación de dos semanas. (Say yes. Then apologize for bringing four suitcases on your two-week vacation!)

Exercise: A Sample Letter

Dear friend,

You don't know how happy I am to receive your new address. Too much time has passed since the last time that we talked. How is everybody? Your mother and father? I hope they are well. What's new? I hope that I see you all the next time that I travel over there.

I also remember all those times that we chatted. I hope to do it again, soon.

With all my affection,

Lisa

Index

THE EVERYTHING SERIES!

BUSINESS

Everything® Business Planning Book
Everything® Coaching and Mentoring Book
Everything® Fundraising Book
Everything® Home-Based Business Book
Everything® Landlording Book
Everything® Leadership Book
Everything® Managing People Book
Everything® Negotiating Book
Everything® Network Marketing Book
Everything® Online Business Book
Everything® Project Management Book
Everything® Robert's Rules Book,
     $7.95($11.95 CAN)
Everything® Selling Book
Everything® Start Your Own Business Book
Everything® Time Management Book

COMPUTERS

Everything® Build Your Own Home Page Book
Everything® Computer Book

COOKBOOKS

Everything® Barbecue Cookbook
Everything® Bartender's Book, $9.95
     ($15.95 CAN)
Everything® Chinese Cookbook
Everything® Chocolate Cookbook
Everything® Cookbook
Everything® Dessert Cookbook
Everything® Diabetes Cookbook
Everything® Fondue Cookbook
Everything® Grilling Cookbook
Everything® Holiday Cookbook
Everything® Indian Cookbook
Everything® Low-Carb Cookbook
Everything® Low-Fat High-Flavor Cookbook
Everything® Low-Salt Cookbook
Everything® Mediterranean Cookbook
Everything® Mexican Cookbook
Everything® One-Pot Cookbook

Everything® Pasta Cookbook
Everything® Quick Meals Cookbook
Everything® Slow Cooker Cookbook
Everything® Soup Cookbook
Everything® Thai Cookbook
Everything® Vegetarian Cookbook
Everything® Wine Book

HEALTH

Everything® Alzheimer's Book
Everything® Anti-Aging Book
Everything® Diabetes Book
Everything® Dieting Book
Everything® Hypnosis Book
Everything® Low Cholesterol Book
Everything® Massage Book
Everything® Menopause Book
Everything® Nutrition Book
Everything® Reflexology Book
Everything® Reiki Book
Everything® Stress Management Book
Everything® Vitamins, Minerals, and
     Nutritional Supplements Book

HISTORY

Everything® American Government Book
Everything® American History Book
Everything® Civil War Book
Everything® Irish History & Heritage Book
Everything® Mafia Book
Everything® Middle East Book

HOBBIES & GAMES

Everything® Bridge Book
Everything® Candlemaking Book
Everything® Card Games Book
Everything® Cartooning Book
Everything® Casino Gambling Book, 2nd Ed.
Everything® Chess Basics Book
Everything® Collectibles Book
Everything® Crossword and Puzzle Book

Everything® Crossword Challenge Book
Everything® Drawing Book
Everything® Digital Photography Book
Everything® Easy Crosswords Book
Everything® Family Tree Book
Everything® Games Book
Everything® Knitting Book
Everything® Magic Book
Everything® Motorcycle Book
Everything® Online Genealogy Book
Everything® Photography Book
Everything® Poker Strategy Book
Everything® Pool & Billiards Book
Everything® Quilting Book
Everything® Scrapbooking Book
Everything® Sewing Book
Everything® Soapmaking Book

HOME IMPROVEMENT

Everything® Feng Shui Book
Everything® Feng Shui Decluttering Book,
     $9.95 ($15.95 CAN)
Everything® Fix-It Book
Everything® Homebuilding Book
Everything® Home Decorating Book
Everything® Landscaping Book
Everything® Lawn Care Book
Everything® Organize Your Home Book

EVERYTHING®
KIDS' BOOKS

All titles are $6.95 ($10.95 Canada)
unless otherwise noted
Everything® Kids' Baseball Book, 3rd Ed.
Everything® Kids' Bible Trivia Book
Everything® Kids' Bugs Book
Everything® Kids' Christmas Puzzle
     & Activity Book
Everything® Kids' Cookbook
Everything® Kids' Halloween Puzzle
     & Activity Book ($9.95 CAN)

All Everything® books are priced at $12.95 or $14.95, unless otherwise stated. Prices subject to change without notice.
Canadian prices range from $11.95–$31.95, and are subject to change without notice.

Everything® Kids' Hidden Pictures Book
($9.95 CAN)
Everything® Kids' Joke Book
Everything® Kids' Knock Knock Book
($9.95 CAN)
Everything® Kids' Math Puzzles Book
Everything® Kids' Mazes Book
Everything® Kids' Money Book ($11.95 CAN)
Everything® Kids' Monsters Book
Everything® Kids' Nature Book ($11.95 CAN)
Everything® Kids' Puzzle Book
Everything® Kids' Riddles & Brain Teasers Book
Everything® Kids' Science Experiments Book
Everything® Kids' Soccer Book
Everything® Kids' Travel Activity Book

KIDS' STORY BOOKS

Everything® Bedtime Story Book
Everything® Bible Stories Book
Everything® Fairy Tales Book
Everything® Mother Goose Book

LANGUAGE

Everything® Conversational Japanese Book
(with CD), $19.95 ($31.95 CAN)
Everything® Inglés Book
Everything® French Phrase Book, $9.95
($15.95 CAN)
Everything® Learning French Book
Everything® Learning German Book
Everything® Learning Italian Book
Everything® Learning Latin Book
Everything® Learning Spanish Book
Everything® Sign Language Book
Everything® Spanish Phrase Book,
$9.95 ($15.95 CAN)
Everything® Spanish Verb Book,
$9.95 ($15.95 CAN)

MUSIC

Everything® Drums Book (with CD),
$19.95 ($31.95 CAN)
Everything® Guitar Book
Everything® Home Recording Book
Everything® Playing Piano and Keyboards Book
Everything® Rock & Blues Guitar Book
(with CD), $19.95 ($31.95 CAN)
Everything® Songwriting Book

NEW AGE

Everything® Astrology Book
Everything® Divining the Future Book
Everything® Dreams Book
Everything® Ghost Book
Everything® Love Signs Book,
$9.95 ($15.95 CAN)
Everything® Meditation Book
Everything® Numerology Book
Everything® Paganism Book
Everything® Palmistry Book
Everything® Psychic Book
Everything® Spells & Charms Book
Everything® Tarot Book
Everything® Wicca and Witchcraft Book

PARENTING

Everything® Baby Names Book
Everything® Baby Shower Book
Everything® Baby's First Food Book
Everything® Baby's First Year Book
Everything® Birthing Book
Everything® Breastfeeding Book
Everything® Father-to-Be Book
Everything® Get Ready for Baby Book
Everything® Getting Pregnant Book
Everything® Homeschooling Book
Everything® Parent's Guide to Children
with Asperger's Syndrome
Everything® Parent's Guide to Children
with Autism
Everything® Parent's Guide to Children
with Dyslexia
Everything® Parent's Guide to Positive Discipline
Everything® Parent's Guide to Raising a
Successful Child
Everything® Parenting a Teenager Book
Everything® Potty Training Book,
$9.95 ($15.95 CAN)
Everything® Pregnancy Book, 2nd Ed.
Everything® Pregnancy Fitness Book
Everything® Pregnancy Nutrition Book
Everything® Pregnancy Organizer,
$15.00 ($22.95 CAN)
Everything® Toddler Book
Everything® Tween Book

PERSONAL FINANCE

Everything® Budgeting Book
Everything® Get Out of Debt Book

Everything® Get Rich Book
Everything® Homebuying Book, 2nd Ed.
Everything® Homeselling Book
Everything® Investing Book
Everything® Money Book
Everything® Mutual Funds Book
Everything® Online Business Book
Everything® Personal Finance Book
Everything® Personal Finance in Your
20s & 30s Book
Everything® Real Estate Investing Book
Everything® Wills & Estate Planning Book

PETS

Everything® Cat Book
Everything® Dog Book
Everything® Dog Training and Tricks Book
Everything® Golden Retriever Book
Everything® Horse Book
Everything® Labrador Retriever Book
Everything® Poodle Book
Everything® Puppy Book
Everything® Rottweiler Book
Everything® Tropical Fish Book

REFERENCE

Everything® Astronomy Book
Everything® Car Care Book
Everything® Christmas Book,
$15.00 ($21.95 CAN)
Everything® Classical Mythology Book
Everything® Einstein Book
Everything® Etiquette Book
Everything® Great Thinkers Book
Everything® Philosophy Book
Everything® Psychology Book
Everything® Shakespeare Book
Everything® Tall Tales, Legends, & Other
Outrageous Lies Book
Everything® Toasts Book
Everything® Trivia Book
Everything® Weather Book

RELIGION

Everything® Angels Book
Everything® Bible Book
Everything® Buddhism Book
Everything® Catholicism Book
Everything® Christianity Book
Everything® Jewish History & Heritage Book

All Everything® books are priced at $12.95 or $14.95, unless otherwise stated. Prices subject to change without notice.
Canadian prices range from $11.95–$31.95, and are subject to change without notice.

Everything® Judaism Book
Everything® Koran Book
Everything® Prayer Book
Everything® Saints Book
Everything® Understanding Islam Book
Everything® World's Religions Book
Everything® Zen Book

SCHOOL & CAREERS

Everything® After College Book
Everything® Alternative Careers Book
Everything® College Survival Book
Everything® Cover Letter Book
Everything® Get-a-Job Book
Everything® Hot Careers Book
Everything® Job Interview Book
Everything® New Teacher Book
Everything® Online Job Search Book
Everything® Personal Finance Book
Everything® Practice Interview Book
Everything® Resume Book, 2nd Ed.
Everything® Study Book

SELF-HELP/ RELATIONSHIPS

Everything® Dating Book
Everything® Divorce Book
Everything® Great Marriage Book
Everything® Great Sex Book
Everything® Kama Sutra Book
Everything® Romance Book
Everything® Self-Esteem Book
Everything® Success Book

SPORTS & FITNESS

Everything® Body Shaping Book
Everything® Fishing Book
Everything® Fly-Fishing Book
Everything® Golf Book
Everything® Golf Instruction Book
Everything® Knots Book
Everything® Pilates Book
Everything® Running Book
Everything® Sailing Book, 2nd Ed.
Everything® T'ai Chi and QiGong Book
Everything® Total Fitness Book
Everything® Weight Training Book
Everything® Yoga Book

TRAVEL

Everything® Family Guide to Hawaii
Everything® Family Guide to New York City, 2nd Ed.
Everything® Family Guide to Washington D.C., 2nd Ed.
Everything® Family Guide to the Walt Disney World Resort®, Universal Studios®, and Greater Orlando, 4th Ed.
Everything® Guide to Las Vegas
Everything® Guide to New England
Everything® Travel Guide to the Disneyland Resort®, California Adventure®, Universal Studios®, and the Anaheim Area

WEDDINGS

Everything® Bachelorette Party Book, $9.95 ($15.95 CAN)

Everything® Bridesmaid Book, $9.95 ($15.95 CAN)
Everything® Creative Wedding Ideas Book
Everything® Elopement Book, $9.95 ($15.95 CAN)
Everything® Father of the Bride Book, $9.95 ($15.95 CAN)
Everything® Groom Book, $9.95 ($15.95 CAN)
Everything® Jewish Wedding Book
Everything® Mother of the Bride Book, $9.95 ($15.95)
Everything® Wedding Book, 3rd Ed.
Everything® Wedding Checklist, $7.95 ($12.95 CAN)
Everything® Wedding Etiquette Book, $7.95 ($12.95 CAN)
Everything® Wedding Organizer, $15.00 ($22.95 CAN)
Everything® Wedding Shower Book, $7.95 ($12.95 CAN)
Everything® Wedding Vows Book, $7.95 ($12.95 CAN)
Everything® Weddings on a Budget Book, $9.95 ($15.95 CAN)

WRITING

Everything® Creative Writing Book
Everything® Get Published Book
Everything® Grammar and Style Book
Everything® Grant Writing Book
Everything® Guide to Writing a Novel
Everything® Guide to Writing Children's Books
Everything® Screenwriting Book
Everything® Writing Well Book

Introducing an exceptional new line of beginner craft books from the Everything® series!

All titles are $14.95 ($22.95 CAN)

Everything® Crafts—Create Your Own Greeting Cards
1-59337-226-4
Everything® Crafts—Polymer Clay for Beginners
1-59337-230-2

Everything® Crafts—Rubberstamping Made Easy
1-59337-229-9
Everything® Crafts—Wedding Decorations and Keepsakes
1-59337-227-2

Available wherever books are sold!
To order, call 800-872-5627, or visit us at *www.everything.com*
Everything® and everything.com® are registered trademarks of F+W Publications, Inc.